KayakCraft

Fine Woodstrip Kayak Construction

KayakCraft
Fine Woodstrip Kayak Construction

by Ted Moores

Photographs by Jennifer and Ted Moores
Illustrations by Ted Moores

A WoodenBoat Book

To all the students with whom I have had the pleasure of building canoes and kayaks. Thank you for the fresh ideas and simple solutions.

Copyright © 1999 by Ted Moores

Cover and Book Design: Lindy Gifford
Printed in the U.S.A.

Published by WoodenBoat Publications
Naskeag Road, P.O. Box 78
Brooklin, Maine 04616 U.S.A.

ISBN 0-937822-56-6

Front and back covers, title page photography: Darel Bridges
Back Cover Paddler: Debbie Castle, Registered Maine Guide
Interior photographs by Jennifer Moores and Ted Moores, unless otherwise noted.

Library of Congress Cataloging-in-Publication Data
Moores, Ted.
Kayakcraft:Fine woodstrip construction/by Ted Moores.
     p.   cm.
   ISBN 0-937822-56-6 (alk. paper)
   1. Kayaks—Designs and construction.   I. Title.
   VM353.M66 1999   99-33080
   623.8'29—dc21   CIP

Acknowledgments

Writing a book is much like building a kayak: the book, or the kayak, may be your creation but it can only come to be through the support and patience of others. Without my partner, Joan Barrett, keeping our family happy and the Bear Mountain Boat Shop running, I could not have stolen enough time to do this book justice. Daisy Moores, my eldest daughter and the scholar of the family, read the first outline and pointed it in the right direction. The highlight of the project has been working with my younger daughter, Jen Moores, doing the photography. She is a pleasure to work with, has a good eye for lighting, and eclectic taste in music.

Steve Killing has made a major contribution to the depth of this book with his four exquisite kayak plans and excellent illustrated chapter on the fundamentals of kayak design.

Glenda Madgwick and Fred Forster, who read the manuscript, were not shy about pointing out the parts they thought were obscure.

I'm grateful to Ron Frenette and his 1996 kayak-building class for working out the rudder and deck hardware details and getting carried away with making plank design features. The pattern on our kayak was stolen from John Slana, but there were many more to choose from.

The Canadian Canoe Museum has been most accommodating in making their collection and archives available for research.

To my neighbor Teresa: thanks for delivering the local paper with stories worth reading marked, and for planting flowers and keeping the grass cut when I should have been cutting it.

WoodenBoat Publications has been great to work with; Editor Matt Murphy has been critical yet kind.

To all of you who have encouraged and helped to make this book happen, thank you.

Contents

1 | Introduction

HISTORY

The craft of backyard kayak building has a long and significant history, and if you are interested, you can be part of it. Over the past 4,000 years or so, the evolution of the kayak has been driven by people like yourself, building to satisfy a personal need. Your need to build a kayak is as important to your existence as it was to the Eskimo hunter's. Our quest today is not narwhal, but sanity and quality of life.

Backyard kayak construction has taken on many forms to satisfy the individual needs of the builder. Different styles of boats have reflected solutions to survival using an ingenious mix of available materials, simple tools, and a building technique that was appropriate to the skill level of the builder.

The Eskimo kayak, built from materials found in the sea, required a high level of skill. This skill was acquired by growing up around someone who was a kayak builder. Since much of the work of building would take place in the same space where the builder ate and slept, exposure to the craft would be a natural process and come at a very young age. At some point, the young builder would be accepted as the village builder and most likely become a kayak builder for life. As the kayak evolved into a vehicle for recreation, the building and using of a kayak was not necessarily a survival tool. Today, contemporary construction techniques, materials, and tools are utilized to produce an appropriate craft without having to dedicate a lifetime to learning skills.

1-1

In the mid-1800s, the Scotsman John McGregor learned about kayaks and turned them into yachts, and so the kayak became a familiar image. Construction was based on traditional English small boats and required a high level of boat-building skill. This "Rob Roy"–style kayak (Photograph 1-1), as it came to be known, was soon embraced by American builders such as John Henry Rushton of Canton, New York. Incorporating the feather-lap joint developed by the Adirondack guide-boat builders (which resulted in a smooth hull surface), Rushton built the Stradivarius of double-paddle and sailing canoes. Construction was a fine balance between strength and lightness, and the boats had a fine furniture finish. They required a very high level of craftsmanship and the best of materials.

Because of the high price of these finely crafted boats, by the turn of the century, canoe sailing had become a sport of the elite. Fueled by the resources of the affluent and the skills of the professional builder, the sailing canoe quickly evolved into a specialized racing craft with the emphasis on sport and speed rather than recreation. By about 1915, the sport began a fast decline as the canoe sailors discovered the outboard motor, the bicycle, and other forms of recreation. Canoe builders like Rushton had to resign themselves to a market demanding less expensive cedar and canvas canoes that require neither skilled labor nor the best materials.

Undoubtedly, there were sailing and double-paddle canoes built during this period by casual builders, but because of the skills required, most would have been professionally built.

In the 1920s, the kayak took a different direction in Germany with the development of the folding kayak. Percy Blandford, in his book *Tackle Canoeing*, relates a story that could explain the beginning of the folding kayak. It seems a German professor was out walking on a wet Sunday and went into a museum to pass the time. As he was folding up his umbrella, he saw an Eskimo kayak and wondered if it could be folded the same way as his umbrella. Kayaking became an extremely popular recreational pursuit in Germany in the 1920s, and the manufacture and use of kayaks spread to other countries, including England. Folding kayaks transformed the aboriginal construction method into a familiar form, with the use of contemporary tools and materials. It was not a big step for the amateur builder to adapt this system to backyard technology.

When Percy Blandford began publishing how-to information in England for the home builder, skin-on-frame kayak construction became accessible to the casual builder of limited resources and simple woodworking skills. Based loosely on traditional skin kayak construction, frames were cut to a pattern from plywood and joined together with sawn longitudinal stringers. The frame was then covered with canvas and waterproofed with paint. The use of precut plywood frames that were set up on a building bed took the place of a lifetime of experience by the aboriginal builder, who built intuitively with the materials that floated into the

bay. This technique flourished because it combined patterns that controlled the shape with easy-to-find material, simple woodworking tools, and basic woodworking skills.

To the 1929 Boy Scout Jamboree in Birkenhead, England, a group of Boy Scouts from Hungary brought a fleet of simple canvas-on-frame kayaks that they had built. This design was later published in *Scouter*, the scoutmaster's newspaper, as the British Scout Kayak. Thus began a movement that would take kayak building from the igloo to the backyards of the world.

There are now numerous variations on the aboriginal skin-on-frame technique being promoted in books by Dyson, Putz, Brinck, and Snaith and in WoodenBoat School classes (Photograph 1-2). These techniques range from basic get-on-the-water-cheap-and-cheerfully, to elaborate reproductions of traditional craft using a mixture of natural and exotic materials.

1-2

Building kayaks from flat plywood sheets probably began about the time waterproof plywood became available. When we look at a skin-on-frame kayak, the skin is stretched flat between the longitudinal battens, making a hard chine hull shape. It is not hard to picture these flat skin surfaces being cut from thin plywood sheets, nor is it hard to imagine why you would want to do this. The downside of skin-on-frame construction is keeping the skin tight to maintain an effective hull shape—not to mention vulnerability to puncture.

Plywood is now a very popular material for home-built kayaks. Kits and plans are available from a number of sources, and these boats go together quickly and

Chris Kulczycki

1-3

require little or no previous woodworking experience. The technique has much in common with stitching a shirt together: plywood pieces are cut to a predetermined shape and the seams sewn together, producing a three-dimensional kayak shape. While this building technique has little to do with traditional boatbuilding, it does produce a very functional and potentially beautiful kayak and doesn't require learning many new skills or investing a great amount of money (Photograph 1-3).

One downside of the tortured plywood technique is that there is a limit to the shape that can be forced into a flat plywood panel. Even with stressing and torturing, the designer of this type of kayak must begin with the limitation of the material and work backwards, rather than from function to design to material. A more sophisticated method incorporates the multi-chine hull shape of many of the traditional skin kayaks. By dividing the hull surface into easy-to-bend pieces, some surprisingly complex and effective shapes may be developed from flat plywood panels (Photograph 1-4).

Chris Kulczycki

1-4

STRIPPERS

Strip-planked boats reinforced with fiberglass and resin (Photograph 1-5) came onto the small-craft building scene in the mid-1960s. It was driven by a combination of old and new technologies and some crazy marathon paddlers in Wisconsin trying to make their cedar-strip canoes lighter and faster. As the story goes, one marathon paddler fiberglassed the outside of his traditional cedar-strip canoe, then split the ribs out of the interior, cut off the nails, and fiberglassed the interior.

The new technology was polyester resin combined with fiberglass fabric reinforcement. This material, billed as "the cure to all wooden boat problems," had been around about ten years and had fired the imagination of a growing number of backyard builders. Perhaps using a roll of cloth and a can of resin was less intimi-

1-5

dating than cutting a stem bevel. Casual builders took to it with a vengeance. The giant fiberglass boatbuilding industry as we know it today began with the backyard builder who could not leave the stuff alone.

Edge-nailed strip planking was familiar by then, having gained some popularity on the East Coast of Canada and the United States. The attraction to this technique was that a lower grade of wood could be used to advantage by cutting around the defects. This reduced the material cost and made the pieces a manageable size for one person to handle. While it did require boatbuilding skills to set up the molds and backbone, it did not require traditional planking and caulking skills. Successful lobster boats, fishing boats, and recreational craft—both power and sail—were built by semi-skilled, nonprofessional builders using this method.

In practice, this technique worked best if the boat could be left in the water to keep the hull from drying out. If the hull was allowed to go through many cycles of wet to dry, eventually the seams would open up. If the seams had been glued, the plank would split along the grain, where it is hardest to find and fix.

1-6

Obviously, this was not a good system for small craft like dinghies and canoes, which are expected to dry out when not in use. In order for strip planking to be effective in small craft, one more step in the evolution was necessary. Marathon paddlers are a competitive and tenacious bunch. When that old cedar-strip boat without the ribs proved to be lighter but not faster, they decided to strip plank a faster hull shape and fiberglass both sides, in place of the ribs. So they discovered the monocoque structure that we use today (Photograph 1-6).

My first exposure to the technique came in 1971. In Trout Creek, Ontario, Ross Ellery had started out building strip-planked, fiberglass-reinforced marathon canoes for his own use. Before he knew it, he was in the canoe business. About this time, I was working as a freelance commercial artist in downtown Toronto, and was looking for a way out. Ellery's canoes would catch my eye as I drove past his place. Being a dreamer, it wasn't hard to visualize a peaceful life in cottage coun-

try, building beautiful boats for people who would line up at the door with money in hand. It pays to be naive; we can do a lot when we don't know any better. Well, 27 years later, I occasionally think about the fantasy; I have forgotten the money part, but I can't help wondering when the peaceful part begins.

Looking back, I can see that the inexperience I began with has become an asset for all of us. Having become involved with the technique when it was still in the experimental stage, plus having no woodworking or boatbuilding skills in the beginning, frustrated me at times and lengthened my learning curve. But because of this, solutions had to be worked out that gave satisfactory results in the shortest time, while using common sense and simple tools. I have to think the technique would be different if my background had been in boatbuilding or engineering. My technique began with the assumption that professional results are to be expected if good patterns are used and the simple steps performed, with care, in the most effective order.

1-7

To begin with, a form representing the shape of the kayak is set up on a flat table. Thin planks about ¼″ x ¾″ are edge-glued and stapled temporarily in place over the form (Photograph 1-7). When the glue has set, the staples are pulled out and the surface is sanded in preparation for the fiberglass cloth that will be saturated with the liquid resin. After fiberglassing, the hull is removed from the mold, and sanded, and the interior is then fiberglassed.

The building technique is simple and approachable, as well as strong and beautiful, but it is neither the fastest nor the cheapest way to build a kayak. I like to think, however, that it can be the most satisfying. There are a lot of steps, but the steps are small, and because of this, mistakes are small and easily corrected.

HOW STRONG AND DURABLE WILL THE KAYAK BE?

One of the questions you should be asking yourself before deciding to build a wood-strip/epoxy kayak is, "How strong and durable will the kayak be?" That is a fair question, and one that, up until recently, would have gotten an answer based on experience rather than scientific data. To illustrate how strong they are, I would use as an example the 30′ C15 sprint-racing canoe we build. The average crew weight of fifteen paddlers is about 2,350 lbs. In spite of this, we use the same ¼″ cedar planking with a single layer of 6-oz. fiberglass cloth as we will use on our Endeavour 17 kayak in this book.

Will it break? Yes, it will—in the same way that your new BMW is happy on a good road doing 130 miles per hour. But, park it in a parking lot where someone opens his door into yours, and your BMW will be damaged. A kayak is intended to be paddled upright in the water, and in this medium, even the most fragile craft will take care of you. So, in terms of durability, we need to consider what will happen when we take the craft out of its intended medium. In the same way that my Volvo will fold up in stages if I hit a tree, the structure of your kayak should be up to the unintended conditions that it could find itself in.

In a kayak, the paddler is sitting at water level, so visibility into the water is restricted to a short distance ahead. In spite of this, kayaks seldom move so fast that there is not time to react before running out of water. The sea kayak has the advantage of being used primarily on open water and is not subject to the same hostile environment as the whitewater kayak. Most damage that will be sustained will be while getting on and off the beach and transporting the boat.

An Endeavour 17 covered with 6-oz. 'glass cloth is strong with a reasonable weight (47 lbs. with seat, rudder, and bulkheads); it may be built lighter if care is taken when the craft is not in the water.

The following article by J. R. Watson appeared in *Epoxyworks*, Number 10, Winter 1998, and is the first scientific testing that I have seen that gives us numbers that relate to the strength of our kayak. One piece of the equation that the numbers do not reflect is the shape of the kayak hull. The shallow arch of the hull should deflect less in practice than the flat 12″ × 12″ test panel. Another consideration is that most damage to the hull will come in the form of a blow from the outside rather than from a sustained load on the edge of the test panel. A blow to a monocoque structure will be distributed and absorbed by a large area of the hull. Because the deflection is being distributed over a larger area, the angle of deflection is reduced; in theory, this should allow the hull to sustain a load greater than the 12″ × 12″ test panel.

How Tough Are They?
by James R. Watson

Once I went over a small falls in my stripper kayak. At the bottom was broken concrete with rebar in it. I clenched my teeth as the little kayak ground over it, hoping I'd built it tough enough. But when I pulled to the bank to inspect the damage, there were only superficial scrapes.

Since then, we have conducted proper tests to aid in estimating strip-plank scantlings. We evaluated and compared the stiffness and ultimate strength of laminates of differing 'glass schedules, layers, wood-core thickness, and weight. The results indicate appropriate scantlings for several popular daysailers and boat components. More important, they suggest how best to build strength and stiffness into stripper-style hulls. Glass fabric is used in wood-strip composite construction to supply cross-grain strength to wood planking. In more

traditional building methods, closely spaced ribs serve this function. While two layers of cloth and ¼″ planking are appropriate for a canoe, it's inadequate for larger hulls. Three good ways to increase strength and stiffness are: increase plank thickness; add more layers of reinforcing fibers; or use stiffer (higher modulus) reinforcing fibers. To measure the effects of these variables, we subjected 12 × 12″ Western red cedar panels to high loads over a short time. This simulated the loads a hull endures in heavy seas, while beaching, and during hauling and launching. We constructed 16 cedar-glass samples, using WEST SYSTEM brand epoxy to bond the fiberglass fabric to the wood panels. We used normal wet lay-up procedures and let the epoxy cure at about 60° F. We built seven marine-grade plywood samples for comparison. We tested four thicknesses of cedar (³⁄₁₆", ¼", ⁵⁄₁₆"and ³⁄₈") with two weights of woven glass fabric (4 oz and 6 oz).

Next, we accurately weighted the samples, and measured and recorded loads and deflections with our MTS machine. To simulate actual structural applications, the machine exerted loads parallel to the grain on the cedar samples, and parallel to the face grain on the plywood panels. We measured loads exerted in pounds, and inches of deflection at specific load-points until panel failure. The ramp (rate of pressure applied) was selected for relatively short duration. The chart shows strength as "pounds to failure" and stiffness as "inches of deflection" at failure. Marine plywood of standard sizes used in small boat construction (with and without fiberglass cloth) is listed on the bottom of the chart as the known quantity for comparison. As expected, the panels became heavier as we added fiberglass cloth and epoxy. However, surprisingly little weight was gained relative to the increase in strength and stiffness. Data indicates that increasing both the number of layers of cloth and the thickness of the wood core will increase the overall strength of the wood strip structure without adding much weight. We found that ¼" cedar sandwiched between layers of 6-oz. glass cloth, the proven schedule for canoes, failed when subjected to a load of 221 pounds. An additional layer of 6-oz fiberglass, as might be applied to a canoe's bottom, increased the failure point by over 100% to 450 lbs, but added just three more ounces per square foot. Most, but not all of the failures were on the tension (bottom) side of the panel. The numbers don't adequately convey just how much energy it takes to cause failure. You'd have to be in the laboratory when it happens to fully appreciate it. The MTS test machine applies forces silently and invisibly (up to 100,000 pounds). At the moment of failure, there is a sound like a rifle shot, then a puff of cedar dust and pulverized glass. We used our Hydromat test fixture in our most recent tests. It shows the stiffness results for a plain weave, E-glass and 3K carbon fiber, applied to one side and both sides of a panel. This data also reveals weight gain per square foot. Examining this data, we may develop practical ways to use wood strip construction. We hope it benefits those who are considering using this nice building method.

COMPARISON OF STRENGTH OF VARIOUS 'GLASS SCHEDULES, LAMINATES, AND PANEL THICKNESSES

Panel thickness cedar strip	Fiberglass schedule	Weight oz/sq ft	Inches of deflection	Pounds to failure
³⁄₁₆"	1 layer 4 oz	6.5	.85	162
³⁄₁₆"	2 layers 4 oz	8.8	.82	309
³⁄₁₆"	1 layer 6 oz	8.0	.73	214
³⁄₁₆"	2 layers 6 oz	10.6	.90	500
¼"	1 layer 4 oz	9.0	.45	150
¼"	2 layers 4 oz	10.3	.70	375
¼"	1 layer 6 oz	9.8	.49	221
¼"	2 layers 6 oz	12.3	.58	450
⁵⁄₁₆"	1 layer 4 oz	10.6	.43	188
⁵⁄₁₆"	2 layers 4 oz	12.6	.66	499
⁵⁄₁₆"	1 layer 6 oz	11.6	.48	300
⁵⁄₁₆"	2 layers 6 oz	14.1	.44	500
³⁄₈"	1 layer 4 oz	12.7	.42	250
³⁄₈"	2 layers 4 oz	14.1	.66	675
³⁄₈"	1 layer 6 oz	13.1	.32	298
³⁄₈"	2 layers 6 oz	15.4	.51	823
Marine plywood				
⁵⁄₃₂"	1 layer 4 oz	8.5	1.47	211
⁷⁄₃₂"	1 layer 4 oz	10.9	1.01	325
¼"	1 layer 4 oz	12.8	.79	429
⁵⁄₃₂"	no 'glass	6.9	1.60	45
⁷⁄₃₂"	no 'glass	9.1	1.20	149
¼"	no 'glass	10.7	.63	225

Darel Bridges

1-8

PROFESSIONAL RESULTS FOR THE CASUAL BUILDER?

How does a casual builder get professional results on his or her first kayak? If you are like most people building a kayak, you want to build one boat and be pleased with the results (Photograph 1-8). You don't aspire to be the village kayak builder, but will instead move on to other experiences and adventures. You want to do many things and do them well, but don't have time to learn everything the hard way or reinvent the wheel.

Is it possible to expect professional results

even if you are still learning to use a hammer and screwdriver? Yes, it is possible, and I see it happening consistently in the classes I teach. Students do it by working on the assumption that theirs is not a practice project; it is their kayak, the real thing.

My system of building marries craft techniques with the control of manufacturing principles. Control is what will bridge the gap between your skill and professional results. If you are considering building a kayak to relieve stress, or you are a rebellious teenager wanting to make a creative statement, control may not have been what you had in mind.

However, one of the big motivations for building or creating anything is to reassure ourselves that we are in control of something. When we live and work with other people, at best we influence and hope for a compromise. When you build something for yourself, you are in control, and it is you who makes the decisions and takes responsibility for the results. Control is not meant to limit creativity, but rather to allow you to concentrate on combining the components in a creative and craftsmanlike fashion.

To understand the connection between craft building and the control of manufacturing techniques, we can look at Peterborough, Ontario, in the early 1800s (Photograph 1-9). Peterborough is centrally located in Ontario, Canada, about 30 miles north of Lake Ontario, on the Otonabee River. Enterprising settlers were attracted to this area by the timber, the abundance of water for power and transportation, as well as by the beauty of the unspoiled wilderness. As their principal vehicle of wilderness travel, the early settlers had adopted the birchbark canoe of the local Algonquin Indians. These canoes were most likely obtained by purchase or barter, as there is no hard evidence of the settlers building many bark canoes for their own use.

The settlers, however, did refine the native dugout with the use of European hand tools. The crude dugout was quick to make and had been useful to the settlers for ferrying supplies and building materials to homesteads along the river. Large basswood and butternut logs were available, and the axe and adze used to produce a dugout were familiar to every settler. The native-style dugout was useful as a barge but far too heavy and crude for serious bush travel.

By the mid-1800s, the settlement was thriving and people had time for recreation. It is not hard to imagine the settler with time on his hands using familiar tools to trim a little weight off the old work dugout and make it look more like the bark canoe he knew could be paddled. With the regatta coming up, why not see how long and skinny we could make it without taking a swim?

Driven by the spirit of competition and the search for a lighter canoe, the dugout was quickly developed into a fine-lined craft. The Canadian Canoe Museum in Peterborough, Ontario, has in its collection a finely crafted 16' basswood dugout canoe that is a consistent thickness of about ½" over the entire surface. The decks are butternut with walnut coamings and thwarts. I believe that the basic visual style of the Peterborough canoe probably evolved at the dugout stage and has remained virtually unchanged to this day. In spite of thinning the walls to the minimum, the dugout canoe was still much heavier than the bark canoe.

Ken Brown Collection

1-9

John Stephenson and Tom Gordon changed all that, if the story we have been able to piece together is true. Around 1857, these gentlemen, who were friends and hunting/fishing partners, got tired of portaging their monstrously heavy, waterlogged dugout canoe. We know that Stephenson was extremely inventive, a blacksmith, millwright, cabinet maker, and partner in a planing mill. Mr. Gordon was 24 years old in 1857 and had just completed a boatbuilding apprenticeship. I like to think that Stephenson came up with the idea and, with the help of Gordon, the boat-builder, worked out how to put it together.

Using their finely shaped dugout as a form, ³⁄₈″ x ⁵⁄₈″ elm or white oak ribs were steamed and bent over it on about 5″ centers and fastened temporarily at the sheer. Wide basswood planks, planed to ¼″ thick, were nailed two per side to the ribs (Photograph 1-10). After all the planks had been fastened, the hull was pried off the dugout and the copper nails were clinched on the inside. The open ends of the planking were nailed to a stem that had been carved from a solid block of softwood. Plank seams were then backed up with short lengths of rib stock nailed over the seam and fit tightly between the ribs.

1-10

This canoe could have been clinker built, as Gordon was, no doubt, familiar with the technique. But the innovation was the use of the dugout as a mold to establish the shape of the hull. As they struggled with picking up the shape of a wide basswood plank that had to be bent in two directions at once, the idea of patterns for all the parts couldn't have been long in coming. These men took the building of a wooden canoe from craft to manufacture by making the process repeatable.

Sometime in the next three years, the early dugout was replaced with a solid form that would accept a keelson and stems. The news of the project must have made great gossip because three years later, in 1861, Tom Gordon in Lakefield, John Stevenson in Ashburnham, William English in Peterborough, and Dan Herald in Gores Landing were all building wide board canoes.

The significance of all this for us is that, in my shop, we have incorporated the

lessons of repeatability into our method of strip planking. The canoe manufacturer capitalized on repeatability by being able to quickly train a new employee to work at a productive level. Cutting a plank to fit a pattern or bending a steamed rib over the form did not require knowing everything about the design and building of the canoe. Although we are not setting up a production line, accurate molds and patterns will control the shape of the kayak and allow us to concentrate on building.

The other component of repeatability is breaking the task into small enough steps that it is familiar to you. Teaching canoe and kayak building courses to about 100 students a year has given me a good idea of the questions the entry-level builder might have. You will notice that some parts of the how-to will put a lot of emphasis on seemingly obvious steps. This is because it is not obvious to everyone. So, if it is something you have known forever, be patient—there might be something that you have missed later on.

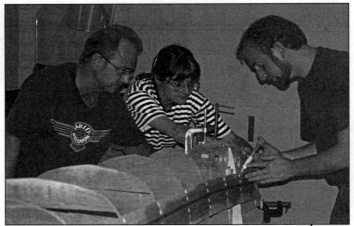

1-11

WHO CAN BUILD, WHY AND WHERE?

One of the motivations for building anything is being involved in the magic of creation (Photograph 1-11). When I see a completed boat that catches my eye, my first thought is usually, "There are a lot of things you can do with a pile of sticks." That's trite, but what I am feeling is much like what one feels when watching the sun set from Negril beach. You know it is going to happen and can anticipate the dynamic beauty, but you don't really have the picture until it happens. When the varnish has been completed, the last of the fittings have been placed, and the light is just right, your kayak will cease to be a series of parts that you have carefully fit together and will become a kayak, a single object of function and beauty. As each component becomes one, something happens that is greater than the sum of the parts. When you paddle your kayak for the first time and find yourself saying out loud, "Did I really build this?"—well, that is the magic.

Both manufactured and hand-crafted objects have their own style of perfection based on how well they fulfill their intended functions and how well their construction has been executed. The thought going into a production-line product happens largely before the item goes into production. The hand-crafted object, on the other hand, will reflect a thought process that accompanies the making of each component from start to finish.

There are other fundamental differences between a hand-crafted and a manufactured object. A well-manufactured object such as a car is the result of complete control over the materials and the process used to put it together. Tolerances for the way pieces are assembled are incorporated into the design, so that misfits appear intentional.

A hand-crafted object, on the other hand, will reveal something of the builder and his or her response to the materials. The way each detail has been developed tells us what mattered most to the builder. As an example, imagine you are shopping for antique furniture, and two chests of drawers catch your eye. Checking the drawers, you see perfectly cut dovetails on one piece and, on the other, layout lines and neatly cut pins that are not all the same width. My guess is that you will choose the one with the layout lines.

There is something special about the piece because we know that somebody got involved in making it. When we see the way the pieces fit together and to what extent each component has been developed, we see a slice of a real person's life. Tight-fitting dovetail joints tell us that the builder had high standards and was skilled in the use of hand tools. The layout lines left on the side of the drawer where it didn't show suggest that the builder, though proud, was also trying to feed his kids.

Who can build a fine wood-strip kayak?

The quick answer is that most people who can tie their shoelaces can build a strip-planked kayak. Anyone can be involved in some, or most, parts of the building process. The question might be better answered by looking at who is building, and why. Sometimes a builder simply wants the best affordable kayak and is willing to put some effort into it. Often, there are other reasons for building, such as dream fulfillment, family bonding, or crisis (stress, identity, marital, job change, retirement, self-esteem, mid-life, etc.) management. Although fulfilling a dream is part of the motivation for most builders, there are many who have been harboring long-time urges to build something beautiful while raising kids and making a living. As they approach retirement, they are finally positioned to do something for themselves.

Then there was the retired airline pilot who was scheduled for a second triple-bypass surgery and wanted to leave something of himself to each of his five daughters. And one of my favorites: The administrator of a juvenile correctional institution was having a communication problem with his rebellious clients. Out of frustration, he began building a strip-planked canoe in his office. Before long, the kids were hanging around, asking questions and offering to help. Having found a mutual interest, with a language they all understood, he was able to expand the communication and eventually change the attitude of the whole institution.

A boatbuilding project of a manageable size is a great family project. In one WoodenBoat School class, I had the pleasure of working with three generations on one canoe. When kids reach their teens, the number of activities that appeal to the whole family is quickly reduced. A strip-planked kayak project has been common ground for many parents and kids—and a way to learn something about each other.

In terms of how old a builder should be, I would think that attention span is more of an issue than years. I have had students as young as 11 and as old as 87 who could do anything that needed to be done. If you are working with someone else and want the project to be a positive experience for both of you, be aware that your buddy's attention span may not be the same as yours. If another's attention is wavering and cannot be subtly stimulated, take a break without making an issue of it. Pushing past this point will make it a negative and potentially dangerous experience, and it will defeat the original purpose.

1-12

I am amazed at the number of people who find building a small boat a pivotal point in their lives. Maybe it is because building a good boat has all the components of a life in control. Working through the building steps, from thoughtful preparation and careful execution to the reward, is a pattern of living that makes sense. Learning to respond to and work in harmony with our materials can teach us something about getting along with ourselves and others. Finding a fair curve will require looking at the line from many different angles before making up your mind that the line is fair; that's not a bad way to live either. There is no computer printout at the end, but your boat will be a graphic illustration of who you are and will remind you that you really are a great person.

Expect to get more out of this building project than just a kayak to paddle. I hope you'll enjoy the process and let it work for you in more than the obvious way.

WHAT SKILLS ARE REQUIRED?
Pride and patience are much more important than skill in handling tools or knowledge of design and materials.

Building a fine wood-strip/epoxy kayak requires a skill level typical of the motivated amateur. I have broken the process down into steps small enough that the next thing to do is always familiar or easily learned. When all the familiar steps are performed in order, you will have built a professional-quality craft (Photograph 1-12).

Begin at a stage of construction that you are comfortable with and that fits your time and budget. This could be anywhere from cutting your own trees to receiving your planking in a shrink-wrapped package. Choose a starting point at which you have confidence that everything up to that point is under control, and take responsibility for it from there. This means buying epoxy you can trust to be predictable and give the expected results. Or, buying planking that you know has been accurately machined and carefully packaged.

Warning for perfectionists: Perfection is elusive, but it is often why we do this kind of project. After more than 27 obsessed years of wooden boats, I have yet to build one that wouldn't be different next time. Perfection is a journey; the point is to take pleasure in where you are today, believing that you will be somewhere else tomorrow. The key is to set a goal that is appropriate to your purpose.

HOW LONG WILL IT TAKE?
It is difficult to come up with an exact estimate for the number of hours required for you to build a wood-strip/epoxy kayak. It will depend on how long it takes to get a shop set up, how easy it is to acquire the materials (and at what stage you acquire them), how fast you work, and what you have to work with—and that is just for starters. About 150 hours is the number I hear most often for a basic kayak, carefully built and nicely finished.

Most people building a fine wood-strip/epoxy kayak will be more interested in the quality of time spent building and the exquisite results than in low build times. Time is certainly valuable to most builders, but the quality of that time should give a fair return.

HOW MUCH WILL IT COST?
In 1998, a complete kit of machined parts sold for about $1,100 U.S. The price will go down if you machine your own parts, or up if you outfit it with all the bells and whistles.

HOW TO USE THIS BOOK

One of the problems with working from how-to instructions is making sure you are not being set up for trouble by too much or not enough information. If the instructions are sketchy, the builder must fill in the missing pieces through research or trial and error. While this will give you a good education, it will be much slower going. On the other hand, if the instructions are comprehensive and easy to follow, you could be tempted to stop doing your own thinking. Besides missing half the fun, it could be a real a problem if a key piece of information happens to be missing and nobody notices until it is too late to be corrected gracefully.

The aim of this book is to give you the steps, in order, and show you what I do to get excellent results consistently. Before each operation is broken into steps, there will be an explanation of the step's purpose. This is your cue to start running through your list of solutions, then have a look at what I do. Looking for your answer first will help to explain information that is unclear to you, and you won't be confused if I have missed a piece of the puzzle. You will be surprised how often we will have the same idea; I have noticed that most people asking for advice already have the answer. The other reason for not letting your guard down is that you never know when the light will come on and you will come up with a new or better way to build your kayak. The craft of kayak build-ing will continue to evolve, and the development will come from builders like yourself who have questioned existing methods and come up with a better way.

Work safely. Throughout this book you will find many references to safety both during construction and in building a kayak that will be safe in the water later. In Chapter 9, I have referred to an important paper on exposure to epoxy resin and the results of overexposure. The paper was prepared by Gougeon Brothers, Inc., the makers of WEST SYSTEM epoxy, and is full of data that will help you make intelligent decisions regarding your health.

Much of the information presented in this book is a foundation for making intelligent and safe decisions on your own. Steve Killing will begin by explaining the fundamentals of kayak design. With this information, you will be able to choose a design that is right for you.

You know that you want to build a kayak, and it must be the boat you always wanted to own and paddle. You also know that the idea is presumptuous, since the word "spokeshave" is still drawing a blank. Well, don't worry. You have the two most important pieces: the beginning and the end. Together, we'll fill in the pieces in the middle.

The design chapter will show you where the kayak shape comes from. After that, you are invited into our shop to watch the Endeavour 17 come alive.

2 | Kayak Design

Text and illustrations
by Steve Killing

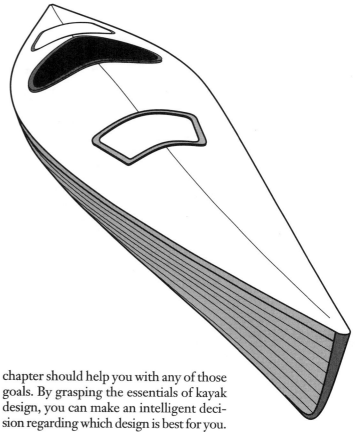

RECIPE FOR A FINE KAYAK

I was fussing over the details of a new kayak drawing when a client stopped by to chat. He peered at my work for a moment and then, with a puzzled expression, said, "I don't get it. How can you still be designing new kayaks? Surely they were perfected centuries ago." It wasn't the first time I had heard that sentiment.

One would think that through decades of paddling on oceans, lakes, and rivers, the possibilities for variation in shapes would have been exhausted. If there were only one use for a boat, one material to build from, and one size and temperament of paddler, that may have been true. But we all paddle in different places for different reasons, and we are anything but identical in our personalities and body shapes, so there are good reasons to have many designs for many purposes.

Assembling the right features to design a kayak that floats is not very difficult, but it takes an innovative designer to create a masterpiece that both satisfies the customer's needs and appeals to the eye. The combination of characteristics is key. There are so many variations in kayak design that it would be hopeless here to try to analyze each one; but it is practical to discuss the components—beam, length, prismatic coefficient, rocker, and section shape—that blend together to form every kayak (Illustration 2-1).

You may wish to design your own kayak, modify an existing design, or build with care and precision a proven model. This chapter should help you with any of those goals. By grasping the essentials of kayak design, you can make an intelligent decision regarding which design is best for you.

READING THE LINES

The fruits of a designer's toil are presented in a lines drawing. This shows the three principal views of the boat: the plan (top) view, the profile (side) view, and the body plan, or sections (viewed from the bow and stern, Illustration 2-2). The concept is simple—much the same as a house plan that shows the arrangement from the top, front, and side. The only complicating factor with a boat is that there are few straight lines and, therefore, the shape is harder to visualize. The stations (also called sections) are the primary curves used to convey the shape to the builder and are created by taking slices across the hull, just like slicing

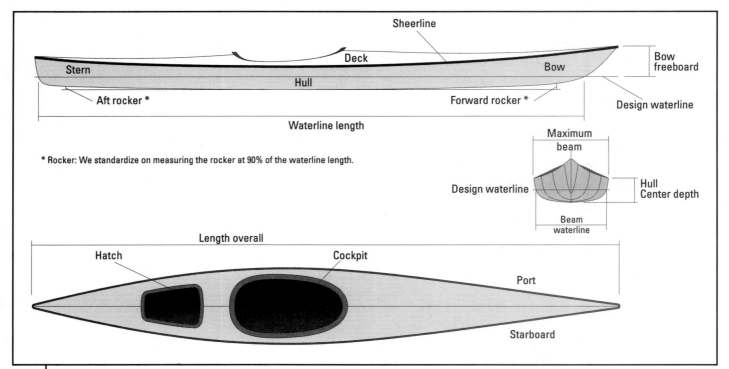

Sheerline

Deck

Stern

Hull

Bow

Aft rocker *

Forward rocker *

Bow freeboard

Design waterline

Waterline length

* Rocker: We standardize on measuring the rocker at 90% of the waterline length.

Maximum beam

Design waterline

Hull Center depth

Beam waterline

Length overall

Hatch

Cockpit

Port

Starboard

2-1

a loaf of bread. When viewed from the side or the top, these stations still appear as straight lines, but when viewed from the bow or stern, they reveal the curved shape of the hull.

For the kayaks described in this book, the section spacing is constant at 12", which is a convenient distance both for visualizing the hull shape and controlling the shape of the wooden strips used to form the boat. It is typical for the two ends of the boat to be separated on the drawing, with the bow on the right side of the centerline and the stern on the left (Illustration 2-2). In the Bear Mountain full-size kayak plans, the bow and stern profiles are drawn on separate sheets.

Buttocks are vertical slices parallel to centerline, which, when viewed from the side, show the long, graceful, underwater curves (Illustration 2-3). Waterlines, hor-

izontal slices parallel to the water, when viewed from above reveal the fineness of the bow and the general form of the boat. Combined, these lines not only convey the shape of the boat, but also help to ensure its fairness (Illustration 2-4).

In my vocabulary, smoothness and fairness are quite different things. The smoothness of a hull is a function of how much sanding and careful varnishing has been done. Glass is smooth, but sandpaper is not, yet both can be shaped to make a fair surface. Much of the goal of the initial careful setup of your kayak mirrors mine throughout the design process: to ensure that the surface is fair (Illustration 2-5). Most would agree, I think, that a hull that oscillates from hollow to bump to hollow to bump is not fair; neither the eye nor the water will flow easily over its surface. Less obvious is a shape that changes its curva-

2-2

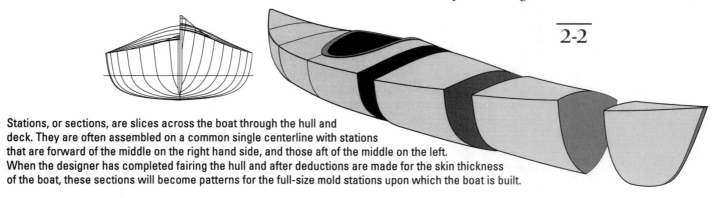

Stations, or sections, are slices across the boat through the hull and deck. They are often assembled on a common single centerline with stations that are forward of the middle on the right hand side, and those aft of the middle on the left. When the designer has completed fairing the hull and after deductions are made for the skin thickness of the boat, these sections will become patterns for the full-size mold stations upon which the boat is built.

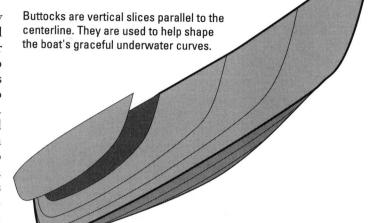

2-3

ture randomly from high to low; it may exhibit no hollows, but some areas will appear a little too flat. The designer doesn't have the benefit of being able to run his hands over the surface to check its fairness, but other tools are available to check the fairness before the hull is built. If the designer is drawing with traditional tools, like plastic or wooden splines, then the force required to bend the spline into an awkward, unfair shape should be an alarm bell. However, if the drawing tool is a computer, the indicator will be a curvature plot that highlights changes in the curvature (Illustration 2-6). This rendered view of the hull and deck highlights areas of positive and negative curvature by plotting them in various colors. A fair hull will have gradually changing hues as the surface flattens toward the ends, but local bumps or hollows will stand out as hot spots in the midst of the smooth contours.

The sheerline, with its gentle, fair curve, is one of the most important components in controlling the look of your boat. If the designer did not draw it with care or the builder did not spend the time to ensure it was as graceful as the designer intended, then the finished boat will be a disappointment. In normal conditions, the sheerline has nothing whatever to do with the performance of the boat—it sel-

Buttocks are vertical slices parallel to the centerline. They are used to help shape the boat's graceful underwater curves.

dom gets wet—but it has everything to do with the appearance and perceived purpose of the boat. A cruising kayak that looks like a high-speed racer or a whitewater kayak that looks likes a freight canoe won't please anyone.

FLOATING A BOAT

Once a kayak is built, it is easy to see how it floats. It is no surprise that without an occupant the boat floats high in the water, and it will sink an inch or two with the paddler in the cockpit. However, determining the flotation level on the drawing board is not so easy. The science goes way back to Archimedes, who discovered that

2-4

The waterlines are horizontal slices through the hull parallel to the water's surface. They are good for fairing the upper three-quarters of the boat, where they are close to perpendicular to the hull's surface. Waterflow around the boat approximates the direction of the waterlines near the bow, and the buttocks in the middle of the boat. Waterlines, buttocks, and sections must all be fair in order that the final hull shape be easy to plank and fast through the water.

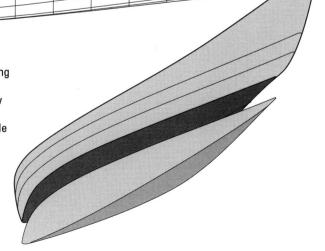

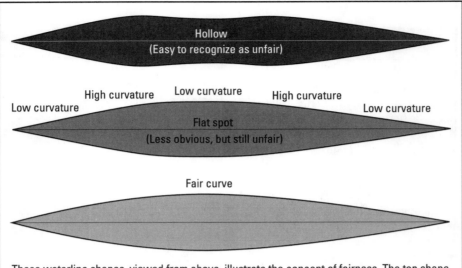

Hollow
(Easy to recognize as unfair)

Low curvature   High curvature   Low curvature   High curvature   Low curvature
Flat spot
(Less obvious, but still unfair)

Fair curve

These waterline shapes, viewed from above, illustrate the concept of fairness. The top shape, with its hollow midsection, would be interpreted as unfair by most kayakers. However, the waterline in the middle drawing has a less obvious problem: the flat spot in the middle, with its significant changes in curvature, is also not fair. The bottom shape, with gradually changing curvature, is the goal for most boats.

2-5

when a body is floating, it displaces its own weight of water, and hence the term "displacement" to refer to the weight of a boat. If our floating kayak with paddler weighs 230 lbs., then the boat will sink down until it pushes aside 230 lbs. of water. If we could now remove the kayak from the picture and leave the depression in the water, we would see an exact mold of the under-water shape of the kayak. If this depression were filled with water, the water would equal the weight of the kayak (Illustration 2-7). This knowledge permits the designer to calculate where the boat will float. If the volume of the hull under the waterline is calculated, then that weight of water equals the weight of the kayak. Adjusting the flotation plane of the boat will alter the weight of water displaced and permit the designer to match the predicted overall weight to the calculated displacement. This final waterline is often termed the "design waterline." Similarly, the incremental change in flotation with added weight is a useful figure for the kayaker to know. Often listed on the drawings as the pounds-per-inch immersion, a typical value of 110 would indicate that for every 110 lbs. added, the boat will float one inch lower in the water.

PRISMATIC COEFFICIENT

The prismatic coefficient is unique in that it indicates something of the shape of the boat, rather than a mere singular dimension such as length or beam. It is a measure of how much volume is contained in the ends of the kayak. The calculation of the prismatic coefficient takes the underwater volume of the boat and compares it to the volume of a container that is the shape of the midsection elongated to the full length of the waterline

A fair kayak bow

An unfair kayak bow

In these curvature plots, the dark areas represent large curvature while the lighter tones indicate near flat areas. The bow sections of the upper kayak show a smooth transition from one area to another. Conversely, the S-shaped edge to the lighter low-curvature area in the bottom image indicates there is an area of unfairness in this hull. In the actual boat, the unfairness could be felt by a mere touch of the hand; however, on the computer screen the designer requires the aid of these curvature maps to let him know how fair the boat is.

2-6

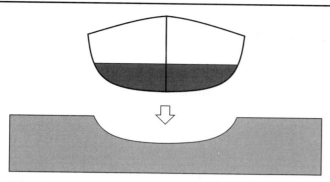

A floating boat will displace, or push aside, a volume of water that equals the boat's own weight. Therefore, if we measure the volume of the underwater portion of a boat, and multiply by the density of water (62.4 lbs/cu.ft.), the resultant weight of water will equal the weight of the boat.

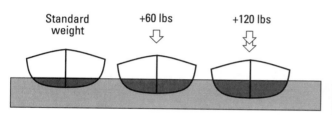

Standard weight   +60 lbs   +120 lbs

The additional depth that a kayak will immerse in the water is termed the pounds-per-inch immersion. The boat above drops 1" for every 60 additional pounds that is added.

2-7

(Illustration 2-8). For comparison, a lake freighter, which has near shoebox proportions, would have a prismatic coefficient hovering around 0.9, because the actual shape is very similar to the projected elongated box, whereas canoes, kayaks, and sailboats (without their keels) range from 0.5 to 0.6. The lower the prismatic, the finer the ends will be.

This provides some rule-of-thumb guidance for the performance strengths of the boat. As the prismatic lowers, the efficiency of the boat in the lower speed ranges improves. A large boat for lightweight paddlers would need a low prismatic to permit them to paddle it with some ease. Conversely, a racing design, which needs to perform its best at high speed, will have a higher prismatic. But the decision to push a lot of volume into the ends of a kayak to increase the prismatic is not as simple as this description might imply; if a high prismatic means a fast boat, one would think that all boats should have a high prismatic. But the problem with a high prismatic hull is that, although efficient near the top end of its speed regime,

it will be difficult to push through the water at lower speeds. As with most design decisions, the choice of prismatic is a matter of degree. Pushing too much volume into the ends of a boat will not continue to increase the upper-end speed, but will become a deterrent to speed. A very bluff aft end will cause turbulence, separated flow, and significant drag. A few successful canoes and kayaks have been designed with prismatic coefficients as high as 0.60, but most boats have prismatics bracketed between 0.53 and 0.58.

STRIVING FOR SPEED
The long and the short of it

Paradoxes abound in the world of boat design, and in no place more than in discussions of length. No hydrodynamicist will deny that length is the ultimate speed-producing factor; and yet, when you suit up and slide into a long kayak, you may not be able to make it move any faster than a short one. As with many complex systems, there are several factors at work, and a common-sense look at the extremes will illustrate the point. If we stretch a kayak to the unrealistic length of 100', there will be obvious problems, not the least of which is the damage to your roof racks. If the awkwardness of the beast seems to be the major drawback, the second surprise

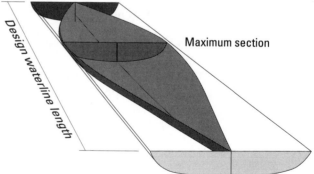

Prismatic coefficient = volume/(maximum section area x DWL)

Design waterline length

Maximum section

The prismatic coefficient is a measure of how much volume is contained in the ends of the boat in relation to the size of the maximum section. This illustration above shows the underwater portion of the boat sitting in a trough formed by stretching the maximum section to the ends of the waterline. The ratio of these two volumes is the prismatic coefficient. A low number, for example 0.5, indicates the ends of the boat are very fine, while a number hovering around 0.7 would indicate very full ends. A comfortable prismatic target would be from 0.53 to 0.60.

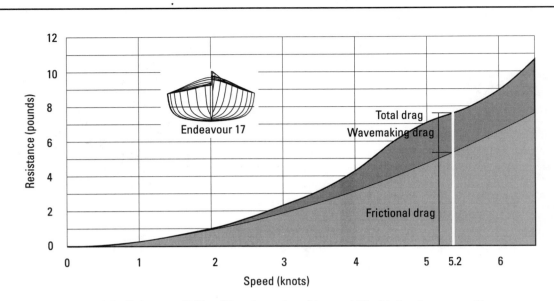

The resistance of the Endeavour 17, like all kayaks, varies with speed. The frictional component increases
in a predictable fashion because it is a function only of the wetted surface of the hull and the speed of motion.
The wavemaking drag, which is plotted above the frictional drag, is less uniform as its value is dependent
upon the interaction of the bow and stern waves. The two drags are added together to give the total drag.
The theoretical hull speed of this boat is shown by the vertical line at 5.2 knots.

2-9

will be the disappointing speeds; the boat is simply so big that even if it is efficient at high speeds (which it will be), you won't have the power in your arms to get it anywhere near that speed, no matter what any theorist says. So for every weight and power of paddler, there will be an optimal length. Determining your ideal length is not practical in the confines of your living room. The best way is to paddle boats, lots of boats. Then you will be able to tell fairly quickly what size is best for you.

It's a drag

The easiest way to learn about drag is to imagine what happens when you first slide into the kayak at the beach. When sitting still, there is no movement of the water relative to the boat, so there is no drag. As you take the first stroke with the paddle, the hull begins to slide through the water and the water resists. This low-speed resistance is primarily due to the wetted area of the hull. The water sliding past the underwater portion of the hull creates friction, which always slows the boat down. If you are paddling forward, the force is pushing you back, and, contrary as drag forces are, if you paddle backwards, it pushes forward. It seems like this frictional drag, as it is called by those who know, has a mission to

displease. Designers will go to great lengths to reduce this drag, because, unlike the wavemaking drag that appears only at higher speeds, it is always present.

If the only goal in kayak design were to make boats easy to paddle at low speeds, then designers would reduce boats' underwater area by making them short and narrow, resulting in much more rounded sections below the water. In fact, the minimum wetted surface would be a beach ball with a cockpit. While such a boat would exhibit low frictional drag, it would have three very limiting flaws. It would be hopeless for high-speed or even moderate-speed paddling because of the high wavemaking drag, the stability would be very low, and it would be next to impossible to steer in a straight line. So most designers, although paying close attention to minimizing the wetted area of the hull, keep a sharp eye open to possible negative effects on stability and steering.

A look at a real-life hull shape will illustrate the point. Let's consider the boat in this book, the 17' Endeavour, as the base boat for our comparison (Illustration 2-9). Its hull shape is a moderate vee when viewed in section. If we wished to reduce the wetted surface more, to eliminate some of the frictional drag for easier low-speed

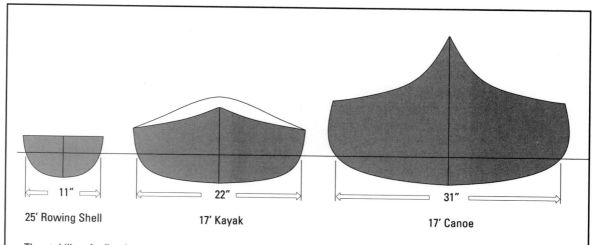

25′ Rowing Shell   11″

17′ Kayak   22″

17′ Canoe   31″

The stability of a floating vessel is proportional to its beam. If one were to enlarge the beam of any of the boats above, the boat would become more stable. The narrow rowing shell on the left has an absolute minimum beam in order to keep the wetted surface, and therefore the frictional drag, low. The penalty, however, is very low stability, which can only be tolerated because of long oars—which the rower can use as a balancing aid on the return stroke.

The kayak is in the mid-range of beam and hull stability. The center of gravity is the other component that affects stability—the lower the weight is placed in a boat, the more stable it will be. Because a kayaker sits lower in the boat than a canoeist, the center of gravity is correspondingly lower, and less hull stability is necessary. The canoe on the right has a significantly greater beam in order to keep the paddler upright even when sitting high on the seats.

2-10

paddling, a more rounded shape would be better. But to keep the volume under the water the same (because we must if it is to float at the same level), a more rounded shape must be both deeper and narrower. Many rowing shells take on this shape for exactly this reason—their designers want to reduce frictional drag to a minimum. The loss, however, is in stability. As the hull gets narrower, stability drops dramatically, and the boat may be fast but nearly impossible to maintain upright—not a useful compromise for a kayak. Rowing shells can stand the reduced stability because they have long oars that act like a tightrope walker's pole, helping to balance the boat (Illustration 2-10).

If we wanted to flatten the boat more, to increase the beam and give the boat more stability, the wetted surface would grow. A comparison of the 16′6″ kayak Resolute with the 17′ Endeavor will show this trend (see page 27-29). The wider 16-footer is more stable and pays a slight penalty in wetted surface.

The length of a kayak has a not-so-obvious effect on the second component of drag, the wavemaking drag. As you start to propel a kayak at slightly faster speeds, say just below your normal cruising speed, waves are created at the bow and stern.

The bow wave first rises and then falls again perhaps a few feet aft of the bow, oscillating up and down, gradually reducing in size until it reaches the stern. There is another quite separate wave produced by the stern that joins in with the bow wave in a rather confused manner. With each increase in boat speed, you can notice that the first trough of the bow wave moves farther aft. Eventually, when you switch into race mode (assuming you have the power to do that), there will be only one wave along the length of the boat, and it will flow smoothly into the wave produced by the stern. You have now reached what has been historically called "hull speed."

This limit to a boat's speed is related to an unalterable property of water. Waves in lakes and oceans travel at a fixed speed relative to their length. Long ocean swells travel fast and a short lake chop travels slowly. Waves produced by a kayak follow the same rules, not because of anything that a designer has done, but because of the natural properties of water; it's just what happens. There is a relationship, therefore, between the speed your boat is traveling and the distance between the crests of the bow waves you produce. The length between crests is given by the simple formula:

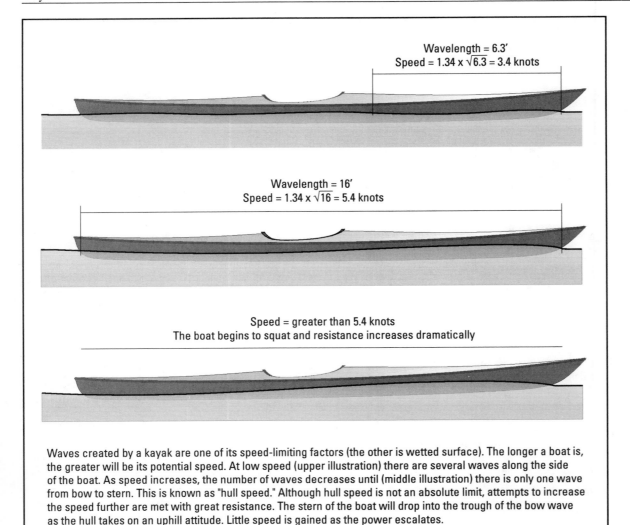

Wavelength = 6.3'
Speed = 1.34 x √6.3 = 3.4 knots

Wavelength = 16'
Speed = 1.34 x √16 = 5.4 knots

Speed = greater than 5.4 knots
The boat begins to squat and resistance increases dramatically

Waves created by a kayak are one of its speed-limiting factors (the other is wetted surface). The longer a boat is, the greater will be its potential speed. At low speed (upper illustration) there are several waves along the side of the boat. As speed increases, the number of waves decreases until (middle illustration) there is only one wave from bow to stern. This is known as "hull speed." Although hull speed is not an absolute limit, attempts to increase the speed further are met with great resistance. The stern of the boat will drop into the trough of the bow wave as the hull takes on an uphill attitude. Little speed is gained as the power escalates.

2-11

Wavelength = 0.557 × speed^2
where the length is in feet and the speed in knots. The equation can also be written as:
$$\text{Speed} = 1.34 \times \sqrt{\text{waterline length}}$$

The length is the length between crests of the wave, but if we substitute in the length of the hull, we get the common equation for the theoretical hull speed. So why is the hull speed related to the speed of a wave? (Illustration 2-11). As one tries to paddle the boat faster than the "one wave along the side of the boat" hull speed, the distance between the crests of the bow wave, one at the bow and the other now at the stern, increases. The second crest is moving beyond the stern, and the aft end of the hull drops into the trough. The hull is now traveling uphill. Attempting to increase the speed more drops the stern

farther, and the resistance climbs (Illustration 2-11).

However, the designer can make your paddling life much easier by making the boat longer, so that the bow and stern waves are further separated. The augmented length increases the potential speed of the boat because the second crest of the bow wave will not reach the stern until a higher speed is obtained. The point of high drag is delayed, and therefore, higher paddling speeds are possible.

Some paddlers will argue that these discussions are not relevant for cruising kayaks because high-speed racing is not the goal. Well, the argument is the same: a higher speed for a given paddling effort equals less effort for a given speed, and I don't know anyone who enjoys working harder than they have to while cruising. Let's take a look at a typical kayak design

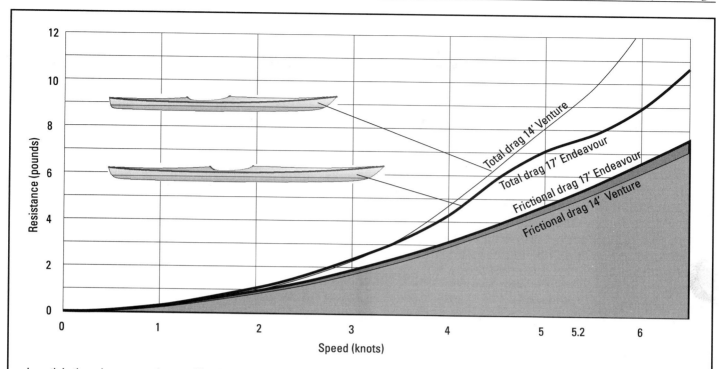

Length is the primary speed-controlling factor. These comparative plots for the 14' and 17' kayaks show how the frictional and wavemaking drags compare. Even though the 17' kayak, because of its large wetted surface, has more frictional drag at all speeds, its lower wavemaking drag more than compensates. In the low-speed range up to about 3 knots, the small kayak has lower total drag. As wavemaking drag plays more of a role at the higher speeds, the larger kayak becomes easier to paddle than the smaller. This analysis is for mid-weight paddlers. If the analysis were done for a light paddler, it would favor the small boat, and for heavier paddlers, it would favor the Endeavour.

2-12

and see how these two drag forces, the frictional and wavemaking drag, trade off against each other.

To make the discussion relevant, let's compare the Venture 14 and the 17' Endeavour. They have been designed for different sizes and strengths of paddlers, but for a fair comparison, we will put the same mid-weight paddler in each. The accompanying plot (Illustration 2-12) of drag versus speed illustrates how the frictional and wavemaking drags vary as the speed of the boat increases. The small boat has a significantly reduced frictional drag because of its lower wetted surface; the short length and narrow width both contribute. As speed increases, the frictional drag of both boats increases proportionately, with the smaller boat always having less. However, the wavemaking drag tells a different story. The small boat's wavemaking drag climbs above the 17-footer's when a speed of 3 knots is reached. This increase is directly related to the short length and its interaction with the waves along the side of the boat.

Of course, when kayakers are out paddling, they only care about the total resistance, not its component frictional and wavemaking parts. The total in this case indicates that the small boat takes less power to propel than the larger boat up to a speed of 3.5 knots. Beyond that speed, the big boat is easier to move. For this mid-weight paddler, either boat might be suitable, depending on expected use and available body strength. However, if we were to perform this same comparative analysis for a 170-lb. paddler, the wavemaking drag would become more pronounced and would indicate that the 17' kayak is a much better bet.

STABILITY: IS IT REALLY AS MYSTERIOUS AS SOME PEOPLE THINK?

Stability is consideration number one when I design a new kayak, because it is so important to the comfort and safety of the paddler. It is convenient that this critical factor is a straightforward, predictable property. By straightforward I mean it is not mysterious, artistic, or controlled by the moon; it is simply the result of adjust-

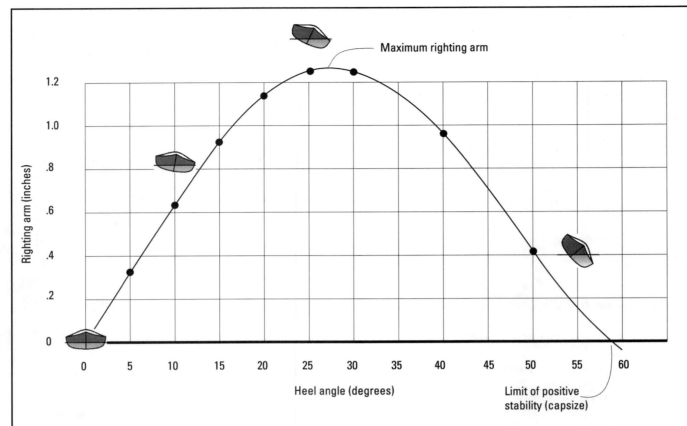

Maximum righting arm

Limit of positive
stability (capsize)

Righting arm (inches)

Heel angle (degrees)

This stability plot for the Endeavour 17 shows the righting arm (tendency to return to upright) for each heel angle. At 25° this kayak has its maximum righting arm; if the boat heels beyond that, the tendency to prevent a capsize reduces. If the heel angle exceeds 58°, the curve indicates the boat will capsize, as the curve crosses the zero axis. This plot is based on a vertical center of gravity, of both the boat and paddler, located 4″ above the waterline. The paddler can alter the effective height of this center of gravity by leaning away from the capsize and thereby further delaying an imminent dunking.

2-13

ing the shape of the boat to meet a mathematical target.

I have heard countless times, from both unknowing designers and misled kayak owners, revering a great kayak shape that had the "magic" feel to its stability, "Man, you can't get a feel like that from any computer-designed boat. You've got to feel the wood when you shape it." Or "getting the stability of a small boat right is more art than science." Well, sorry to burst the bubble, but stability is one thing that can be predicted exactly and reproduced from one boat to another (Illustration 2-13).

The hard science defining stability should not be confused with your personal impression of what good stability is. A boat that you consider very stable may be simply too tippy for your partner. How comfortable you are in a boat, the length of time you have spent playing around on the water, and even your swimming ability all weigh into the impression of "sta-

ble enough." Although the determination of what degree of stability is appropriate is subjective, once that figure is determined, it is just a matter of shapes and math to match it dead-on.

There was a time when the calculation of righting moment, the usual measure of stability, was tedious. Although manual calculations would give the designer a good feel for the factors that influence stability, the answer arrived at through a series of refinements to an initial estimate wore off after the tedium of the tenth iteration set in. So now, with computer software that can calculate stability in less time than it takes you to read this sentence, the designer can spend more time shaping the boat to achieve the goals. Most of you won't have software to do the calculation, so I will describe the basics and provide a few examples.

The greatest influence on stability is beam, meaning the width of the hull not

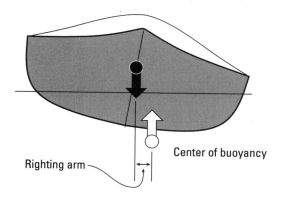

Weight acts through center of gravity

Righting arm

Center of buoyancy

As a boat heels, the center of buoyancy moves to one side. The distance between the center of gravity and the center of buoyancy is called the righting arm.

2-14

just at the middle, but all along the length of the boat. It is somewhat intuitive that a wide boat will be more stable than a narrow one (Illustration 2-14). We have all walked down a wide dock with no thought of capsize, and many have stepped unsuspectingly into a narrow canoe or kayak and demonstrated to the delight of bystanders that narrow boats have little stability. But it is not just the width of the boat in the midsection that influences stability. Two boats, both with a maximum beam on the waterline of 25″, but one diamond-shaped in plan view and the other much more rounded, will have quite disparate stabilities (Illustration 2-15). Those mathematical stability calculations I discussed earlier include, as one of their primary factors, the width of the boat on the waterline at each station. Those values are then cubed (multiplied by themselves three times). That gives a heavy weighting to the larger values near the center of the boat, but the beam at the ends is still significant. You can also appreciate that since the cube of the beam influences stability, a small increase in the width of a boat makes a significant change in stability. Take heed that the difference between two similarly shaped boats, one with a beam of 23 inches and the other with a beam of 24 inches, is very significant.

The surprising fact is that there is almost no effect on the transverse (side-to-side) stability when the length is changed. The discussion of the influence of length on stability is a bit unfair, because so many other things change with length, like the volume under the water and the overall weight. However, if we were to examine two boats, one just a slightly stretched version of the other, the righting moment—the factor that is so important to you when you step in at the dock—would be the same. If the beams are the same, the stability will be the same.

Secondary stability is a rather loose term that describes how the boat feels when it gets near the point of capsize. (Illustration 2-16). Some descriptions of canoes and kayaks may mention, "This boat has a moderate initial stability and very high secondary stability." The dis-

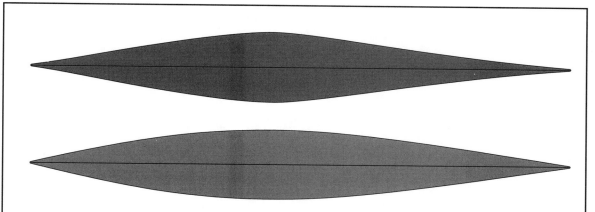

The entire waterline shape needs to be analyzed to correctly calculate stability. Both these underwater views of a kayak hull show the same waterline beam of 25″, but the more diamond-shaped hull with the finer ends has significantly less stability. Although beam of the waterline at the widest point is of significance, widening the waterline either side of the midsection will increase the stability.

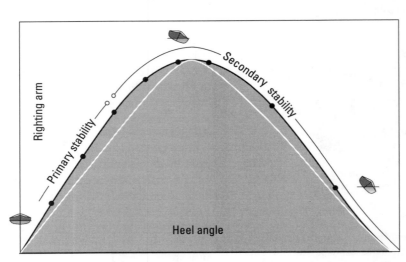

Righting arm

Primary stability

Secondary stability

Heel angle

The loose terms "primary" and "secondary" stability are often used to describe the characteristics of the righting-arm curve. The primary segment occurs in the linear portion of the curve, often up to about 15° of heel. At this point the rate of increase of stability that the kayaker feels as the boat heels begins to taper off. The boat starts to feel less secure. This is the beginning of the secondary portion of the curve. A boat that is described as having good secondary stability would have a gradual top to the curve; this permits the paddler to sense when the boat is becoming unstable. The white curve, although reaching the same peak as the dark line, has a very abrupt top that gives little warning of the change in stability. This kayak would not be forgiving.

2-16

cussions are usually rather inexact in nature, but they are trying to describe the shape of the righting moment curve as the boat heels. You can appreciate that, as the boat begins to tip (heel), the width of boat immersed in the water will vary. A boat with a lot of flare above the waterline will pick up width and stability as it heels. A boat with tumblehome above the waterline, typical of many whitewater kayaks, will quickly reduce its stability. All kayaks will reach a point (the limit of positive stability) when the stability curve slides through zero. At that point, the boat is quite happy to turn upside down.

SYMMETRY: I THOUGHT ALL BOATS WERE SYMMETRICAL

Most traditional canoes are symmetrical—both from side to side (assuming a competent builder) and front to back. With the stern the same shape as the bow, it can be paddled in either direction with acceptable results (Illustration 2-17). The boat was shaped this way to make the craft more versatile. With the seats shifted slightly toward the rear of the canoe, two people could paddle it for-

ward, or a single paddler facing aft could enjoy the boat on his own. As modern canoes were developed for specific purposes—tripping, whitewater, or solo travel—so their shapes have become more specialized. The ability to paddle efficiently either forward or backward was given up to improve the forward performance. Canoe shapes are now much like kayak shapes in that the forward and aft ends are different. I would hazard a guess that most boats are like mine—fuller in the aft end than the bow—although I know of few that are the other way around. By slimming the bow somewhat and filling out the stern sections, the upper-end speed can be enhanced; this is effectively the same phenomenon as lengthening the hull. This fuller aft end pushes the stern wave farther aft and allows a higher top speed; if you are a cruiser, it gives easier paddling at lower speeds. Like most things in life, moderation is the key to success here. If the stern, and by that I mean the last four feet or so of the boat, is made too wide and/or deep, then the drag will begin to increase again. If the water flow behind

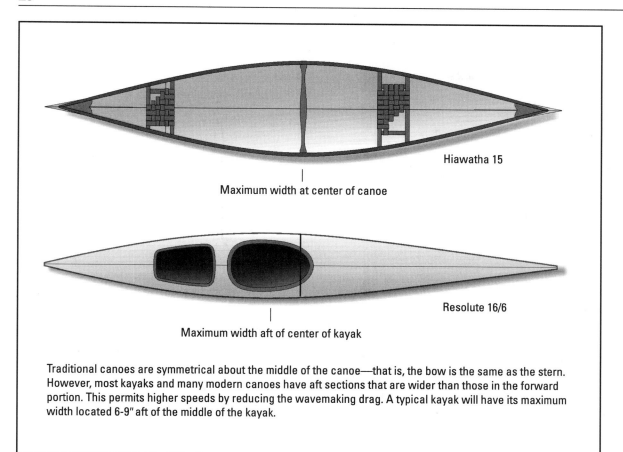

Hiawatha 15

Maximum width at center of canoe

Resolute 16/6

Maximum width aft of center of kayak

Traditional canoes are symmetrical about the middle of the canoe—that is, the bow is the same as the stern. However, most kayaks and many modern canoes have aft sections that are wider than those in the forward portion. This permits higher speeds by reducing the wavemaking drag. A typical kayak will have its maximum width located 6-9″ aft of the middle of the kayak.

2-17

your kayak is reminiscent of the washing machine rinse cycle, then chances are the stern is too full.

WHY SKINNIER THAN A CANOE?

The width of a canoe hovers around 36″, and yet kayaks average out at a slim 24″. They both carry one or two people and have comfortable stability for average paddlers. How can that be? (Illustration 2-18). We have already discussed the science of stability and discovered that beam is very important—the kayak, with its narrower beam, must have less stability. An empty kayak hull is less stable than a beamy canoe's hull. However, when one adds a person to each vessel, the pictures meld into one. The canoeist sits eight or more inches above the floor, while the kayaker is virtually sitting on the bottom of the boat. This lowers the center of gravity of the kayak at least seven inches compared to that of a canoe. That change makes a world of difference to the real stability of the boat and permits kayaks to be much slimmer than canoes. Narrower means faster, because of the reduced skin friction and wavemaking drag. If you are heading out for a race, take a kayak.

TOURING VERSUS WHITEWATER: WHY THE DIFFERENCE?

The destination of a touring kayak and a whitewater kayak are about as far apart philosophically as one can get. They share water, but that is about all. The whitewater kayaker is looking for the bumps, turns, and excitement of fast river water, while the touring sea kayak finds peace in the lakes and ocean swells. The design of the two vessels, therefore, has to be distinctly different. The whitewater kayak is designed not for speed, but for maneu-

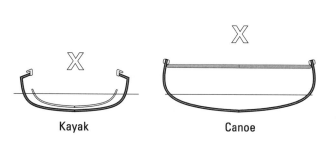

Kayak   Canoe

Because of the substantially higher seats in a canoe, the paddler's center of gravity (marked by the X) is correspondingly higher. This raised CG requires more beam on the canoe relative to the kayak to provide adequate stability.

Touring cross section   Whitewater cross section

Boats are purpose-designed. Since whitewater kayaks spend a good deal of their lives heeled, they don't have sharp sheer corners; this reduces the possibility of catching on eddies or debris. Their sections below the waterline are rounded to ease turning. This combines with the exaggerated rocker, when viewed from the side, to make their strength maneuverability rather than all-out speed.

2-19

verability. It is short, with significant rocker (curvature of the centerline fore and aft) and a rounded sheerline that will not catch rocks, branches, or eddies when the boat is dramatically heeled in tight turns. With a focus on agility, the boats will have rounded hull sections and exaggerated rocker (Illustration 2-19).

In order to keep a cruising kayak pointing forward, the rocker is straightened aft and the hull's sectional shape is generally more vee-shaped. Everything that the whitewater kayak was striving for is ignored here. The short length is stretched and the rocker flattened to favor speed over turning ability. The sheerline and deck are raised to provide more interior space for legs and storage.

The significance of small changes in rocker at the aft end of a canoe or kayak cannot be ignored. A change in depth of the hull of less than half an inch in the last two feet of a kayak will change a wandering kayak into a straight tracker.

RUDDER OR NO?
Rudders may be installed on kayaks for two reasons. The first is admirable; the second is not. Paddlers who will spend a great amount of time cruising on the open water of lakes and oceans will find that a rudder is their savior on windy days, when the prevailing breeze will make your life miserable. Maintaining a straight course becomes difficult and tiring as the wind or waves continually swing you around, but a rudder can change all that. The foot-

controlled rudder lets the paddler concentrate on paddling and sightseeing while the rudder maintains a course. When cruising in closer quarters or investigating a small river, the rudder flips up out of the way to permit quicker control.

A second reason to install a rudder is to correct a fundamental design flaw that makes it difficult to steer the kayak in a straight line in any condition. The real solution here is to change the hull shape, not to add a rudder.

TRY ONE ON FOR SIZE
The value in understanding the theory of what makes boats go fast, and in fact what makes them turn, stay upright, make waves, and keep you dry, is in rounding out the experience of kayaking. When testing various kayaks or paddling your very own, you will have more enjoyment and be able to paddle better if you know why the boat performs as it does.

Before starting your kayak-building project, think about the stability and performance that is appropriate for you and make some informed decisions on length and beam. If you would like someone to compare with, consider this: I am 165 lbs., 5'10" inches tall, and am comfortable in boats (but definitely am not an Olympic paddler). The 17' Endeavour is the boat for me. Pick a boat for you, and don't hesitate—you'll be glad you started the project.

CHOOSING A KAYAK
The four kayak designs presented in the remainder of this chapter have already found approval in the workshop and on the water. When you glance at the drawings you will realize that the boats are all of a family; the profiles are similar in both the hull and deck centerlines, and the cockpits in some cases are identical. But even though they appear similar, they have been carefully designed for different purposes.

Full-size patterns are available for each of these designs, as well as for others (see "Sources," page 173). You can also build from the tables of offsets presented here with each set of lines. If you require instruction in this process, consult the Sources list on page 173.

ENDEAVOUR 17

Length 16'11"
Beam 23½"
Center Depth 12½"
Bow Height 14"
Prismatic .56
Pounds/inch
Immersion 97
Optimum Disp. 130-250 lbs

The Endeavour 17 was the first design of this family and is still the most popular. With a length that makes paddling easy and a stability that hits the mid-road between a rock-solid platform for the beginner and a slim performance kayak, this hull suits just about everyone. If you have never paddled before, you will feel confident in this boat after a couple of morning outings, and will be ready to enjoy it for the rest of your life.

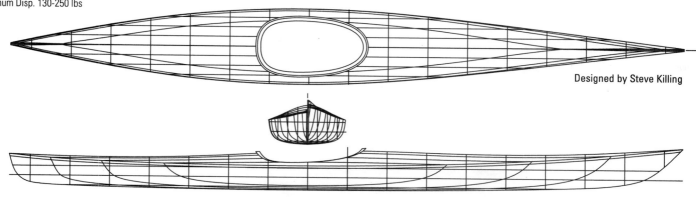

Designed by Steve Killing

ENDEAVOUR 17 HULL
Table of Heights

Station No.	16	15	14	13	12	11	10	9	8	7	6	5	4
Sheer	0-04-7	0-05-6	0-06-2+	0-06-5+	0-07-0	0-07-1+	0-07-2	0-07-2+	0-07-1+	0-07-0	0-06-5+	0-06-2+	0-05-6
2" Buttock		1-00-6+	1-01-6+	1-02-2	1-02-3+	1-02-4+	1-02-5	1-02-5	1-02-4+	1-02-4	1-02-3	1-02-1	1-01-6
4" Buttock			1-00-7	1-01-6+	1-02-2	1-02-3+	1-02-4	1-02-3+	1-02-3	1-02-2+	1-02-0+	1-01-5+	1-00-7+
6" Buttock				0-07-2+	1-00-7+	1-01-6	1-02-0+	1-02-1+	1-02-1	1-01-7+	1-01-4+	1-00-5	0-09-6
8" Buttock					0-07-4	1-00-5	1-01-3	1-01-5+	1-01-5+	1-01-4+	1-01-1+	1-00-0+	0-07-0
10" Buttock						0-11-2	1-00-2+	1-00-4	1-00-0+	0-10-0+			
Profile	1-00-6+	1-01-6+	1-02-1	1-02-3	1-02-4+	1-02-5	1-02-5+	1-02-6	1-02-5+	1-02-5	1-02-4+	1-02-3	1-02-1

(continued below)

Station No.	3	2	1	0
Sheer	0-05-0	0-04-1	0-03-0	0-01-5+
2" Buttock	1-01-1	0-11-2+	0-03-5	
4" Buttock	0-10-5+			
6" Buttock				
8" Buttock				
10" Buttock				
Profile	1-01-7	1-01-3+	1-00-2+	0-06-2

Table of Half Breadths

Station No.	16	15	14	13	12	11	10	9	8	7	6	5	4
Sheer	0-01-1+	0-03-6	0-06-0+	0-08-0+	0-09-5	0-10-6	0-11-2+	0-11-4	0-11-1+	0-10-3+	0-09-3	0-08-0+	0-06-5
4" WL													
6" WL	0-01-1	0-03-6											0-06-5
8" WL	0-00-7+	0-03-4+	0-05-7	0-07-7+	0-09-4	0-10-5	0-11-2	0-11-3+	0-11-1	0-10-2+	0-09-1+	0-07-6+	0-06-2+
10" WL	0-00-6	0-03-2+	0-05-5	0-07-5	0-09-1+	0-10-2+	0-11-0	0-11-1	0-10-6+	0-10-0	0-08-7	0-07-3+	0-05-7+
12" WL	0-00-2	0-02-5+	0-04-7+	0-06-7+	0-08-4	0-09-5	0-10-2	0-10-3	0-10-0	0-09-1+	0-08-0	0-06-4+	0-05-0
14" WL			0-01-3	0-03-3+	0-05-1+	0-06-3	0-07-0	0-07-0+	0-06-5	0-05-6+	0-04-4	0-02-7	0-01-0

(continued below)

Station No.	3	2	1	0
Sheer	0-05-1	0-03-5	0-02-0+	0-00-4
4" WL			0-01-7+	0-00-1+
6" WL	0-05-0+	0-03-3	0-01-5	-0-00-0
8" WL	0-04-6	0-03-0+	0-01-2	
10" WL	0-04-2	0-02-4	0-00-6+	
12" WL	0-03-2	0-01-4+	0-00-0+	
14" WL				

(Endeavour 17 Deck Offset Tables on following page.)

ENDEAVOUR 17 DECK

Table of Heights

Station No.	16	15	14	13	12	11	10	9	8	7	6	5	4
Sheer	0-04-6+	0-05-1	0-05-2	0-05-1+	0-04-7	0-04-2+	0-03-5	0-03-0+	0-02-6+	0-02-7+	0-03-2	0-03-4+	0-03-5+
2″ Buttock		0-05-3+	0-05-4	0-05-3+	0-05-1+	0-04-5	0-04-0	0-03-3	0-03-1+	0-03-2+	0-03-5+	0-04-0	0-04-0+
4″ Buttock		0-06-0	0-06-0	0-05-6+	0-05-4+	0-05-1	0-04-4+	0-04-1	0-04-0	0-04-1	0-04-3	0-04-5+	0-04-6
6″ Buttock			0-06-4	0-06-2+	0-06-0+	0-05-6	0-05-3	0-05-0+	0-05-0	0-05-1	0-05-2+	0-05-4+	0-05-5
8″ Buttock				0-06-7	0-06-5+	0-06-3+	0-06-1+	0-06-0	0-06-0	0-06-0+	0-06-2	0-06-3+	
10″ Buttock						0-07-1	0-07-0	0-06-7	0-06-7	0-07-0			
Profile	0-05-1	0-06-0+	0-06-5	0-07-0	0-07-2	0-07-3+	0-07-4+	0-07-4+	0-07-4	0-07-2	0-07-0	0-06-4+	0-06-0

(continued below)

Station No.	3	2	1	0
Sheer	0-03-4+	0-03-2	0-02-4+	0-01-6
2″ Buttock	0-04-0	0-03-5+	0-03-1	
4″ Buttock	0-04-6			
6″ Buttock				
8″ Buttock				
10″ Buttock				
Profile	0-05-2+	0-04-3	0-03-2	0-02-0

Table of Half Breadths

Station No.	16	15	14	13	12	11	10	9	8	7	6	5	4
Sheer	0-01-4	0-04-0	0-06-2	0-08-2	0-09-6+	0-10-7	0-11-4	0-11-5	0-11-2+	0-10-4+	0-09-4	0-08-1+	0-06-6

(continued below)

Station No.	3	2	1	0
Sheer	0-05-2+	0-03-6+	0-02-2+	0-00-6

RESOLUTE 16'6"

Length	16'6"
Beam	25½"
Center Depth	12"
Bow Height	13½"
Prismatic	.57
Pounds/inch Immersion	102
Optimum Disp.	150-260 lbs

The Resolute 16'6" may surprise you. Although shorter than the Endeavour, it has a greater capacity (because of its greater beam) and is a more stable boat. It was developed after some specific requests for a boat that would be easy to handle on land (hence the shorter length), would have a wide cockpit opening for easy entry and exit, and could carry a great load. If you are a larger person, but don't want to deal with the extra length of the Endeavour, then the Resolute will fit your needs.

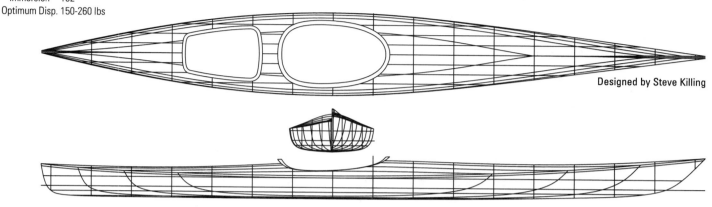

Designed by Steve Killing

RESOLUTE 16'6" HULL

Table of Heights

Station No.	16	15	14	13	12	11	10	9	8	7	6	5	4
Sheer	0-04-5	0-05-5	0-06-2	0-06-5+	0-07-0	0-07-1	0-07-2	0-07-2+	0-07-1+	0-07-0	0-06-5+	0-06-2	0-05-5+
2" Buttock		1-00-6	1-01-5+	1-01-7+	1-02-0+	1-02-1	1-02-1	1-02-1	1-02-1	1-02-0+	1-01-7+	1-01-5+	1-01-3
4" Buttock			1-00-7	1-01-4+	1-01-6+	1-02-0	1-02-0	1-02-0	1-02-0	1-01-7	1-01-6	1-01-3+	1-00-6+
6" Buttock			0-07-7+	1-00-7+	1-01-4	1-01-6	1-01-6+	1-01-7	1-01-6+	1-01-5+	1-01-3	1-00-6	0-10-6
8" Buttock				0-09-6	1-00-6+	1-01-3	1-01-4+	1-01-4+	1-01-4	1-01-2	1-00-4+	0-10-0+	
10" Buttock					0-08-7+	1-00-2+	1-00-7	1-01-0	1-00-6	0-11-7+	0-07-6+		
Profile	1-00-3+	1-01-7+	1-02-0+	1-02-1	1-02-1+	1-02-1+	1-02-2	1-02-2	1-02-1+	1-02-1+	1-02-0+	1-01-7+	1-01-5+

(continued below)

Station No.	3	2	1	0
Sheer	0-05-0	0-04-0	0-02-6+	0-01-3+
2" Buttock	1-00-6+	0-11-1+	0-03-2	
4" Buttock	0-11-0			
6" Buttock				
8" Buttock				
10" Buttock				
Profile	1-01-3+	1-01-0+	0-11-6+	0-04-2

Table of Half Breadths

Station No.	16	15	14	13	12	11	10	9	8	7	6	5	4
Sheer	0-00-5+	0-03-4+	0-06-1+	0-08-3+	0-10-2	0-11-4	1-00-2	1-00-3+	1-00-1	0-11-2+	0-10-1	0-08-5+	0-07-1
4" WL													
6" WL	0-00-5	0-03-4+											0-07-0+
8" WL	0-00-4	0-03-2+	0-06-0	0-08-2	0-10-1	0-11-3+	1-00-1+	1-00-3	1-00-0+	0-11-1+	0-10-0	0-08-3+	0-06-6
10" WL	0-00-2+	0-03-0+	0-05-5	0-07-7+	0-09-6	0-11-0+	0-11-6+	1-00-0+	0-11-5+	0-10-6+	0-09-4+	0-08-0	0-06-2+
12" WL	0-00-0	0-02-4	0-04-7+	0-07-1	0-09-0	0-10-2	0-11-0	0-11-1+	0-10-6+	0-09-7+	0-08-4+	0-07-0	0-05-1
14" WL			0-00-4+	0-01-5	0-02-6+	0-03-7	0-04-4+	0-04-5	0-04-1	0-03-0+	0-01-3		

(continued below)

Station No.	3	2	1	0
Sheer	0-05-3+	0-03-6	0-02-0+	0-00-2+
4" WL			0-01-7	0-00-0
6" WL	0-05-2+	0-03-3+	0-01-4+	
8" WL	0-05-0	0-03-0+	0-01-1+	
10" WL	0-04-3+	0-02-4	0-00-5+	
12" WL	0-03-2	0-01-3+		
14" WL				

(Resolute 16'6" Deck Offset Tables on following page.)

RESOLUTE 16'6" DECK

Table of Heights

Station No.	16	15	14	13	12	11	10	9	8	7	6	5	4
Sheer	0-04-5+	0-05-0+	0-05-2	0-05-2	0-05-0	0-04-3	0-03-5+	0-03-0+	0-02-6+	0-02-7+	0-03-2	0-03-4+	0-03-5+
2" Buttock		0-05-3	0-05-4	0-05-3+	0-05-1+	0-04-5	0-04-0	0-03-3	0-03-1	0-03-2+	0-03-5	0-03-7+	0-04-0+
4" Buttock			0-05-7	0-05-6	0-05-4+	0-05-0+	0-04-4	0-04-0	0-03-6+	0-04-0	0-04-2	0-04-4+	0-04-5+
6" Buttock				0-06-3+	0-06-2	0-06-0	0-05-5	0-05-1+	0-04-6+	0-04-5+	0-04-7	0-05-1	0-05-2+	0-05-3+
8" Buttock					0-06-6	0-06-4+	0-06-2	0-06-0	0-05-6	0-05-5+	0-05-6+	0-06-0	0-06-1+
10" Buttock						0-07-1	0-06-7	0-06-5+	0-06-4+	0-06-4	0-06-5	0-06-7	
Profile	0-04-7	0-05-7	0-06-4	0-06-7+	0-07-2	0-07-3+	0-07-4+	0-07-4+	0-07-4	0-07-2+	0-07-0	0-06-4	0-06-0

(continued below)

Station No.	3	2	1	0
Sheer	0-03-4+	0-03-1+	0-02-4	0-01-5
2" Buttock	0-03-7+	0-03-4+	0-03-0	
4" Buttock	0-04-5			
6" Buttock				
8" Buttock				
10" Buttock				
Profile	0-05-1+	0-04-2	0-03-0+	0-01-6

Table of Half Breadths

Station No.	16	15	14	13	12	11	10	9	8	7	6	5	4
Sheer	0-00-7+	0-03-6+	0-06-3	0-08-5	0-10-3+	0-11-5+	1-00-3+	1-00-5	1-00-2+	0-11-4	0-10-2	0-08-6+	0-07-2

(continued below)

Station No.	3	2	1	0
Sheer	0-05-4+	0-03-7+	0-02-2	0-00-4+

VENTURE 14

Length 14'0"
Beam 22"
Center Depth 12"
Bow Height 13"
Prismatic .56
Pounds/inch
  Immersion 74
Optimum Disp. 90-200 lbs

For smaller paddlers, the Venture 14 has all the looks of the large kayaks, but in a compact sporty little package. The stems are more vertical to fit the aesthetics of a smaller boat by maintaining a reasonable waterline length, even though the overall length has been reduced. If you weigh 150 lbs or less, this is the boat for you.

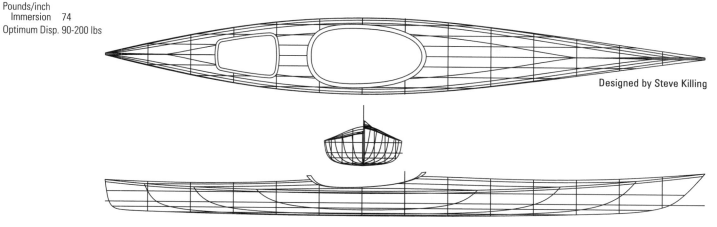

Designed by Steve Killing

VENTURE 14 HULL

Table of Heights

Station No	13	12	11	10	9	8	7	6	5	4	3	2	1
Sheer	0-04-7	0-05-5	0-06-0	0-06-2+	0-06-4	0-06-4+	0-06-3+	0-06-2	0-05-6+	0-05-2+	0-04-4+	0-03-4+	0-02-2
2" Buttock	0-10-4+	1-00-4+	1-01-0	1-01-2	1-01-3	1-01-3	1-01-2+	1-01-2	1-01-0+	1-00-5+	1-00-0+	0-10-0	
4" Buttock		0-11-1+	1-00-5	1-01-0+	1-01-1+	1-01-1+	1-01-1	1-01-0	1-00-5+	1-00-0	0-09-6		
6" Buttock			0-11-3+	1-00-4+	1-00-7	1-00-7+	1-00-6+	1-00-4+	0-11-7	0-09-3+			
8" Buttock				0-11-1	1-00-1	1-00-2+	1-00-1	0-11-3+	0-08-1				
10" Buttock					0-09-0	0-10-2	0-09-4						
Profile	1-00-4+	1-00-7	1-01-1	1-01-2+	1-01-3+	1-01-3+	1-01-3+	1-01-3	1-01-2	1-01-0	1-00-5+	1-00-2	0-10-5+

Table of Half Breadths

Station No	13	12	11	10	9	8	7	6	5	4	3	2	1
Sheer	0-02-7+	0-05-4+	0-07-6	0-09-3	0-10-3	0-10-6	0-10-4	0-09-5	0-08-2+	0-06-6	0-05-0+	0-03-3	0-01-5
4" WL												0-03-2+	0-01-3+
6" WL	0-02-6+	0-05-4							0-08-2	0-06-5+	0-04-7	0-03-0+	0-01-1
8" WL	0-02-4+	0-05-1+	0-07-3+	0-09-1	0-10-1+	0-10-4+	0-10-2	0-09-3	0-08-0	0-06-3	0-04-4+	0-02-5	0-00-5+
10" WL	0-02-1+	0-04-5	0-06-7	0-08-5	0-09-5+	0-10-0+	0-09-6+	0-08-7	0-07-3+	0-05-6	0-03-7	0-02-0	0-00-1+
12" WL	0-01-1	0-03-1	0-05-2+	0-07-0+	0-08-1+	0-08-4+	0-08-2	0-07-2+	0-05-6+	0-04-0	0-02-1	0-00-4	

VENTURE 14 DECK

Table of Heights

Station No.	13	12	11	10	9	8	7	6	5	4	3	2	1
Sheer	0-04-3+	0-04-5	0-04-4+	0-04-1	0-03-3	0-02-5+	0-02-2+	0-02-4	0-02-7	0-03-1	0-03-1	0-02-6	0-02-0
2" Buttock	0-04-6+	0-04-7+	0-04-6+	0-04-3+	0-03-6	0-03-0+	0-02-6	0-02-7+	0-03-2+	0-03-4+	0-03-4	0-03-1+	
4" Buttock		0-05-3	0-05-1+	0-04-7	0-04-2+	0-03-6	0-03-4	0-03-6	0-04-0+	0-04-2	0-04-2		
6" Buttock			0-05-6	0-05-3+	0-05-0+	0-04-5+	0-04-4+	0-04-6	0-05-0	0-05-1			
8" Buttock				0-06-0+	0-05-6+	0-05-4+	0-05-4+	0-05-5+	0-05-7				
10" Buttock					0-06-4	0-06-3+	0-06-3+						
Profile	0-05-1+	0-05-7	0-06-2+	0-06-4+	0-06-6	0-06-6+	0-06-5+	0-06-4	0-06-1	0-05-4+	0-04-6+	0-03-6+	0-02-4

Table of Half Breadths

Station No.	13	12	11	10	9	8	7	6	5	4	3	2	1
Sheer	0-03-1	0-05-5+	0-07-7+	0-09-4+	0-10-4+	0-10-7	0-10-5	0-09-6	0-08-3+	0-06-7	0-05-1+	0-03-4	0-01-6+

RELIANCE 20'8"

Length	20'8"
Beam	28½"
Center Depth	16"
Bow Height	16"
Prismatic	.56
Pounds/inch Immersion	145
Optimum Disp.	250-500 lbs

It is always more fun travelling with a friend, and the Reliance tandem kayak does this well. The boat has lots of storage capacity, comfortable stability, and good looks. During construction, you'll probably wonder why the deck has such an odd shape—but when you cut in the holes for the cockpits, the rise and fall of the deck centerline will make total sense. For serious tripping with a partner, this is your boat.

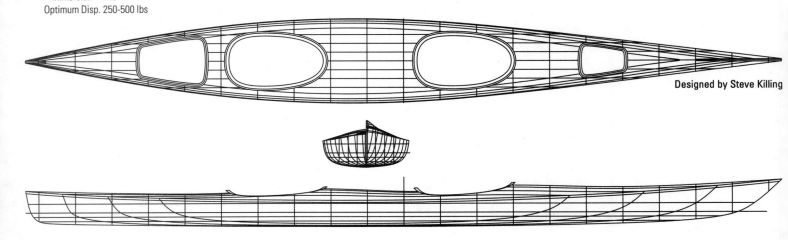

Designed by Steve Killing

RELIANCE 20.5 HULL
Table of Heights

Station No.	20	19	18	17	16	15	14	13	12	11	10	9	8
Sheer	0-05-0	0-05-7	0-06-4	0-06-7+	0-07-2	0-07-4	0-07-5+	0-07-6+	0-07-7	0-07-7	0-07-6+	0-07-5	0-07-3
2" Buttock		1-02-0+	1-03-3+	1-03-7	1-04-1	1-04-2+	1-04-3+	1-04-4	1-04-4	1-04-4	1-04-3+	1-04-3	1-04-2
4" Buttock			1-02-0+	1-03-2+	1-03-7	1-04-1	1-04-2+	1-04-3	1-04-3	1-04-3	1-04-2+	1-04-1+	1-04-0+
6" Buttock				1-02-0+	1-03-1+	1-03-6	1-04-0	1-04-1	1-04-1+	1-04-1	1-04-0+	1-04-0	1-03-6
8" Buttock				0-08-2	1-02-0	1-03-0+	1-03-4	1-03-6	1-03-6+	1-03-6+	1-03-6	1-03-4	1-03-1
10" Buttock					0-07-6+	1-01-4+	1-02-5	1-03-0+	1-03-2	1-03-2	1-03-0+	1-02-5+	1-01-6+
12" Buttock							1-00-1	1-01-4+	1-02-0+	1-02-0+	1-01-5	1-00-3+	0-07-7+
14" Buttock									0-08-2	0-08-5			
Profile	1-02-6+	1-03-6	1-03-7+	1-04-1	1-04-2	1-04-3	1-04-4	1-04-4+	1-04-4+	1-04-5	1-04-4+	1-04-4	1-04-3+

(continued below)

Station No.	7	6	5	4	3	2	1	0
Sheer	0-07-0+	0-06-5	0-06-1	0-05-4	0-04-5+	0-03-6	0-02-5	0-01-3+
2" Buttock	1-04-1	1-03-7	1-03-4	1-03-0	1-02-0	0-11-1+	0-02-6+	
4" Buttock	1-03-6+	1-03-3+	1-02-6+	1-01-5	0-10-3+			
6" Buttock	1-03-3	1-02-5+	1-01-2	0-09-2+				
8" Buttock	1-02-3	1-00-5+	0-06-7					
10" Buttock	0-11-4							
12" Buttock								
14" Buttock								
Profile	1-04-2+	1-04-1	1-03-7	1-03-4+	1-03-1	1-02-2+	1-00-4	0-05-0+

Table of Half Breadths

Station No.	20	19	18	17	16	15	14	13	12	11	10	9	8
Sheer	0-00-7	0-03-4	0-06-0	0-08-1	0-10-0+	0-11-5	1-00-6+	1-01-5	1-02-0	1-02-0+	1-01-6	1-01-0	1-00-0+
4" WL													
6" WL	0-00-6+	0-03-4											
8" WL	0-00-6	0-03-2+	0-05-6	0-08-0	0-10-0	0-11-4+	1-00-6	1-01-4+	1-02-0	1-02-0+	1-01-5+	1-01-0	1-00-0
10" WL	0-00-5	0-03-1	0-05-4	0-07-6	0-09-5+	0-11-2	1-00-4	1-01-2+	1-01-6	1-01-6	1-01-3+	1-00-5+	0-11-5
12" WL	0-00-3+	0-02-7	0-05-1	0-07-2+	0-09-1+	0-10-6+	1-00-0	1-00-6+	1-01-2	1-01-2	1-00-7+	1-00-1+	0-11-1
14" WL	0-00-1	0-02-0+	0-04-0	0-06-0+	0-08-0	0-09-5	0-10-6+	0-11-5	1-00-0+	1-00-0+	0-11-5+	0-10-7+	0-09-6+
16" WL				0-01-4	0-03-3	0-05-0	0-06-1+	0-07-0	0-07-2	0-07-1+	0-06-5+	0-05-6+	0-04-5

(continued below)

Station No.	7	6	5	4	3	2	1	0
Sheer	0-10-6+	0-09-4	0-08-0+	0-06-5	0-05-0+	0-03-4+	0-02-0	0-00-4
4" WL						0-03-4	0-01-6+	0-00-1
6" WL				0-06-4	0-04-7	0-03-1+	0-01-4	
8" WL	0-10-5+	0-09-2+	0-07-6+	0-06-2	0-04-4+	0-02-7	0-01-1	
10" WL	0-10-3	0-09-0	0-07-3+	0-05-6+	0-04-1	0-02-3	0-00-5+	
12" WL	0-09-6+	0-08-2+	0-06-6	0-05-0+	0-03-3	0-01-5+	0-00-1	
14" WL	0-08-4	0-07-0	0-05-2+	0-03-5	0-02-0	0-00-3		
16" WL	0-03-0+	0-01-1+						

RELIANCE 20.5 DECK

Table of Heights

Station No.	20	19	18	17	16	15	14	13	12	11	10	9	8
Sheer	0-05-0	0-05-2+	0-05-5	0-05-6+	0-05-7+	0-05-5+	0-05-0	0-04-2	0-04-2	0-04-5+	0-05-1	0-04-5+	0-03-4
2" Buttock		0-05-5	0-05-6+	0-06-0	0-06-0+	0-05-7	0-05-1+	0-04-4	0-04-4	0-04-7	0-05-2+	0-04-7	0-03-6+
4" Buttock			0-06-1+	0-06-2	0-06-2+	0-06-1	0-05-4+	0-05-0	0-05-0	0-05-2+	0-05-5+	0-05-2+	0-04-3
6" Buttock			0-06-6	0-06-5+	0-06-5	0-06-4	0-06-0	0-05-4+	0-05-4+	0-05-6+	0-06-1	0-05-6+	0-05-1+
8" Buttock				0-07-1	0-07-0+	0-06-7+	0-06-4+	0-06-1+	0-06-1+	0-06-3+	0-06-5+	0-06-4	0-06-0+
10" Buttock					0-07-4	0-07-3	0-07-1	0-06-7	0-06-7	0-07-0	0-07-1+	0-07-1	0-06-7
12" Buttock							0-07-5+	0-07-4	0-07-4	0-07-4+	0-07-5	0-07-5	0-07-4+
14" Buttock									0-08-0+	0-08-0+			
Profile	0-05-2	0-06-1	0-06-6	0-07-1+	0-07-4+	0-07-6+	0-08-0	0-08-0+	0-08-1	0-08-1	0-08-0+	0-07-7+	0-07-5+

(continued below)

Station No.	7	6	5	4	3	2	1	0
Sheer	0-03-1	0-03-2+	0-03-5	0-03-5+	0-03-4	0-03-0	0-02-2+	0-01-4+
2" Buttock	0-03-4	0-03-5+	0-04-0	0-04-0+	0-03-7	0-03-3+	0-02-6+	
4" Buttock	0-04-1	0-04-3	0-04-5	0-04-5+	0-04-4			
6" Buttock	0-05-0+	0-05-1+	0-05-3+	0-05-3+				
8" Buttock	0-06-0	0-06-1	0-06-2					
10" Buttock	0-06-7							
12" Buttock								
14" Buttock								
Profile	0-07-2+	0-06-7	0-06-3	0-05-6	0-05-0	0-04-0	0-02-7+	0-01-6

Table of Half Breadths

Station No.	20	19	18	17	16	15	14	13	12	11	10	9	8
Sheer	0-01-1+	0-03-6+	0-06-1+	0-08-2+	0-10-2	0-11-6+	1-01-0	1-01-6	1-02-1+	1-02-2	1-01-7+	1-01-2	1-00-1+

(continued below)

Station No.	7	6	5	4	3	2	1	0
Sheer	0-11-0	0-09-5	0-08-1+	0-06-6	0-05-2	0-03-6	0-02-2	0-00-6+

3 | Getting Organized

BUILDING TECHNIQUE

Before getting into the details of starting this project, we should look at the building technique we are going to use, the major components, and how they fit together.

There is a variety of methods for building strip-planked kayaks—some that you may be familiar with. To avoid confusion, it is worth looking at the features that are unique to our method. Notice the hull-to-deck joint using a sheer clamp bonded to the deck, the use of station-mold extensions on a combined hull-and-deck mold, and the use of cradle forms for working on the deck.

Hull-to-deck joint

The system we use for attaching the deck to the hull was devised for building our Rob Roy–style decked sailing canoes. It

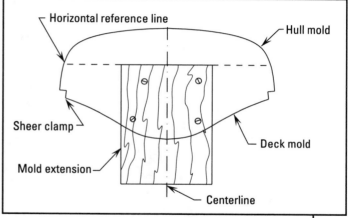

3-2

allows the deck to be removed and easily replaced in the same position, eventually being glued and fastened from the outside of the hull (Illustration 3-1).

A study of the aboriginal kayak structure will reveal that longitudinal strength and stiffness were achieved with the use of substantial sheer clamps. This technique produced maximum stiffness with the least amount of weight, using available materials. While the sheer clamp is less important to our building technique than it was to the structure of the Eskimo skin kayak, it does contribute to the integrity of our kayak and makes a convenient way to join the hull and deck with precision.

Station mold extension

The station mold extension is a temporary extension attached to each station mold to raise the molds an equal distance above the strongback. Extensions are all

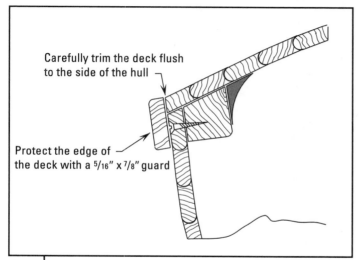

3-1

the same length and extend from the 4"
waterline (horizontal reference line) to
the strongback (Illustration 3-2).

Cradle forms

Cradle forms are used to hold the hull in
a comfortable position while the deck and
interior of the hull are being worked on.
Since the shape and elevation of the cradles are taken from the plans, the hull is
supported evenly, with no chance of dis-
tortion or stress (Illustration 3-3).

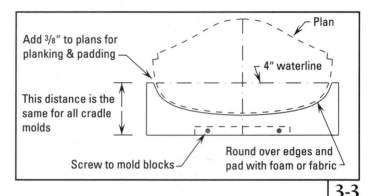

Add 3/8" to plans for
planking & padding

Plan

4" waterline

This distance is the
same for all cradle
molds

Screw to mold blocks

Round over edges and
pad with foam or fabric

3-3

ORDER OF ASSEMBLY

Building our kayak is a series of simple steps.
When each of these familiar operations is
executed in the most effective order, the
reward will be a finely crafted kayak. It is
important to be aware of the order in which
the steps are performed.

The following is a quick look at the major
steps and the order in which the pieces go
together.

1. Cut and machine planking or purchase it
precut.

2. Build and set up the strongback.

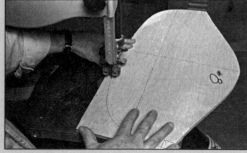

3. Cut out and prepare the station molds.

4. Steam bend and laminate
the inside and outside stems.

5. Set up the station molds
on the strongback.

6. Shape the stems and install the sheer
clamps.

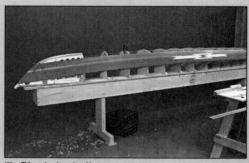

7. Plank the hull.

8. Shape and sand the hull.

9. Apply the fiberglass cloth with epoxy resin.

10. Turn the kayak and molds over, and plank and fiberglass the deck.

11. Remove the deck and molds; shape, sand, and fiberglass the inside hull and deck.

12. Cut openings for the cockpit and hatches, and trim the openings.

13. Fit the bulkheads, seat, rudder, and foot braces.

14. Attach the hull to the deck; install the guards; sand and varnish the boat.

15. Permanently install the bulkheads, rudder, foot pegs, seat, deck tiedowns, etc.

16. Get the bottom wet.

THE WORKSHOP

The winter of 1975, our first year on Bear Mountain, came fast. Living in a 16′ x 20′ A-frame cabin with Joan and two big Afghan hounds was close and getting closer. We framed an 8′ x 16′ shed with 1″ x 2″ strapping. Plastic was fastened tightly over both the inside and the outside of the 1x2s. This kept the wind out and created a dead air space for insulation of sorts; plus, it held the whole contraption together. The natural light was great if the sun wasn't too bright, and with the lights on at night, it looked like something from outer space.

With the woodstove sweating its way through a load of green maple and the shavings building up on the floor, I was laughing at the −40°F temperature outside. This was supposed to have been a winter of trying not to think about boats after having sold my business, Sundance Canoe Company, to Greavette Boat Works the previous year. Things were going just fine, and I was really trying to get interested in The Mother Earth News.

Then a friend from the city brought up the first three issues of *WoodenBoat* magazine. Suddenly, it didn't matter that I thought I was nuts for building wooden boats. It was nice to know that there were other people out there who were as crazy as I was, so I happily admitted my addiction. That plastic shack was a great place to rethink canoe building and plan another run at the boat business.

The point here is not to wait for the perfect workshop with a level wooden floor before getting your kayak started. I know people who have taken the time to have the ideal shop built, and bought all the tools, but they still can't get started. We hear of canoes and kayaks being built in some very bizarre places by those who can't resist the urge to build something. If you are creative and resourceful, there is a place for you to build.

To get the project started, finding a place to work is often as big a problem as stealing a block of time. You can get away with little more than an awning and a work bench, but most casual builders will be looking at the garage or the basement if the project will continue over several seasons.

Basic requirements for a work space

- Dry and out of the direct sun
- Able to maintain temperature between 65° and 85°F while working with epoxy resin
- A bench and a place for tools
- Controllable ventilation if the space is enclosed
- Good lighting of an even intensity
- Comfortable; a place that you look forward to working and relaxing in
- Electric power supply adequate for lighting and the power tools that you will be using

3-5

Workshop size

Photograph 3-5 shows the shop where we built our Endeavor 17. Well, it's actually part of our shop. While the photographs may have been more interesting if shot with a working boat shop in the background, the variety of tools and equipment we use in boatbuilding and restoration could be overwhelming if you don't know how much (or how little) of it you need to build your kayak. In the interest of using photography as illustration, we have kept the junk out of the background.

Our building space was limited to 10′ x 24′, which meant that the bench had to be placed across the end. A better arrangement would be a longer bench along one or both sides. The majority of pieces going into the kayak are long and limber and hard to work with if not well supported. When you arrange your shop, think long and skinny. If this is your first boat, chances are you will have to adapt a space for the project. Even the well-equipped shop set up for furniture making may not fit a kayak and will require rearranging.

A space with about 3′ clear all around the mold is just enough, assuming the parts have been machined beforehand. Since his retirement, Walter Walker, the renowned cedar-strip canoe builder, has been building in a basement room that is so narrow that the mold must be shifted to the opposite wall to work on the other side of the hull. It can be done, but I hope you won't be that restricted. A large space is nice because it allows you to get back far enough to see the kayak in profile.

The length of space required for machining planking in a basement could be a problem. A little more than twice the length of the longest plank plus the machine is required to pass the plank through the machine. Doing the operation outside would be a good solution as it would also take care of the dust.

This is so obvious and the subject of so many jokes that I hate to mention it, but give some thought to getting the kayak out of the basement. Those skinny planks that bent around the corner coming in will be a ridged kayak going out.

Ventilation

A basement workshop will require good ventilation to keep dust and fumes from invading the house. We worked in a shop that was built off the back of the house for about 12 years without a problem with dust and fumes. Using two exhaust fans to direct the air flow, in addition to cleaning up at the end of each day, was an easy solution. A fan in the basement window drawing air from inside the house will keep dust and fumes moving away from the interior of the house. Much of the time spent building the kayak will produce very little dust or noise, so it is possible to work without undue interruption to the household, as long as you plan for the dusty and noisy stages.

Building outside under an awning or fixed roof can be quite pleasant and offers many advantages, assuming climate and security are appropriate. On the downside, while it may solve the ventilation problem, you will attract attention and may have to put up a fence and charge admission.

Work bench

If you don't already have a shop set up, take the time to make some sort of bench and hang up your tools where they can be picked up without walking in circles (Photograph 3-6). Nothing interrupts both the rhythm of working and your train of thought more than searching for the next tool. Sure, some people can stay organized in a mess, but they must be working alone. Unless you are the only one using the work area, you will save a lot of stress and aggravation if everything has a place and is returned to that place.

3-6

If you are like me and you aren't 25 years old anymore, the floor seems to get farther away every year. As one old fellow put it, "Getting down is not the problem; it's getting back up that hurts."

Working on a good, solid bench is obviously easier on the back, but more important is the matter of working safely. Standing at the bench, your body is in a natural, balanced position, with good visibility for maximum control of the tools you are using.

A vise of some kind is your third hand. In the photos, we are using a small clamp-on vise that was quite adequate for building our kayak. Being able to slide it out of the way when not in use is a handy feature. The "ShopMate"-type portable clamping work bench will do all the clamping duties, as well as make a convenient, portable work surface.

Our 2′ x 8′ bench was built from one sheet of ¾″ plywood. It was fast to build and made a great work surface. In addition, we used a pair of saw horses with a third of a sheet of plywood on top as a planking bench.

TOOLS AND SUPPLIES

The tools and supplies shown in Photograph 3-6 were all used in the building of our kayak. There are a few things under the "nice-to-have-but-not-essential" category, but the majority of what you see would be used to build from a kit of machined parts. You will notice that if the parts are purchased ready to be assembled, very few power hand tools and no stationary power tools are required.

The following tools, shop supplies, and materials were used in the building of our kayak. Use it as a guide and begin scrounging what you can and buying what you must. As you follow us through building our kayak, tools and materials will be introduced and their use explained as they are required. This will give you an idea of what is needed and when. If Christmas is coming, mark your wish list in the Lee Valley tool catalog and leave it lying around where everyone can find it.

3-7

Safety supplies (Photograph 3-7)
- Fan that will fit into a window, if building inside
- Apron
- Disposable gloves/work gloves
- Dust masks or respirator
- Rags/wipers
- Solvent bottles (e.g., plastic shampoo bottles)
- Eye protection
- Broom/dust pan

- Bench brush
- Garbage can and bags
- Stool or chair

3-8

Shaping and cutting tools
(Photograph 3-8)
- Jig saw
- Bandsaw (optional)
- Dozuki (Japanese razor saw), back saw, or coping saw
- Portable circular saw with blade for plywood (optional)
- Router and ¼" radius roundover bit (optional)
- Scissors
- Utility knife and blades
- Sharpening stone
- Block plane (low angle preferred)
- Rabbet plane (optional)
- Spokeshave (flat sole)
- Chisels (¼" and 1"+)
- Mill file
- Flat rasp
- Rat tail rasp (optional)
- Paint scraper and blades
- Cabinet scraper and burnisher (optional)

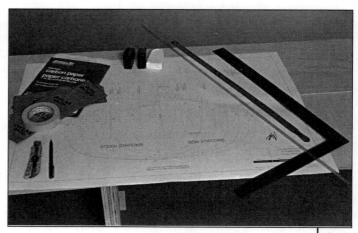

3-9

Measuring and setup tools
(Photograph 3-9)
- Steel ruler (16" or 24")
- Tri-square
- Framing square (optional)
- Level (24" preferred)
- Sliding bevel gauge (small)
- Measuring tape
- Dividers
- Marking gauge (optional)
- String line
- Straightedge and fairing battens

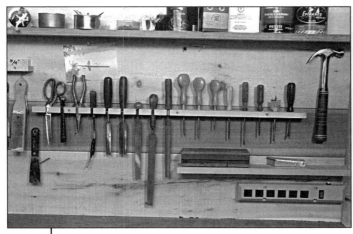

3-10

Fastening tools
(Photograph 3-10)
- Electric drill/driver and bits
- No. 6 taper drill with countersink/counterbore
- 1¼" Forstner bit or spade bit
- Clamps (at least one dozen 3" C-clamps and, optionally, two or three short pipe clamps or bar clamps)
- Staple gun (medium crown)
- Staple puller
- Screwdrivers
- Putty knife
- Light hammer

3-11

Sanding tools and materials
(Photograph 3-11)
- 5" or 6" random-orbit sander
- Sanding block
- Sanding long board (optional)
- Sanding discs (size and backing to fit sander; 80- to 120-grit)
- Sandpaper (sheets 80-, 120-, 220-grit)

3-12

Tools for machining planking
(Photograph 3-12)
- Table saw
- Sharp ripping blade
- Thickness planer (optional)
- Router and router table
- ¼" bead-and-cove cutting router bits
- Calipers

3-13

Fastenings (Photograph 3-13)
- ⁹⁄₁₆" staples
- 1" finishing nails
- 1½" × No. 6 flathead wood screws (100 pieces; use either steel or drywall screws)
- ½" or ¾" × No. 4 or No. 5 flathead wood screws (100 pieces; stainless steel, brass, or silicon bronze)

- Carpenter's glue (yellow; 500ml)
- Paraffin wax (one piece)
- Plastic packaging tape (one roll)
- 1″ masking tape (one roll)
- Black electrical tape (optional)
- Two-sided carpet tape (optional)

Wood components (Photograph 3-15)
- Planking
- Stems
- Sheer clamp
- Guard
- Cockpit and hatch trim

3-14

3-16

Sheathing materials and supplies
(Photograph 3-14)
- 2 gallons of epoxy resin with hardener
- 4-oz. or 6-oz. fiberglass cloth
- Filler and additives (small quantities of WEST SYSTEM #403 Microfibers and #410 Microlite, or similar)
- Five-minute epoxy (optional)
- Solvent (lacquer thinner)
- Brush cleaner
- Color-free rags or wipers
- Mixing containers (plastic, paper, or tin cans)
- Glue brushes (½″ acid brushes)
- Epoxy brushes (2½″ natural bristle)
- Glue syringe
- Squeegee

Finishing materials and supplies
(Photograph 3-16)
- Varnish (2 U.S. quarts premium spar varnish with UV inhibitor)
- Varnish brushes (foam or natural bristle, 1″ and 2″)
- Solvent (paint thinner/mineral spirits or solvent recommended by varnish manufacturer)
- Tack cloth
- Rags or wipers

3-15

3-17

Miscellaneous tools and materials
(Photograph 3-17)
- Tweezers
- Needle nose pliers
- Awl
- Vise
- Extension cords
- Vacuum cleaner
- Electric kettle

4 | Machining the Planking

Since the availability of perfect boards has been steadily declining over the past 100 or so years, you may have to use some planks that are less than the required length. One of the greatest challenges facing wooden boat building in the future will be to find suitable wood. Fortunately for us, a big feature of the wood-strip/epoxy boatbuilding technique is that it does not depend on traditional high-quality boat-building woods to be effective. This means that we will be able to adapt to what is available and learn to make the best of it.

One of the ways we will learn to deal with poor-quality wood will be to find better ways of cutting around defects and then gracefully join the pieces back together. Finger joints have a lot of potential for joining short pieces into full-length planks. Short planks, after being end-matched, are glued into full-length planks on the bench. Although we have seen this technique used by manufacturers of planking, the cutters are readily available for the router, so this joint may now be machined in the home workshop on a simple router table setup.

The only real problem with having to build with short planks is the loss of control over the color scheme. Unless care is taken to color-match the planks at the joint, the finished craft will have a busy, unplanned look to it. If this is not your style, keep the planks together, in order, when cutting and machining. When you glue them back together, turn one piece around so that the ends that grew together

come together at the joint. The color and texture will match and, with a clean cut, will be virtually invisible.

SAFETY
- Read and understand the safety information for each machine you are using.
- Know where the danger is and stay away from it. On a stationary power tool, the cutter is generally in a predictable place; in order to hurt yourself, you must move into the cutter. That said, do not underestimate less predictable dangers like kickback and flying chips.
- Be aware of the direction the cutter is rotating and always feed into the cutter. You must feel the resistance as the cutter cuts its way through the wood. Anticipate the direction and forces the cutter will put on the piece being fed into it. Never feed in the same direc-

4-1

sticking out to get hold of. If not, start them out with a sterile needle.

- Protect your hearing. Machining planking is a noisy job with one or more power tools running at the same time. Wear ear muffs or ear plugs if the noise you are making feels at all uncomfortable (Photograph 4-1).

- Protect your eyes. Always wear eye protection while operating power tools. Protective goggles and full face shields are inexpensive and readily available. Use them.

- Control the dust. Ripping and machining the planking for our kayak produced about three garbage bags of dust and shavings. Think about this when choosing a location for milling. Cutting outside is worth consideration, as it also solves the problem of finding a space 40' long (or double the length of the longest plank being cut) to work in.

Do what you can to control the dust at the source, but at the very least, have good cross ventilation and wear a dust mask.

Watch for dust building up on and around motors, as this will contribute to their overheating.

Clean up before leaving for the day. Yours wouldn't be the first shop to burn down from a bad extension cord shorting out under a pile of dry shavings.

WHERE TO FIND WOOD AND HOW TO CHOOSE IT

Finding a good source of planking material could be one of the more challenging aspects of getting this project started. Don't give up; it is out there.

Of all the materials used in the building of this kayak, planking presents the most possible choices. Some people will want to cut their own trees out of their own wood lots, while others will want to purchase planking completely machined and ready for the boat. Where you fit in will depend on your natural resources, skills, equipment, and time. The cost of planking will be anywhere from gas for the bandsaw mill, to about $500 (1998) for finished bead-and-cove, old-growth red cedar. We hear from people around the world who have used their local wood, so if you don't have access to old-growth Western red cedar, look around and find out what is available in your area that

tion that the cutter is turning; the wood will climb the blade and try to catch up to the speed of the blade. This is a dangerous situation, as it could turn the work piece into a missile. Be cautious while returning boards on the table saw if the back of the blade is not protected by a guard or splitter; the piece could climb the back of the blade and take off in the direction of the operator.

- Try to recognize the optimum feed rate. If fed too slow, the cutter heats and burns the wood; too fast, and the bite gets so big that the machine bogs down, overloading the motor.

- Use a sharp blade of an appropriate design turning at the recommended speed for the cut you are making. (A sharp blade will be safer because it gives you more predictable control.)

- Wax the saw table, fence, and feather boards to reduce friction. For maximum control, the only resistance you feel should be from the cutting portion of the blade and the wood.

- Protect your hands. Wear gloves for handling splintery wood such as cedar. You may not pay much attention to splinters in your hands when you are having fun, but if you forget to dig them out, the infection will give you a bit of pain and itch until they grow out on their own. Keep a pair of tweezers around for pulling splinters. If you pull them right away, there may be a bit would have the appropriate characteristics. Some common alternatives are: other types of cedar, redwood, cypress, basswood, pine, and spruce.

Characteristics to look for
- Weight (about 25 lbs. to 30 lbs./cu. ft.)
- Workability (should machine clean and be workable with hand tools)
- Color (should be pleasant)
- Priced to fit your budget
- Available in the longest possible lengths

Where to look
- Lumber yards selling fence and deck cedar
- Wood specialty suppliers
- Local boatbuilders or cabinet shops
- Advertisements in magazines (e.g., *WoodenBoat*)
- Local sawmills
- Demolition companies for recycled wood
- See Sources, page 173

How to buy lumber
Lumber may be purchased either rough-sawn or dressed. Rough-cut lumber will give you the best yield as well as the most control over grain orientation and dimensions, but it does require access to a thickness planer. We buy rough-sawn 2″ × 8″ lumber, from which we cut about 44¼″ × ⅞″ edge-grain planks per board. Beginning at a full 2″ thick, the plank can be cut either way, so we always end up with edge-grain planks. Beginning with a large dimension also gives us many pieces that look the same, making it easy to control the color scheme.

Dressed lumber will generally be kiln dried and planed down to a nominal ¾″ thick. This is the most convenient way to buy lumber; it is easy to see what you are buying, and the wood is ready to be run through the table saw. Check the thickness of the plank with calipers, looking for a consistent thickness on all the planks you are cutting. If the rough plank was dressed before the moisture content stabilized, the thickness could have changed as the plank continued to dry. This will affect the width of the planking and could be a problem if short lengths of different widths must be joined together.

If planks of inconsistent width are run through a two-router setup, machining both the bead and the cove at the same time, the machining on one side will be inconsistent. Typically, a slight variation in width will not be significant if the planks are full length and machined on a single router setup—that is, if the bead and cove are milled in separate operations.

When possible, choose flat-grain boards so that ripping ¼″ off the edge will yield an edge-grain plank.

Taking the time to cut the planking accurately and cleanly cannot be overemphasized. Nothing will contribute more to a good building experience and a fine boat than will properly machined planking. Once you have to start compromising for poorly machined planks, the extra work and confusion will last until the hull has been sanded and 'glassed. There is enough to think about without having to deal with planks that don't fit together. Remember that if there is a ¹⁄₁₆″ step between two planks on one side, there is also another ¹⁄₁₆″ step on the other. Cleaning up the joint on both sides will take off ⅛″, or half the thickness of the plank.

How much to buy
The Endeavor 17 we are building required about 80 planks or about 65 board foot (bf). The retail price at the time (1997) was about $4.50 per bf for select and better 2″ × 8″ rough-sawn Western red cedar. (One board foot is 1″ thick × 12″ wide × 12″ long.) To calculate the number of planks for the kayak you are building, measure the perimeter of the widest station mold and divide by the width of plank you will be using. Be sure to add the width of the saw cut when calculating the amount of rough lumber required to produce a finished plank.

If there are defects that must be cut around, take this into account when deciding on quantity. An extra 20% is safe for good stuff if you have allowed for the waste from machining; more if the quality is marginal. Use your judgment after seeing the available wood to make a final decision on quantity. Don't hold your breath looking for perfect boards; I'm sure they exist, but they are extremely rare.

TOOLS AND EQUIPMENT FOR MACHINING PLANKING
Table saw

The table saw is the preferred tool for ripping planking. It doesn't have to be anything fancy as long as the blade runs true and the fence can be locked securely into position.

An inexpensive HSS hollow-ground blade designed for ripping will be adequate for cutting enough planking for one kayak. It will make a decent cut but will dull quickly. If you can invest a little more, look for a thin kerf carbide-tipped planer blade. This tool removes a minimum amount of wood, so it will give you a better yield per plank and require less horsepower for continuous cutting. The cut can be very smooth if a feather board is used.

Bandsaw

A bandsaw will rip planking if the guides are set up right and the blade is sharp. We use a ½" × 4tpi blade on a 14" Rockwell with a ¾-hp motor. We find it most useful for resawing from ⁸⁄₄ down to ⁴⁄₄ but have ripped miles of planking on it in the past. It means an extra pass through the planer, so I use it only when I can't stand the noise of the table saw any longer. Although the bandsaw makes a thinner cut, after planing, the waste would be similar to the cut from a regular ⅛" ripping blade.

The problems with cutting planking on the bandsaw are the rough surface it produces and the inconsistent (though slight) thickness to be expected. If a cove is machined on this plank, the thin edges that should be crisp will be ragged and will fall apart when the plank is handled.

Portable circular saw

It is possible to build a jig that would adapt the portable circular saw for ripping planking. The saw is mounted over the rip fence with the blade set square, ¼" from the fence. As the board is fed into the blade, the blade will try to lift the board, so a feather board on top as well as the side would be a good idea.

Thickness planer

A thickness planer is a handy tool to have around but is not imperative for this kayak unless you are using rough-sawn lumber. If you are slowly acquiring power tools, consider a good 6" jointer first.

Infeed/outfeed plank supports

Ripping and machining planking requires level support for the plank on both the infeed and outfeed ends of the machine. It does not work having someone holding the other end of the board. As the operator, you must be in full control of feeding and directing the board.

Cobble the supports together from what you have—saw horses, ladders, cardboard boxes, plywood off-cuts, roller stands, or anything that will make a long, level, low-friction surface (Photograph 4-2). Use paraffin wax to reduce friction between the board and the support to make it easy to feed and control the plank.

4-2

Dust collector

Unless you earn a living in your shop, the dust collector might be another of those nice-to-have tools that stay on the bottom of the list. Dust collectors used to be high-priced industrial machines but are now quite affordable. Tool catalogs are a good source of low-cost, portable dust collectors, which begin at about $150. They do make a big difference when working in a confined space, for both machining and sanding.

Feather board

The purpose of the feather board is to keep consistent pressure between the board being cut and the fence on the table (Photograph 4-3). It is impossible to do this by hand, as the pressure will change every time your hand is repositioned. Consistent pressure to the fence and a steady feed rate are necessary if a clean, straight cut is expected.

Make the feather board from a piece of scrap hardwood with the fingers cut

4-3

long enough to be flexible. Do not try to make this cut on the table saw. Besides being dangerous, the saw kerf is quite wide; use either a bandsaw or jigsaw. Wax the business ends of the fingers to reduce friction.

There are several other anti-kickback jigs (Photograph 4-4) on the market such as the yellow wheels we are using here. They have the advantage of not having to be reset for each cut, as well as holding the board down to the table.

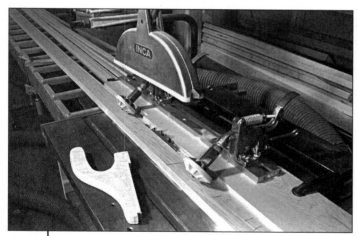

4-4

Push stick

Every stationary power tool should have a push stick appropriate to the tool. Think of the safest way to control the end of the board as it passes the blade while keeping your fingers a safe distance from the danger, and design your stick accordingly.

Router and bits

Machining the bead and cove will require a router mounted in a router table. A simple router of at least ¾ hp and a simple table are all that are required, as the cut is small and the bit is light.

Bead-and-cove router bits are available from a number of manufacturers. They come in both ¼" and ½" shank, and cost from about $35 to $100 per set. Frankly, I think that the ½" shank bits at $100 per set are more bit than you need for the cut, and more money than you should have to pay. For excellent quality and fair price, consider Lee Valley Tools. (See Sources, page 173.)

MAKING THE CUTS

Ripping and machining planking for the kayak will take about one day if you are well set up, or longer, depending on how much cobbling you have to do to get started and the time it takes to clean up afterwards.

Begin by setting the infeed and outfeed supports level with the saw table. The plank must be supported and under control if a consistently accurate cut is expected. Assuming that the plank is dressed to the desired plank thickness and the edge trimmed, set the fence for exactly ¼" and make the cut.

Check the cut in several places along the length for thickness and consistency. Calipers will tell you exactly what is happening, but a ruler along the edge will work, too. It is a good idea to keep checking the occasional plank as ripping progresses. Take your time, making sure every cut is the best you can make it. Any problem with the cut now will be a problem until the kayak has been planked and sanded.

When feeding the board through the saw, watch the edge of the plank as it glides along the fence. In theory, there should not be any space between the board and fence. In practice, the space will open and close slightly as the board passed through. If it opens up more than slightly, try to identify the cause and do what you can to correct it.

Paraffin wax on the table and fence, as well as on the feather board, will make a big difference in cutting down the friction, and will give a better feel for controlling the plank.

If you are interested in controlling the color or must join short planks, keep the planks in order as they come out of the saw.

MACHINING THE BEADS AND COVES

A router table setup will look something like Photograph 4-5. Keep a pair of feather

4-5

Check the cove by fitting two pieces together and feeling the way they line up.

Handle the planking carefully after machining. I find that taping the planks together in bundles of 10 or 12 pieces makes them safe and easy to handle and makes the colors easier to see.

4-6

boards close to the cutter head to hold the plank up to the fence and to dampen the vibration. Position loose guides at the infeed and outfeed ends of the table so that the plank is always under control when it reaches the feather board at the cutter head.

Machine the bead on the first pass, as the feather board will ride on this edge during the second pass through the router; the fragile edges on the cove side could not survive the pressure of the feather board.

Watch the depth of the cut. Shaping the edges should not reduce the width of the plank. Leave a very slight flat (about 1/64″) in the middle of the bead edge as a depth reference. Keeping the flat portion in the middle will confirm that the bead is centered.

There may be a slight chipping on one edge of the plank caused by the table saw blade. Machine the bead on this edge and save the crisp edge for the cove. Marking the bottom of the plank with a lumber marker before ripping will make this edge easy to identify.

The edges on the cove side should also have a slight flat (again, about 1/64″) rather than going all the way to a feather edge; such an edge would be too fragile to handle. These flat edges will also tell you that the cove is centered if they are the same width on both sides.

Pay attention to the feed rate, as this can have an effect on the quality of the cut. If fed too slow, the cutter will burn the plank and shorten the life of the cutter. Too fast, and it will splinter the edge rather than cut it clean. Remember that each broken edge will require filling and sanding before the fiberglass/epoxy can be applied. Watch for changes in grain pattern and direction, and adjust the feed rate accordingly.

Photograph 4-6 shows an example of the router being mounted above the table. For a single-router setup, it is probably faster to set up from the bottom in a router table.

In photograph 4-7 we are using the second router as part of a cobbled-up multiple-cutter shaper— called a "sticker" in the trade—using two routers plus the planer. The plank enters the planer and is dressed to 1/4″, then is powered by the planer past the two routers at about 30′ per minute. With this jig, one person can shape about 2½ miles of planking a day, but it does require considerable setup time.

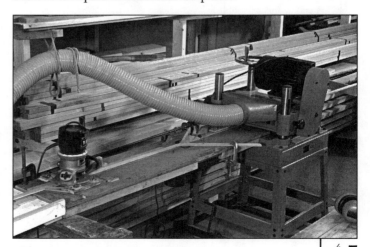

4-7

BUYING MACHINED PLANKING

If you lack the necessary machines and space to work in, buying finished planking with the bead and cove accurately machined on the edges is worth consideration. Unless you are willing to make a long-term shop investment, buying planking can be quite cost-effective. When the costs of a new planer blade for the table saw and a set of router bits are added to the cost of the raw wood, there will be little saving if you are building only one kayak.

Be careful buying machined planking. A fancy advertisement does not guarantee a good product. The suppliers that I use for WoodenBoat School and other building courses are listed in the Sources. If you can't see the planking before purchasing, ask to see some samples and, if possible, talk to someone who has used it.

If you are trying to save money, ask for a price on less than full-length planks, but don't settle for less-than-perfect machining.

What to look for

- Have a clear idea of what good planking is, so you know what to ask for and what to expect.
- Insist on edge-grain planks. Flat grain is really miserable to shape and sand and should only be used for a contrast of texture or as a last resort.
- Consistent machining is paramount. The slight flats on the edges of the cove should be the same on both sides and be consistent over the length of the plank. When the bead is fitted into the cove, the planks must be flush on both sides; fit two pieces together and feel the fit with your fingers.
- The width and thickness must be consistent. If either of these measurements is off, suspect that there will be inconsistent machining on the edges.
- Ask about packaging for handling or shipping. This is very important, as each edge that is broken off must be dealt with in some manner. The safest package will have all the planks fit carefully together into a block about 6" × 6"—enough for one kayak. The package must be bound together tightly to keep the edges from working against each other.

Although the bundle is bound up tightly with the edges protected, try not to let it flex more than necessary. To transport the bundle on roof racks, think of some way of supporting the full length (such as a ladder or long plank). Keep it dry. If there is a danger of rain, wrap the wood tightly in plastic, using lots of tape.

If the planking is being shipped via common carrier, it must be well protected from damage as well as moisture. The most reliable package is a cheap particle-board crate with 1" × 3" strapping on the outside. Heavy corrugated cardboard is usually effective if it is tightly bound together with straps and lots of tape. Cardboard shipping tubes work well as long as the contents are well protected before inserting them into the tube and the fit is tight enough that things don't rattle around inside. Remember that the package is heavy and awkward, and the shipper will hate having to move it by hand; assume that it will be abused.

Joining short planks

The simplest way to join two planks is to cut the ends of the planks square, apply glue to the end of the plank, and join in position on the mold. There is no need to make the joint over a station mold, as the next plank will keep the top edge of the bead and cove planks in line. Personally, I prefer not to make the joint over the station mold. It means that there is an extra pair of staple holes to draw the eye to the joint. If the joint is by itself, with no staple holes, it is less likely that the joint will be seen.

Although the top of the plank is held together with the edge of the next plank, if the glue is fast, you may not get to this in time. It's best to staple a piece of scrap planking (about 3' long) in the position of the next plank to hold it in line until the glue grabs. Sometimes a joint will fall in an area where there is a lot of twist in the plank and the ends won't line up. If that is the case, splint the joint between two short pieces of plank and clamp until the glue sets. (Be sure to wax the splints, so you don't glue them to the boat.)

The technique we are using to create the feature pattern on our kayak (see below) could also be used to deal with short planks. I love solutions like this, where a problem is not considered a dead end but rather an opportunity to develop in a new and creative direction.

4-8

MAKING A FEATURE PLANK

This idea originated at Ron Frenette's Canadian Canoe Company, inspired by the need to make use of a surplus pile of short, dark planks. Some of the gentlemen building Endeavour 17s in Ron's shop picked up on the idea and began doing variations of the pattern we are using here (Photograph 4-8). When the dust had settled, there must have been a dozen or so variations on this theme used in both hull and deck. The possibilities are endless, limited only by the color of the available materials and your imagination.

The crew at Canadian Canoe assembled the pieces for the feature planks on the mold, one piece at a time, and found the process quite fussy. I have taken the idea a step further by gluing all the pieces together in a jig on the bench, then instal-

4-9

ling it as a full-length plank. This worked out slicker than I had imagined it would. The pieces went together quickly, and none of the glue joints let go on the way to the mold.

A custom planking detail, placed judiciously, will personalize your boat. To make one, begin by drawing a full-sized pattern that will include the plank lines and the design. Keep in mind that the width of the plank lines you are going to draw is the width of the plank coverage rather than the width of the plank (i.e., subtract the bead or cove). The angle of the bevel will depend on your design, but a longer bevel will suggest a feeling of forward motion and the larger gluing area will result in a stronger joint. You might want to tape the pattern into position on the mold to be sure the scale is appropriate to the size of the hull.

Basswood and dark Western red cedar are used in Photograph 4-9 for a high contrast, but less of a contrast can be just as effective if that suits your style. Try to choose a contrasting wood of a similar density to the planking. As the surface is being sanded, the harder wood will sand slower and end up being higher than the surrounding surface. If you must use a denser wood, finish up with a scraper to bring it down to the level of the soft wood. Finish by hand with a firm sanding block. Whatever wood you choose, for a clean fit, cut and machine all the planks at the same time and on the same machine setup.

If you don't have access to a power saw capable of making accurate, repetitive cuts at an angle, it is possible to make the cuts by hand. Make up a miter box that will give you a reasonably consistent angle and vertical cut. To compensate for the lack of precision that the miter box will give us, cut both pieces at the same time; lay the planks parallel and one on top of the other to make the cut.

Cut all the parts and lay them out on the pattern to be sure that they fit together and look like what you had in mind.

Putting the pieces together

Make up a jig that will keep all the pieces in a straight line and facilitate clamping the pieces together (Photograph 4-10). For a guide, staple a piece of planking parallel to the edge of the bench, with the cove side facing the edge of the bench.

4-10

Position this guide in about two plank widths to accommodate the plank being made up. Another short clamping piece will fit into the cove of the glued-up plank and hold everything in place. Before fastening the fence down, it might be a good idea to cover the gluing area of the bench with plastic film or tape so that the plank doesn't become part of the bench.

Before applying the glue, do a dry run with all the pieces and clamps in place. You don't want any surprises with wet glue on the parts. When the two bevels are fit together and the edges parallel, draw a reference line across the joint so that you won't have to fumble with it with glue on the joint. Use a fast-setting carpenter's glue so you don't have to wait forever to assemble the next plank. Leave the pieces clamped up long enough for the glue to grab. You may need to do a destruction test with some scrap wood to find out what the glue's drying time is. After taking the glued-up plank out of the jig, check the joints and clean up any glue that has squeezed out of the joint.

When the planks are all glued up, arrange them in order and draw a reference line across all the planks. Use this reference to position the planks on the mold.

5 | The Building Jig

ome definitions are needed before we set up the strongback and begin cutting and setting up the molds (Illustration 5-1).

Station mold: Temporary forms that, when set up in order at predetermined heights and intervals, define the shape of the kayak. Bear Mountain plans are drawn full size for ¼" strip planking on 12" centers. Use these plans as given; the ¼" planking thickness and 1" inside stem have been deducted. Make one mold for each station plus stem molds for the bow and stern. Most plans will use a system similar to ours, but check your plans before marking out the mold.

Horizontal reference line: On our plans, the 4" waterline is used as the horizontal

reference line, but any convenient waterline will do. Measure from this line to determine the height of each mold above the strongback. If the plans you are using do not have this line, draw one by striking a line through the sections parallel to the base line. (Note: This line must define a horizontal plane that intersects all the station molds as well as the stem molds.)

Sheer line: The top edge of the hull, where the hull and deck meet.

Mold extension: An accurately cut piece of board that is used to raise all the molds to a consistent height above the strongback.

Strongback line: This line runs parallel to the horizontal reference line and should appear as the lowest horizontal line

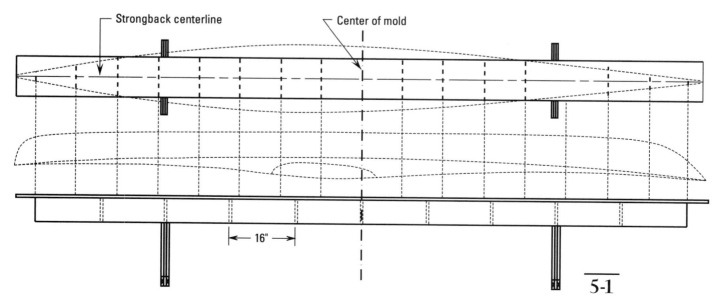

Strongback centerline

Center of mold

16"

5-1

on the plans. The bottom edge of the mold extensions will land on this line.

Note: This line is drawn on the plans and is common to all station and stem molds.

Centerline: The vertical reference line on the station molds. The plans show only one side of each section; when transferring the plans to the mold material, the plan is flopped on this line to draw the opposite side of the station molds.

It is important to draw a centerline (and waterlines) on both sides of the mold material.

Some plans will have everything on one sheet; in this case, the centerline could be the vertical reference line for the stem molds.

Station line: Station lines show the position of the station molds on the strongback. These lines run at right angles to the strongback centerline and are usually located on 12″ centers.

BUILDING THE STRONGBACK

Assemble the strongback parts in this order:
- Rip the boards to size.
- Assemble the two 8′-long portions of the box beam.
- Assemble the 4′-long inner portion.
- Combine these three portions to make up the 16′ box beam.
- Assemble the legs around the gables.
- Level the beam and attach the top.
- Stabilize the strongback by attaching it to the floor.

The strongback is a long, low table that is used as the foundation for the molds. It must be level, straight, steady, and firmly anchored, for all of the steps involved in making and setting up the mold will relate back to the strongback. Accuracy at this stage will simplify the process later on and allow you to double-check each step using a level and the centerline.

In the past, we have recommended using solid wood for building the strongback, but the odds of finding dry, straight 2″ × 10″ planks 16′ long are slim. If you were lucky enough to find them, you probably wouldn't want to waste them on a strongback.

Plywood and particle board are available and relatively inexpensive. The material we are using here is ¾″ poplar plywood, good one side. I found the poplar very pleasant to work with compared to spruce

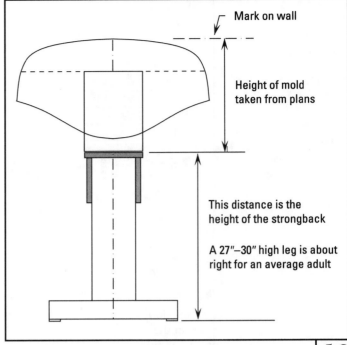

Mark on wall

Height of mold taken from plans

This distance is the height of the strongback

A 27″–30″ high leg is about right for an average adult

5-2

or fir. Because poplar is light in color, fine black pencil lines are easy to see. As an added bonus, the wood is soft enough that slivers are not a great problem.

Particle board is plenty strong, and durable enough for building a few kayaks on. Being smooth and light in color, fine black lines show up well. The only restriction I see to using particle board is that it must be kept dry; if it gets wet, it swells up and falls apart. Of course, sealing it with varnish or paint is a possibility, but if you balance the time and expense against the price of plywood, plywood might be the better deal.

The strongback design we are going to build here has gone through a half dozen or so versions and is about as simple is it can get. It is economical, is easy to build and set up, and will give you predictable results, even with warped boards and an uneven floor.

If you are considering using another type of strongback, be sure it will give you a predictable surface to build on, and will remain this way for the duration of the project.

Determine the height of the strongback

Before you cut the parts for the strongback legs, consider the ideal working height of the mold. There will be times when you will either have to bend over or climb up on something in order to work effectively on all of the hull surface. Decide what height will be most comfortable for you.

Try putting a mark on the wall where you visualize the maximum comfortable working height to be (Illustration 5-2). This will be about 6″ to 8″ below your shoulder height. Pick up the depth of the building jig from the plans and measure down this distance from the mark on the wall. This will give you the height of the strongback from the floor. Visualize this line as being the lowest height you will have to work at. If you can live with this position, good; if not, play with some different combinations.

Determine the length of the strongback

While a strongback that is the same length as the kayak is ideal, a shorter boat may be built on a longer base if the mold is raised about 2″ above the top of the strongback (Illustration 5-3).

A box beam may be lengthened, within reason, by extending the top past the ends of the box. It need not be as long as the boat; the bow and stern molds, within reason, can overhang the strongback.

Specifications

Note: These specifications are for a strongback 17′ long × 30″ high. Adjust these measurements for the strongback you are building.
- Length of box beam: 16′
- Depth of beam: 8″
- Length of top: 17′
- Width of top: 10″
- Height of strongback: 30″

Materials
- 2: (4′ × 8′) sheets ¾″ plywood or particle board
- 2 lbs.: 1⅝″ steel drywall screws
- ½ lb.: 1¼″ steel drywall screws

Cutting list
- Top: 10″ × 96″, 2 pieces; 10″ × 12″, 1 piece
- Sides: 8″ × 96″, 4 pieces; 8″ × 48″, 2 pieces
- Gables: 8″ × 7″, 8 pieces; 8″ × 5½″ (approximate), 3 pieces
- Legs: 7″ × 25¼″, 4 pieces, or adjust to fit; 7″ × 21¼″, 2 pieces
- Feet: 4″ × 24″, 4 pieces
- Filler blocks: 4″ × 8½″, 4 pieces

Cutting the parts

If the parts for this strongback are cut accurately and straight, assembly will be straightforward. Consistent widths are more important than exact numbers. And, if all the 8″ and 10″ parts are slightly undercut because of the width of the saw kerf (7⅞″ and 9⅞″), there will be very little waste from the 4′ × 8′ board.

A table saw with the appropriate blade is the tool of choice for making long cuts. It is very important to support the board on both the infeed and outfeed ends. Besides the obvious safety considerations, you will get the most accurate cut if all your energy and concentration are on guiding the board rather than doing a dangerous balancing act with an awkward 4′ × 8′ sheet.

If you don't have a table saw capable of

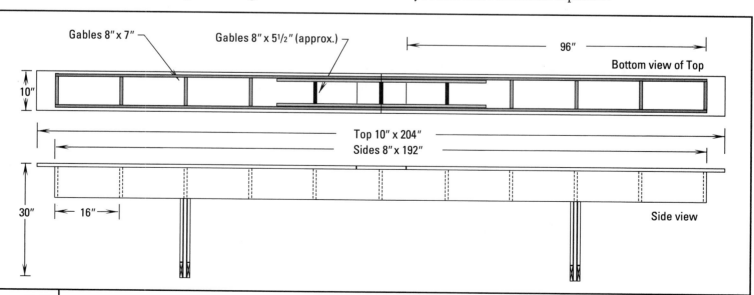

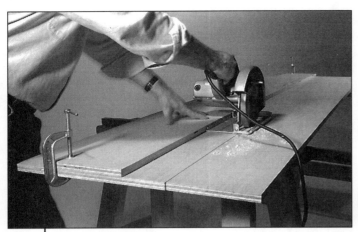

5-4

making accurate cuts on 4' × 8' sheets, consider having the board sectioned into the required 8" and 10" widths at the lumber yard. Many yards have a panel saw or large table saw and will perform this service for a small charge.

Another possibility is to use a portable circular saw (Photograph 5-4) or router to make the cuts. Use a stiff straightedge or the factory edge of another board as a guide for the tool. This is an effective method that will give you an accurate cut and will simplify the handling of the large sheet.

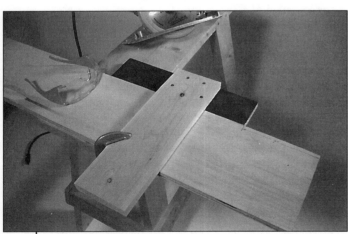

5-5

The handy T-square jig in Photograph 5-5 is easy to make and will give you consistent right-angle cuts using a portable circular saw or router. Make the T-square jig from 1" × 4" softwood or plywood. Clamp the parts together and confirm the angle with a square before fastening with screws.

Having to add or subtract the width of the machine base for each measurement could get confusing and become a source of cutting error. To simplify the process, put the jig together leaving the top of the "T" longer than the distance to the cut-

ter (Photograph 5-5). When you make the first cut, the top of the "T" will be trimmed to a length that represents the exact distance from the edge of the machine base to the inside edge of the cutter. On subsequent cuts, line up the end of the T-square with your cutting mark, and the cut will be exactly where you want it to be. If measuring from the right, add the width of the cut.

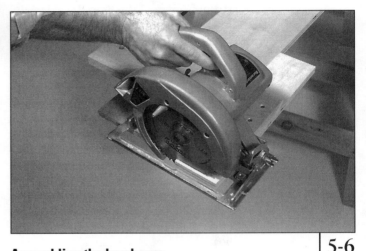

5-6

Assembling the box beam

Our beam is made up of two 8' open-ended box sections that are joined together on the inside with a 4' inner box section. If a longer or shorter beam is required, adjust the length in the middle where the inner box section will span the joints.

Begin by assembling the three sections. If the boards for the sides are warped, position them so they will work against each other to become straight when fastened to the gables.

To lay out the positions of the gables, clamp two side pieces together and mark both sides at the same time; if your dimensions happen to be off, the parts will still go together square. Project lines down the inside face of each board and mark the side of the line that you want the gable to be positioned on. A line drawn down the outside and centered on the gable position will show you exactly where the screws should go.

Assemble the inner section in the same manner, but note that the exact width of these gables will depend on the thickness of the material being used for the sides. Measure and cut these parts carefully to ensure a snug fit of the inner box inside the main boxes.

Unless the parts are clamped tightly

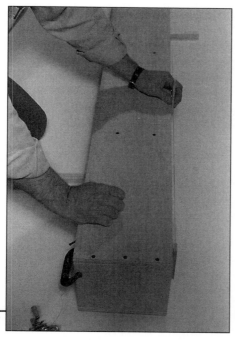

5-7

together, there is a good chance that a screw being driven without a pilot hole will strip in the end grain of the gable before the parts are drawn together. To be sure this doesn't happen, clamp the parts together, and to keep the direction of the screw under control, drill a pilot hole that fits the screws you are using.

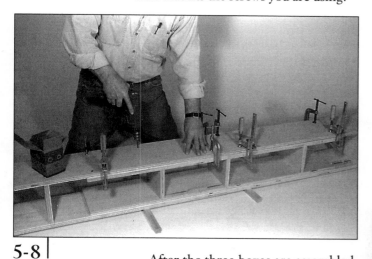

5-8

After the three boxes are assembled, set up the two 8' sections on the floor, and then slide the 4' inner section into position. Roll the three components together onto their sides and block up the entire beam until it is level from end to end. Shims should raise the beam enough to get a few clamps on the bottom side of the beam. Try to get it level enough that the joints in the middle fit together tightly, then clamp it in this position. The beam

will be flexible from side to side until the top is attached, so final straightening will be done at that time.

Before fastening the components together, it is most important that the top side be straight from end to end. Since the top of the strongback becomes the baseline for the mold, any problems with the top will become problems with the mold.

Use a string line stretched tight from one end of the beam to the other with a ¼" spacer under each end of the line (Photograph 5-6). This will raise the line a measurable distance above the beam and allow you to use a ¼" spacer to check the beam at frequent intervals along its length.

When you are sure that the beam is as straight as you can make it, fasten it together with 1¼" drywall screws (Photograph 5-7).

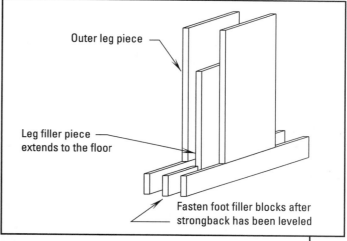

Outer leg piece

Leg filler piece extends to the floor

Fasten foot filler blocks after strongback has been leveled

5-9

Assembling the legs

Turn the beam bottom-side up on the blocks and assemble the legs around the appropriate gables (Illustration 5-9). (It will be difficult to slide the leg over the

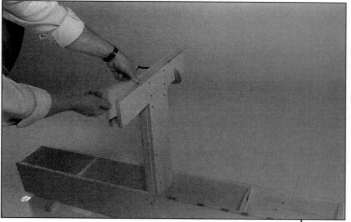

5-10

5-11

gable if the leg is assembled beforehand.)

Clamp the parts together, making sure that the leg is flush with the top of the beam. Screw the parts together from both sides with 1⅝″ drywall screws.

5-12

Consider leaving the foot filler blocks unfastened for now (Photograph 5-10). After the strongback has been leveled, you can adjust these blocks to contact the floor, then fasten them to the feet. This will simplify leveling and stabilizing the strongback, regardless of the irregularity of the surface you are setting up on.

One of the first Endeavor 17s was built in a WoodenBoat School class on the cambered deck of the ferryboat *Eureka*, a floating exhibit at the National Maritime Historic Park in San Francisco. The blocks on one side raised the mold about

¾″. Since "plumb and level" were at the mercy of harbor traffic, the mold was set up and fastened to the deck early on a quiet Sunday morning.

Building in the dirt-floored boat shed at the Mariners' Museum of Newport News, Virginia, we drove stakes into the ground in place of the filler blocks. Once leveled, the feet were screwed to the stakes, effectively stabilizing the strongback for the duration of the course.

After turning the strongback over, clamp the top of the leg around the gable and fasten the legs to it (Photograph 5-11).

Leveling the beam and attaching the top

Turn the beam over and set it up where you intend to build, then check it for level (Photograph 5-12). The beam must be level across its width and reasonably close to level lengthwise. Shim under the feet where necessary, then stabilize the strongback in position with the filler blocks.

When you are satisfied that the beam is level, fasten the top to the box. Use one edge of the top as a guide and straighten the beam to it. Clamp a few blocks (Photograph 5-13) that are the same width as the overhang along one edge of the top as a guide. Press the beam up to the blocks, clamp, and fasten. You could do this with lines drawn on the bottom face of the top, but they will be awkward to see.

5-13

Since the top is one of two reference planes used in setting up the mold, it is important that you have confidence in its accuracy. After fastening it, do a final check with the level.

What tolerances are acceptable? Although you have been carefully controlling all the variables up to this point, there is still the possibility that there are small waves in the top. Discrepancies up to about ¹⁄₁₆″ may be compensated for when the mold is set up. If it is off more than this, the problem should be identified now and corrected.

5-14

It is a good idea to fasten the strongback to the floor in some manner (Photograph 5-12). There will be a certain amount of pushing and pulling as the kayak goes together, and you would like to be sure the strongback is not inadvertently pushed out of level.

On concrete, a glob of thickened epoxy under the feet works well. On a wooden floor, make a cleat that fits around the feet and screw it to the floor. Should you have to move the strongback from the setup position during the building process, the cleats will show you where to reposition it when work resumes.

If attaching the feet to the floor is out of the question, at least mark their positions with masking tape. Putting some weight on the feet will help to keep things in place, as will gluing sandpaper to the bottom of the feet.

Laying out the centerline

Establishing the centerline is the first step in setting up the strongback and mold (Illustration 5-15). It is the first in a series of steps that must be performed accurately in order for the mold to fit together smoothly and reproduce the kayak's shape. (If you have confidence in the accuracy of each step, then when something looks wrong, you won't have to backtrack through all the steps to find the problem.)

Expect to spend the better part of a day setting up the mold. Building this kayak will be an exercise in patient preparation, but there is a bonus. The time you spend attending to details and working each step through to conclusion is also time spent preparing for the next step, and will become a big part of what has to happen later.

5-16

Use a tight string line to lay out the position of the centerline (Photograph 5-16). After stretching the line down the centerline of the strongback, mark under the line at intervals convenient for joining the points with your straightedge.

Choose a thin string line that can be pulled tight without breaking. Fishing line works well, but avoid the light monofilament that is meant to be hard for fish to see...it is hard to see. (Note: The line

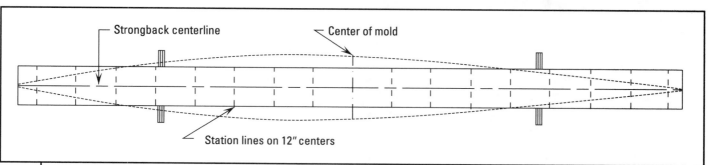

Strongback centerline   Center of mold

Station lines on 12″ centers

5-15

produced by a snapped chalk line is too wide to be accurate for this purpose.) Use a fine ball-point pen to make a good, strong impression.

To double-check the line for straightness, sight down it with your eye lined up with the centerline and slightly above the strongback. Close one eye and squint. This will filter out distracting images, allowing you to concentrate on the line.

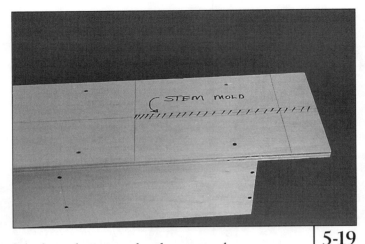

5-19

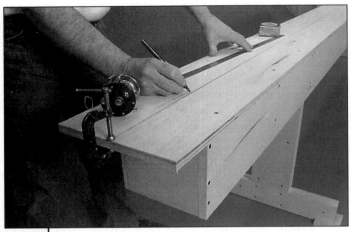

5-17

Laying out station lines

The station lines are drawn perpendicular to the centerline at intervals given on the plans (Photograph 5-17). We have tried a variety of spacing, from 10″ to 18″, and find 12″ to be just right. While less than 12″ is overkill, as the distance increases over 12″ extra staples must be used to tie the plank edges together between station molds. If the spacing on the plans you are using is over 14″, watch that the plank doesn't develop a flat curve between the station molds.

Begin measuring at the midpoint of the strongback, and measure out towards both ends. Use a tape measure along the entire

length, as the accumulated error resulting from measuring from point to point with a ruler will be significant. If you are worried about the tape shifting from position, tape it to the strongback, or put a weight on it.

Draw the station lines perpendicular to the centerline (Photograph 5-18). While you *could* use the edge of the strongback top to guide the square, the centerline is a more reliable reference.

Draw the positions of the stem molds over the centerline. Pick up this width from your stem mold material (Photograph 5-19).

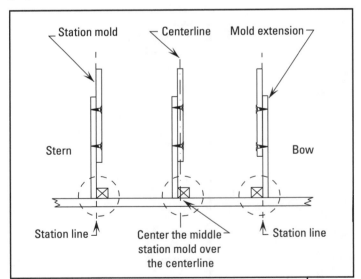

5-20

Attaching mold blocks

Before attaching the blocks to the strongback, it is important to know which side of the line the station mold will be positioned on (Illustration 5-20). As the planks on either side converge at the bow and stern, the plank will land on only one edge of the mold. This is the edge to line up

5-18

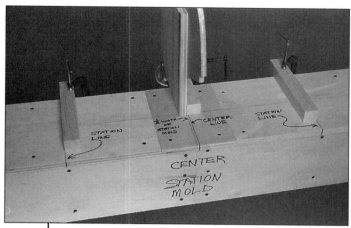

5-21

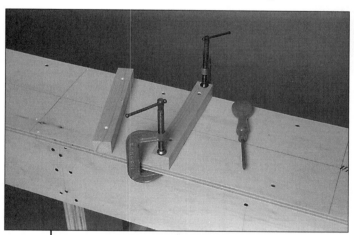

5-22

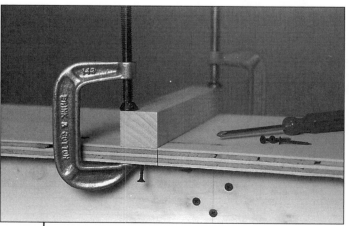

5-23

the sides of each block are at right (90°) angles to the bottom faces in order for the molds to stand plumb to the strongback.

Before putting in the screws, clamp the block to the strongback to keep it from shifting out of position. If you are fastening the blocks from the top, pilot holes in the block will allow the screw to draw the block tight to the strongback. (Use drill size $1\frac{1}{64}$" for 2" × No. 8 screws.)

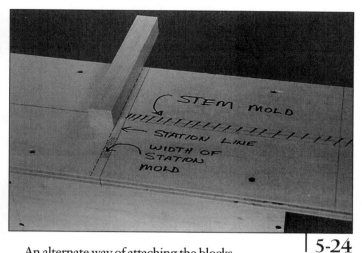

5-24

An alternate way of attaching the blocks is to fasten them up from the bottom with $1\frac{5}{8}$" screws (Photograph 5-23). If you are using a power driver, drywall screws will have a good bite without a pilot hole.

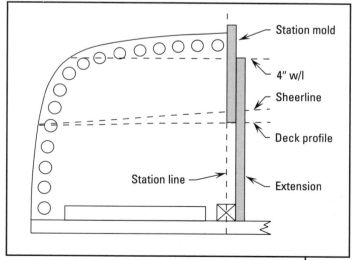

5-25

with the station line.

The block for the middle station is off-set one-half the width of the mold material; this will place the station line in the middle of the station mold (Photograph 5-21). Fasten the remaining blocks on the side of the line that faces the middle of the kayak.

Make the mold blocks from softwood and dimension them about $1\frac{1}{2}$" × $1\frac{1}{2}$" × 10" (Photograph 5-22). It is important that

The blocks for the bow and stern molds (Photograph 5-24) are handled a little differently from the station molds. This is because the mold extensions (see page 65) on these pieces must be removed from the planked boat without disturbing the station molds. Set up the bow and stern molds as in Illustration 5-25; note

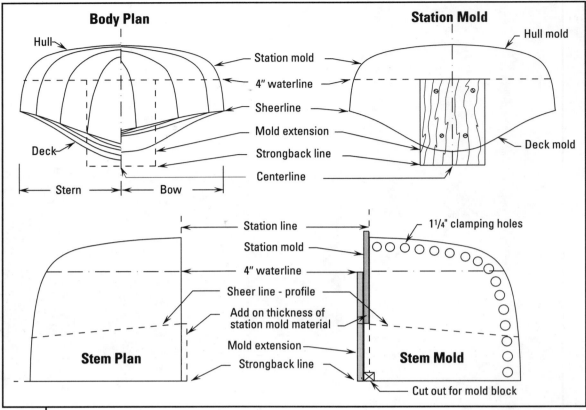

Body Plan

Hull
Deck
Stern
Bow

Station mold
4" waterline
Sheerline
Mold extension
Strongback line
Centerline

Station Mold

Hull mold
Deck mold

Stem Plan

Station line
Station mold
4" waterline
Sheer line - profile
Add on thickness of station mold material
Mold extension
Strongback line

Stem Mold

1¼" clamping holes
Cut out for mold block

5-26

the relationship between the station line, station mold, mold extension, and block at these section molds in the ends (Illustration 5-26).

TRANSFERRING THE PLANS TO THE MOLD MATERIAL
(Illustration 5-27)
Materials and tools for transferring plans (Photograph 5-28)
- 24" carpenter's square
- Ruler
- Masking tape
- Carbon paper
- Ball-point pen
- Pencil
- Batten (⅛" × ⅜" × 32")
- ¾" finishing nails or weights

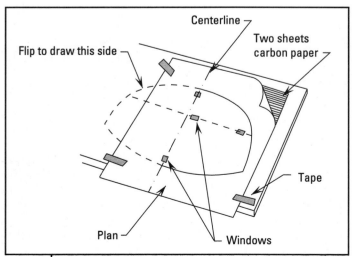

Centerline
Two sheets carbon paper
Flip to draw this side
Tape
Plan
Windows

5-27

5-28

Materials for the molds
Two 4′ x 8′ sheets of ½" plywood were used in building the molds and extensions for the Endeavor 17. Measure the plans you will be using to determine how much material will be required for your molds.

Molds have been made from particle board, plywood, and solid wood with equal success. Particle board is the most cost-

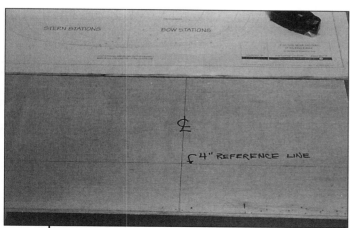

5-29

effective, available, and easy to use. Half-inch particle board is easier to cut and to fair than ¾″ plywood, and should be good for about ten boats. If you anticipate building a large number of kayaks on your molds, plywood will be the best choice. MDF (medium density fiberboard) is sometimes used, but would be my last choice for mold material. Although it is slightly easier to shape than particle board, it is very dense and has a tendency to split when fastenings are driven into its edges. It is expensive, and staples are difficult to pull out of it.

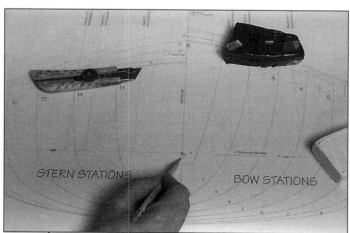

5-30

Preparing the plans and mold material

To avoid fighting with the full 4′ x 8′ sheet, consider ripping the board to width before transferring the plans to the mold material (Illustration 5-28).

Prepare the board for the plans by drawing a centerline and the 4″ waterline/reference line (Photograph 5-29).

Cut windows (¼″ x ¼″) across the centerline and the 4″ waterline or baseline of the plan sheet. This will allow you to see the reference lines on both the plan

and the board at the same time.

Lay the plan on the board and, looking through the window, line up the reference lines on the board with the reference lines on the plan sheet. Hold the plan in place with masking tape, but leave one side open for placing carbon paper (Photograph 5-30).

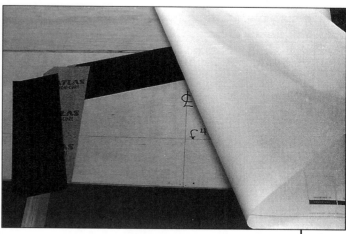

5-31

When the plan is flipped over for drawing the other half of the mold, we need to have a mirror image of the first line on the back side of the plan. To get this line, use two sheets of carbon paper—one sheet carbon side up, one sheet carbon side down. When you trace the line on the plan, the image will be transferred to the back side of the plan as well as to the board (Photograph 5-31).

While you could trace the line with a simple sketching motion, using a batten will result in a cleaner, more fair curve. Use ¾″ finishing nails driven through the plan into the board to guide the batten. Placing the nails so that one side of each is flush with the line will put your batten in the right place. Hold the batten in place

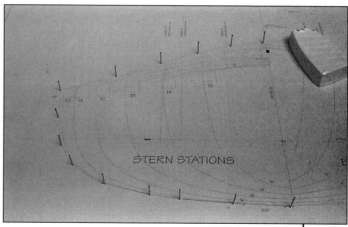

5-32

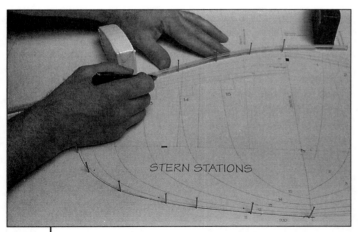

to the hull and the ¾″ top will eventually be shaped to follow the curves of the deck (Photograph 5-34).

After lining up the reference lines and securing the plan with masking tape, position a single layer of carbon paper with the carbon side down. Then, trace the hull and deck lines for the other side of the mold as you did for the first side, and cut out the notch for the sheer clamp (Photographs 5-35 and 5-36).

with a few nails or weights. Then, draw the line with a fine ball-point pen, and use firm pressure to make a good impression (Photograph 5-32 and 5-33).

Before you flip the plan over, it is necessary to transfer the reference lines to

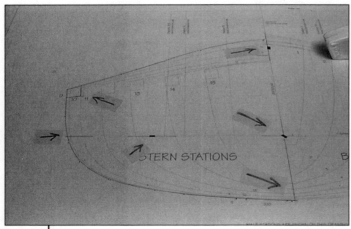

the back of the plan sheet. These include the centerline, the horizontal reference line, and the cutout for the sheer clamp. Mark the cutout for the sheer clamp ¾″ wide by ⅞″ deep. The ⅞″ side will fit up

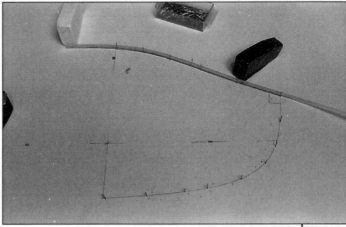

Since the stem profiles do not need to be flopped, use a single layer of carbon paper with the carbon side down. Be sure to transfer all relevant information, including the sheerline, deck line, and horizontal reference line, to the mold material (Photograph 5-37).

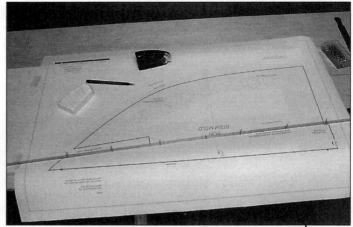

CUTTING OUT MOLDS

Take your time cutting out the station molds. If the plans are accurate and the molds are cut out with care, you shouldn't have to do anything more to them (Photograph 5-38).

Try to leave half the thickness of the

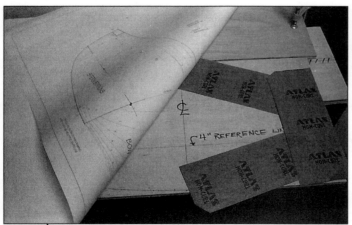

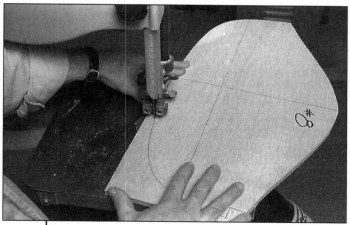

5-38 |

line on the board. If you remove all of the line, you won't know by how much you are off. If you leave all of the line, it is easy to be off the width of the line, plus enough to make a difference. It is better to be outside than inside; you can shape to the line later (Photograph 5-39).

5-39 |

After cutting the section, make a shallow saw cut (¹⁄₁₆″) at both ends of the centerline and at the 4″ horizontal reference line. This cut will transfer the lines to the

back of each board.

Cut the notch for the sheer clamp (Photograph 5-40). Check it carefully; a sloppy fit here will be reflected in the way the deck and sheer clamp fit to the hull. Expect a little more fine tuning later, when the sheer clamp is attached to the mold.

Identify each mold by its station number and draw a centerline and 4″ reference line on the back side of each station mold (Illustration 5-41).

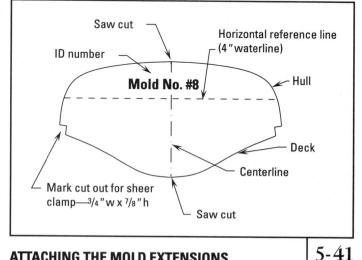

5-41 |

ATTACHING THE MOLD EXTENSIONS

The mold extension is used to raise the mold to a consistent height above the strongback (Illustration 5-42).

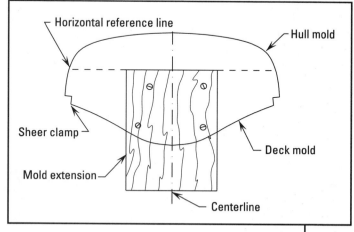

5-42 |

Cut the ¹⁄₂″ plywood (or particle board) exactly the same height for each station mold. The width will be the same as the strongback width except for those molds near the ends. As the hull tapers to the bow and stern, its width will be less than the full width of the strongback; size the extension to fit the station mold.

If the plans you are using do not suggest

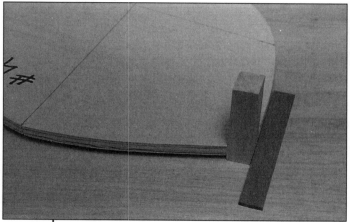

5-40 |

a height for the extensions, choose a height that will raise the lowest point of the building jig about 2″ off the strongback. The lowest point will most likely be the stem.

When you calculate the height of the extension, be sure to add it to the stem molds, too.

Draw a centerline on each extension that is exactly 90° to the ends. Project the line across the ends and join these projections with a line on the other side of the extension (Photograph 5-43).

5-43

Line up the extension centerline with the station mold centerline and flush to the horizontal reference line (Photograph 5-44).

5-44

Clamp the pieces together and check both sides of the mold to be sure that all the lines are where they should be (Photograph 5-45).

When you fasten the extension to the mold, keep in mind that the screws you use will have to be removed without disturbing the station mold before the deck is planked. Choose a screw size slightly

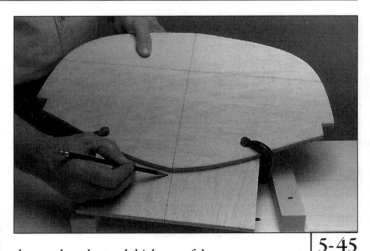

5-45

shorter than the total thickness of the two layers. If the points of the screws protrude, you can be sure that somebody will get hurt by them, and it might be you. Drilling pilot holes for the screws will make them easier to remove.

PREPARING THE STEM MOLDS

Drill clamping holes 1¼″ or larger around the perimeter of the stem mold (Illustration 5-46). Size the holes to fit your clamps. The holes should be about 1″ in from the edge and on about 3″ centers. In order to make a good lamination, the clamps should be as close together as possible. If you don't have this many clamps, make as many holes as you have clamps for (Photograph 5-47).

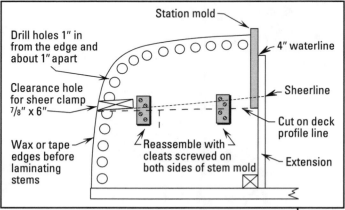

Drill holes 1″ in from the edge and about 1″ apart

Station mold

4″ waterline

Sheerline

Clearance hole for sheer clamp 7/8″ x 6″

Cut on deck profile line

Wax or tape edges before laminating stems

Reassemble with cleats screwed on both sides of stem mold

Extension

5-46

When the planked-up hull is turned over in preparation for planking the deck, the portion of the stem molds that extends above the deck line will have to be removed. To facilitate this, cut the mold now along the deck profile line and reassemble with temporary cleats.

When you screw the cleats on, keep in mind that they will have to be removed

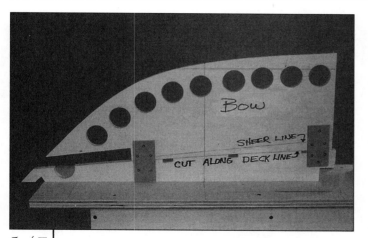

5-47

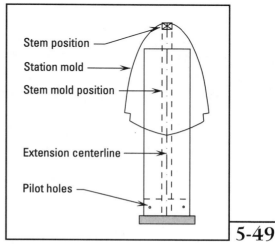

5-49

only tricks are to get started right and to do the steps in a logical order.

Begin by setting up the bow/stern assemblies. They in turn will become the reference for setting up the remaining station molds. Expect it to take longer to set up the ends than it does to fill in the middle station molds.

The first station mold to set up is the one that joins up to the bow or stern stem mold, forming a "T" shape (Illustration 5-49).

Line up the centerline on the station mold with the strongback centerline,

Stem position

Station mold

Stem mold position

Extension centerline

Pilot holes

clamp it to the block, and plumb it with a spirit level (Photograph 5-50). Take your time with this one, as all future measurements relate back to this reference line. If this centerline is off, you will have to deal with a lot of annoying problems relating back to an unknown point.

If the mold isn't plumb, raise a corner, shim, clamp, and check it again. Pilot holes are a good idea here, as you want the parts to be drawn tightly together with the least possibility of being shifted from position. Keep in mind that the screws must come out later when the hull and mold are removed from the strongback.

from inside the hull before planking the deck. Softwood cleats work best because they can be split away from the screws where there is no space to use a screwdriver.

The ³⁄₄″ x ⁷⁄₈″ sheer clamp fits inside the hull and butts up to the inside face of the stem. To accommodate the sheer clamp, cut a loose ⁷⁄₈″ x 6″ clearance slot in the stem mold. Don't cut this slot before laminating the stems, if you can help it, because it will make the mold less rigid.

SETTING UP THE BUILDING JIG

As you build your kayak, there will be some simple steps that seem to take forever to work through, and others that look complicated or tedious but change the boat before your eyes, as if by magic. Setting up the mold is in the latter category (Illustration 5-48). It is one of the more exciting steps, giving you the first three-dimensional look at your kayak and making all your patient preparation worthwhile. If the parts have been prepared with care, expect to spend three to four hours setting up and checking the building jig.

Although setting up the jig is a significant step, it is as simple as lining up the station mold centerlines between an upper and lower centerline along the strongback and fastening each mold to its block. The

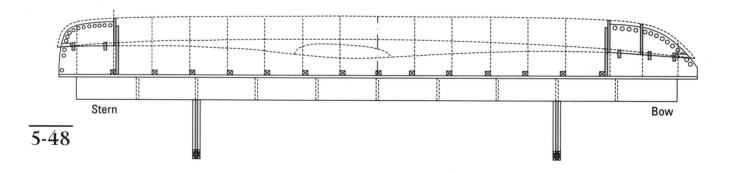

Stern

Bow

5-48

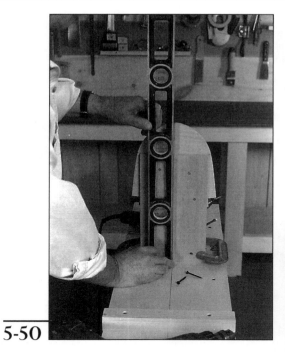

5-50

Slant the screw slightly upwards to give your screwdriver working room.

Stern stem assembly

To complete the stern setup, attach the stern stem mold (Illustration 5-51). Fastened in this "T" shape, the ends will be self-supporting and will become anchors for the upper string centerline.

Put the stem mold into position and clamp it to the station mold. If you do not have a clamp deep enough to fit through the clamp holes in the stem mold, try a small block clamped to the station mold. It will not only act as a guide for the stem

mold, but will also accommodate a small-size clamp (Photograph 5-52 and 5-53).

Position the end stem mold over the strongback centerline and clamp it to the strongback. Note that this end is not fastened to the strongback until the position has been confirmed with the string line. Before fastening the stem mold to the station mold, check for plumb at both ends. If the stem mold happens to be warped, plumb the outboard end, as this will be the reference for positioning the stem.

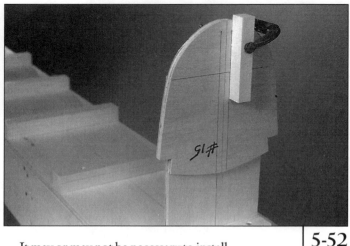

5-52

It may or may not be necessary to install a corner brace (see Illustration 5-54) on the stern section. The brace will stiffen up the assembly and give you control over

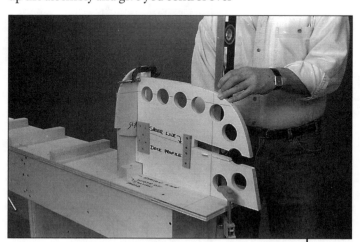

5-53

the end of the stem mold, should it have to be adjusted. It is important to make the cuts on the corner brace exactly 90°, as any degree that it is off will be magnified by the length of the stem mold.

To find the locations of the pilot holes for the corner brace, hold the piece in position and trace its outline, drill holes

Corner brace

Station mold

Screw size: 1¹/₂" x #6

Extension

³/₄" x ³/₄" block

Corner brace

³/₄" x ³/₄" block

5-51

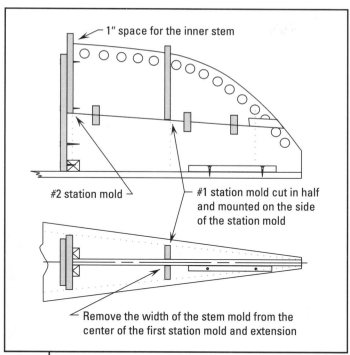

1" space for the inner stem

#2 station mold

#1 station mold cut in half and mounted on the side of the station mold

Remove the width of the stem mold from the center of the first station mold and extension

5-54

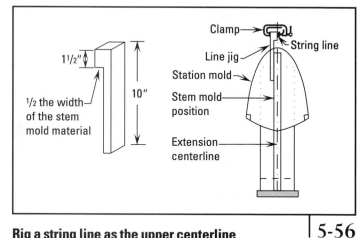

1½"

½ the width of the stem mold material

10"

Clamp

String line

Line jig

Station mold

Stem mold position

Extension centerline

5-56

inside the traced lines, put the piece back into position, and drill pilot holes from the other side of the stem mold into the edge of the brace.

Check the stem mold again to be sure it is still plumb.

Bow stem assembly

The bow assembly is made up of the first two station molds and the stem mold. Set up the stem mold against the second station mold using the same procedure as used on the stern stem (Illustration 5-54). Cut the first station mold in half and remove half the width of the stem mold material from each side of the split station mold; then fasten the pieces to the sides of the stem mold. Use the horizontal reference line and the station line to

establish the position, then attach the pieces with ¾" × ¾" softwood corner blocks (Photograph 5-55).

Check both ends of the stem mold with a level to be sure that they are still plumb. If there is a problem, identify the cause and adjust where necessary.

Rig a string line as the upper centerline

The purpose of the upper centerline is to create a second reference line for positioning the remaining station molds (Illustration 5-56). While it is possible to line the station molds up with the strongback centerline and plumb each one, this does leave room for some discrepancies to creep in. Also, the line will be used to confirm that the stem molds are in line with the centerline and to check the rocker (the fore-and-aft curvature of the bottom).

Clamp the jig that supports the string

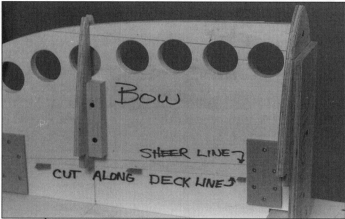

5-55

5-57

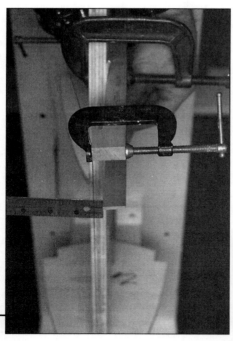

5-58

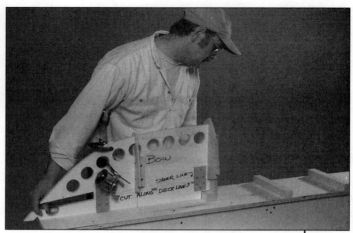

5-59

from the line to the straightedge should give you a number half the width of the stem mold. If the number is off, shim the line-supporting jig until it is centered.

Check that the string line is centered over the station mold centerline (Photograph 5-59). Position your eye directly over the string line and sight down the station mold centerline. If everything is where it should be, the lines will be superimposed over each other, and you will see only one line. If the lines do not match up, shift the end of the stem mold until they do.

to the stem molds, as close to the ends as is practical (Photograph 5-57). If the line is set up parallel to and sufficiently above the strongback, you will have an accurate look at the rocker and know that the line will not get hung up on a station mold. To find the right position for the string, measure the height of the middle station mold plus its extension and add ¾". This will be the distance from the strongback to the top of the line-supporting jig. Positioning the line ½" down from the top of the line-supporting jig will put the line ¼" above the middle station mold and parallel to the strongback.

Clamp the line to the jig rather than tying a knot. The clamp will make it easy to fasten the line and adjust its tension.

After rigging the string line, the first thing to check is that the line is centered over the stem molds (Photograph 5-58). To do this, lay a straightedge vertically along the side of the stem mold and extending past the string line. Measuring

Now check the line at the other end. Getting one end positioned may throw the other end off, so work both ends until they are both lined up to your satisfaction.

Fasten the stem molds to the strongback with ¾" × ¾" blocks cut to an appropriate length.

Set up the remaining molds

With the upper reference line in place and its position confirmed, you can go ahead and set up the remaining molds (Illustration 5-60). Begin by setting up the middle station mold and work out towards the ends. This gives you space to work; otherwise, you might be confined to a 12" space.

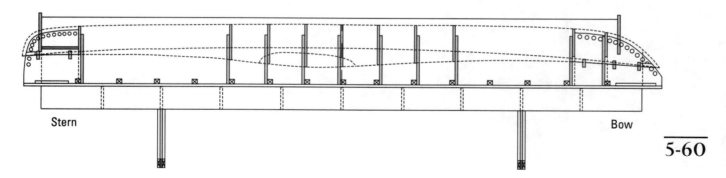

Stern   Bow

5-60

Line up the centerline on each mold and extension so that it is directly under the string line and over the strongback centerline. Clamp the station mold to both sides of the strongback block and check again.

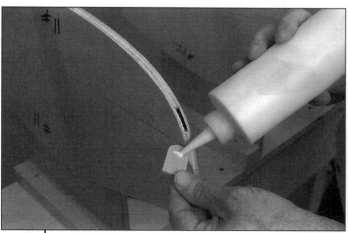

5-61

Stand on something that allows you to look straight down the mold's centerline from above. You should see only one line when all three lines are superimposed.

If it is necessary to adjust a mold, lift the low corner, shim it, and reclamp. The shim is optional, but it will help to hold the mold plumb and steady. When you are happy with each mold's position, screw it to the strongback block.

Install the remaining station molds in the same manner, being sure that they are on the correct sides of the blocks.

When all of the station molds are set up, double-check their positions by standing at the end of the building jig and sighting down the centerline. If you squint just right, you can superimpose all the centerlines over one another and pick out any molds that are out of line.

If cheap plywood is used for the molds, there is a good chance there will be a few voids along the edges of the boards. Voids large enough to hinder stapling the planks to the mold should be filled. Shape soft-

wood plugs to fit the holes and glue them into place. After the glue has set, trim the plugs flush to the edges of the molds (Photographs 5-61 and 62).

To stabilize the tops of the station molds, lay a batten (scrap planking works well) down the keel line of the building jig and tack it to each station mold (Illustration 5-63). Use a small square or the level to plumb each of the molds. Fasten the batten with a 1″ finishing nail at each station, leaving the head protruding about ⅛″ so it can be pulled out later.

5-62

Are the molds fair?

Before going any further, take time to check that the molds all relate to each other in such a way that the lines will be fair curves from one end of the kayak to the other. If the plans are good and you have been careful cutting out and setting up the molds, this step should be a pleasant formality.

Check the rocker. Stand back and sight down the stabilizing batten along the keel line. It should lie in a fair curve from one end of the mold to the other.

Take a short (6′ to 8′ long) piece of planking, and, with your hands as far apart as possible, bend it around the molds parallel to the plank line. The batten should

⌐ Batten tacked to top of station molds

Stern   Bow

5-63

touch each mold with no spaces between the batten and the station mold (Photograph 5-64).

Out-of-fair stations may be corrected by shaving down one or more stations. If the error is extreme, move the mold back and forth or up and down as necessary.

It is possible to be off by about $^1\!/_{16}''$ on the flat sections of the sides or bottom before it becomes a problem. In these flatter areas, the planking will find a fair curve after the staples are pulled out. At the turn of the bilge when an unfair curve is molded in, there will be little change in the molded shape after the staples are pulled.

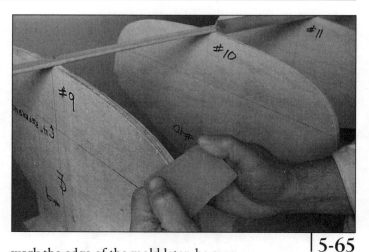

5-65

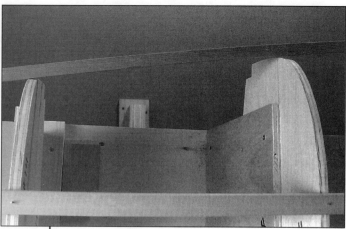

5-64

Wax the molds

This is as good a time as any to treat the edge of the molds so that the completed hull can be gracefully removed from the mold. Paraffin wax on the edge of the station molds and stem molds will keep the glue from bonding the planking to the mold (Photograph 5-65). If you have to

work the edge of the mold later, be sure to touch up the wax in these places.

An alternative to wax is clear plastic packaging tape. While it does take longer to apply, you won't have to worry about wax contaminating the edge of the plank or the inside edge of the stem (Photograph 5-66).

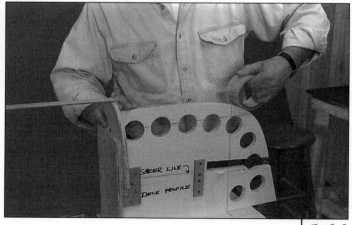

5-66

6 | The Skeleton: Stems and Sheer Clamps

The stems are the first to be made of the many pieces that will eventually become your kayak. After making all the parts that went into getting this project started, it's good to finally make something that stays in the boat.

Stems are an important part of the kayak for structural as well as aesthetic reasons. Visually, the outer stem defines the profile of the kayak and makes a logical conclusion to the plank lines. This gives the kayak a crisp look rather than the mushy feeling that would result if the plank lines simply ended, causing your eye to wander aimlessly out into space. When an outer stem of a contrasting color is used, the effect is even more dramatic.

Structurally, the stems do many things. The force of a blow to the end of the kayak is transmitted through the stem and distributed evenly into the hull structure. Together, the inner and outer stems tie the sides of the hull together, making further reinforcement unnecessary. During the planking process, the inner stem provides a place for the plank ends to land,

effectively controlling their positions while the glue dries. The inner stem also acts as an accurate reference for trimming the planks to an exact length and angle.

In addition to the visual benefits mentioned above, the outer stems cover and seal the ends of the planks and, being of a denser hardwood, protect the softwood planking at the end of the kayak.

In case you are wondering whether you should omit the stems, a number of sources will show you how to build small craft without them. Personally, I have a few problems with this method of construction, not the least of which is pride. When the time it takes to shape and install stems is balanced against the frustration and inconvenience of building without stems and the inherent less-than-professional results, I don't think there should be enough time or weight saved to tempt you.

If the plans you are using do not provide for inner stems, deduct 1″ from the full-size drawing of the stem and stern profile to create the shape and dimensions of the forms for the inner stems.

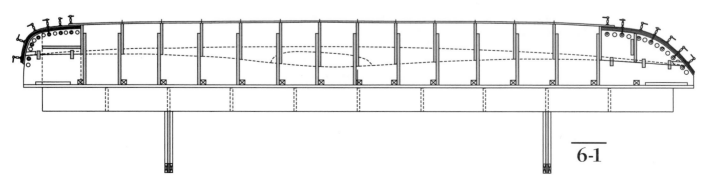

MAKING THE STEMS

A laminated stem is made by ripping the stem stock into thin pieces, steaming and bending, and gluing the pieces back together around a form (Illustration 6-1). A laminated stem should exceed the strength of a solid stem of the same material, and it is well suited to cobbled-up steamers and low-tech bending jigs.

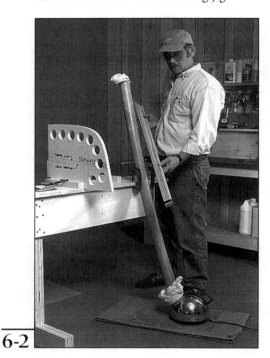

6-2

There seems to be a mystery surrounding steam bending, but there's really nothing to it. In order for wood to assume a new shape, the fibers must be softened with a combination of heat and moisture. When the fibers have become pliable, the wood is slowly but firmly bent around a form, fastened, and allowed to cool. After the moisture content of the piece has stabilized, it will hold its new shape—with some degree of springback.

Steam bending can be a quirky business full of vicissitudes, some real and some questionable (some folks like to consider what is the most favorable position of the moon for bending). The truth is, successful bending depends mostly on the species and quality of the wood being bent, and how quickly the bend is executed.

Since our purpose here is to build a professional-quality kayak using low-tech skills and equipment, rather than to master the art and science of steam bending, laminated stems are recommended. If you are fascinated by steam bending

and would like to learn more, check the Sources (page 173) for more detailed information.

Equipment and Materials

A steam generator can be anything that will produce wet steam and has a means of directing and containing the steam around the wood. Whatever system you come up with, keep it simple, and, most of all, keep it safe. Steam is hot, and it burns quickly with no slow warmup warning signs. Wear gloves for handling the hot pipe and for handling the wood while bending. Watch that body parts don't wander above escaping steam.

The electric kettle steamer we are using here (Photograph 6-2) is about as simple as it gets. Although we have a large steamer in our shop, the kettle would be my first choice for one pair of stems. Not only is it fast to set up, but it does the same job as the big cooker. To direct and contain the steam, a piece of 2"-diameter plastic pipe slightly longer than the stems, and several rags to contain the steam, are a cheap solution.

When you are shopping the yard sales for an old kettle, look for one that does not shut itself off when it reaches a boil. If this is the type you have, it is possible to rewire it, bypassing the thermostat. Keep an eye on the water level while the kettle is boiling. If this is allowed to get below the heating element, the element will destroy itself.

After steaming, it's a good idea to rinse the kettle before returning it to the cook or making the next pot of tea.

The **bending forms** we are using in the photos are the bow/stern stem molds. While you could make and use separate forms, the stem molds work just fine.

Traditionally, stems are steam bent from **solid hardwood.** But this required good, straight-grained, air-dried stock, lots of steam, and a heavy-duty bending jig. Cutting the stock into thin pieces has made the need for ideal materials and equipment less imperative.

I would suggest using a **bendable softwood** such as white cedar or pine for the inner stems, and a hardwood such as ash or cherry for the outer stems. A softwood stem is plenty strong for our purpose, and is lighter and easier to shape than a hardwood stem. As a bonus, it will accept staples better than hardwood. Use hardwood on the outside for its greater density and durability.

Although laminating will allow us to get away with less-than-ideal bending stock, choose the best straight-grained stock you can find. Straight grain not only bends better, but is much easier to shape with hand tools.

Wood that is only partially air-dried will bend the most consistently, but go with the best you can find.

Stock dimensions

- Inner stems: Finished dimension is 1″ wide × 1″ thick × appropriate length of the curve of the stem mold. (Four laminates are required, ¼″ thick × 1″ wide × 4″ to 6″ longer than needed.)
- Outer stems: ⅞″ wide × ½″ thick × appropriate length of above. (Two laminates are required, ¼″ thick × ⅞″ wide × 4″ to 6″ longer than needed.)

Steaming the laminates

Both the inner and outer stems should be formed at the same time; this ensures a perfect fit when the outer stems are installed and avoids the need to make a second bending form for the outer stems.

If the wood you are using is very dry or has been kiln dried, getting some moisture into the wood prior to steaming will increase the chances of a successful bend. This could be done by any means, from wrapping the pieces in a wet towel and plastic, to sinking them in the river. Soaking overnight should be long enough for the ¼″ laminations.

The bow stem on the Endeavor 17 is an easy bend and could probably be made dry. Steaming about 15 minutes will take some tension out of the wood and make it easier to handle.

The stern stem is a much harder bend and will require good bending stock and good heat and moisture. If you put both of the stems to the steam at the same time and bend the bow stem first, this will leave the stern in steam for about 20 to 25 minutes, which is about right for a bend of this radius.

Bending

Once the wood has been removed from the steambox, the optimum bending time will be about 45 seconds. Being thin, the laminations heat up fast, but they also cool down fast, so there is not a lot of time to get the pieces out of the steamer, arrange them on the mold, place the first clamp, and begin to make the bend.

Organization is everything here, and an extra pair of hands for fastening the clamps would be a big help. It is a good idea to have the clamps adjusted to size beforehand, and a quick rehearsal so everyone knows his or her job and when to do it also helps.

Arranging the pieces in order beforehand and securing one end with a piece of plastic electrical tape will save a lot of fumbling between the steamer and the form.

To fire up the steamer, set up the pipe over the kettle spout and prop it against the bench. Tie a rag around the base of the pipe and stuff another into the top to help contain the steam. When the steam is up and the pipe feels hot, place the laminates inside the pipe and replace it over the kettle. The reason for preheating the pipe is to give us an accurate point at which to start timing.

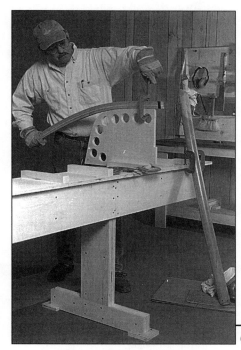

6-3

After steaming for the required length of time, remove the laminates from the steamer and place the first clamp at the end of the stem mold that will be inside the kayak (Photograph 6-3). Let the ends of the strips extend slightly past the end of the mold; these should be trimmed off neatly after gluing. As soon as the first

to dry. Tie their ends together so they can't straighten out and allow air to circulate around all sides. If you have had to soak the laminations prior to bending, expect them to take a little longer to dry before gluing.

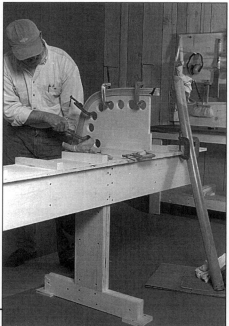

6-4

6-5

clamp is set, immediately begin bending the laminates around the mold with a steady, firm motion. Move slowly enough to let the wood fibers stretch and compress into their new shape, but not so slowly that the wood cools off before the bend is complete.

Try to keep up to the bend by adding a few clamps in strategic places as the bend progresses (Photograph 6-4). It isn't necessary to use a clamp in every hole for this step; four or five clamps will suffice. To keep from mashing the softened wood fibers, tighten the clamps only enough to hold the laminates to the mold. If you can't resist cranking down on the clamps, use clamping pads to protect the steam-softened wood. (Frankly, I find the pads just one more thing to juggle, and they add confusion to a process that depends on speed to be successful.)

Gluing the laminates together
Allow the wood to dry before gluing. The wood fibers that were softened for bending must now harden up before the wood will hold the new shape. In order to create a good structural joint with epoxy glue, the glue must be able to penetrate the surface of the wood; the glue will not displace moisture.

Leave the stems on the stem mold overnight to allow them to get accustomed to their new shape, then remove them and allow another 24 hours for them

Since the stems are a major structural member of the kayak, **they should be laminated using epoxy glue** (Photograph 6-5). Use the same epoxy that you will use later to lay up the fiberglass, and read the manufacturer's instructions regarding thickening agents. Avoid using fillers that contain abrasives such as silica on anything that must be worked with an edge tool; this stuff will take the edge off carbide blades so the edge of your plane won't last long.

6-6

Work clean! If you get glue on your gloves, wipe it off with a dry rag (lacquer thinner will eat most plastic gloves). If you don't, it gets on your tools, then all over your hands and the bench. Work clean; it is the easiest way!

Work safe! Read and understand the

technical and safety information relevant to the epoxy system you are using.

Lay out all the pieces in order on a piece of plastic and brush a thin coat of glue (catalyzed epoxy resin with adhesive thickener added) on all mating surfaces.

Do not apply glue between the inner and outer stems; the outer stem will be installed after the planking is complete, so you need to separate the inner and outer stems after the laminations are made (Photograph 6-6). To be sure the pieces will separate, consider covering the inside of the outer stem or the outside of the inner stem with plastic packaging tape.

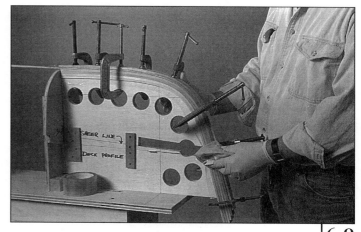

6-9

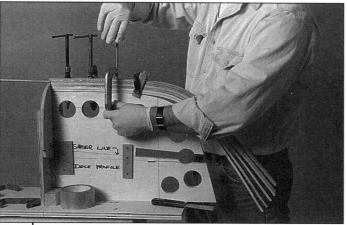

6-7

Begin clamping at the end of the form nearest the station mold, and continue around, placing a clamp in each hole (Photograph 6-7). The clamps should be as close together as possible to get even clamping pressure over the full length.

After you get the first clamp on, clamp two short pieces of planking or scrap wood, one on either side of the stem, to draw the laminates into line (Photograph 6-8). Then place the next clamp. Move this

clamping jig around the stem ahead of the clamps. Using this trick, you should be able to glue up the stems without getting glue all over everything. It is a good idea to place the clamps on alternating sides of the form to counteract the tendency for the stem to roll if all the clamps are on one side. This will also leave a larger space between the clamps for cleaning up the squeezed-out glue.

When all the clamps are on (Photograph 6-9), clean off the excess glue with the putty knife and wipe clean with a rag dampened with lacquer thinner. This will make it easier to separate the inner and outer stems and save having to sand off the excess glue later.

6-10

Drape the thinner-soaked rags over something to let the thinner completely evaporate before discarding them. Spontaneous combustion is possible if solvent-soaked rags are rolled up in a ball and discarded in a garbage can.

Leave the clamps on until the glue has cured, then remove them and separate the inner and outer stems. Clean up the inside

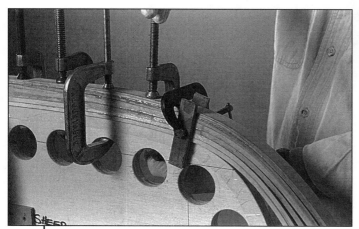

6-8

of the stems and round off the corners that will be exposed on the inside of the boat. While the inside of the stem is not visible after the deck is attached, you know it is there, so you might as well feel good about it (Photograph 6-10).

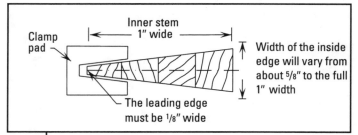

Inner stem 1" wide

Clamp pad

Width of the inside edge will vary from about 5/8" to the full 1" width

The leading edge must be 1/8" wide

6-11

SHAPING THE STEMS

Shaping the stems is another of those steps that look complicated but turn out to be quite straightforward (Illustration 6-11). It is a simple matter of removing all the wood from the side of the stem that interferes with the planking lying fair on them while leaving a 1/8" face on the forward edge of the stem back.

Using one of the most ancient of boat-building tools, the fairing batten, it is easy to see the exact bevel and how much wood must be taken off. Although it is a pleasant job, it can drag on, so take your time and look at it as spokeshave practice—or patience building, if you need that more.

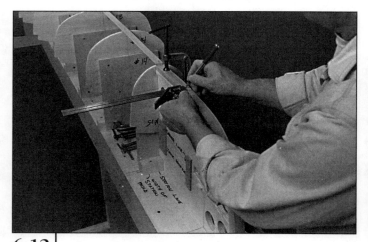

6-12

Cutting the stem bevels

Begin by **drawing a centerline** around the outside edge of the stem using a marking gauge or combination square set to half the stem width (Photograph 6-12).

Draw two more lines parallel to the centerline to show the width of the leading edge (Photograph 6-13). The 1/8"-wide face will narrow down to the centerline

when the stem begins to flatten out as it turns into the bottom of the boat. Exactly where this happens will be obvious as the stem is shaped, and will be confirmed with the fairing batten. To keep things simple, mark the centerline in red and the parallel line in a contrasting color.

6-13

The most difficult part of **shaping the stems** is hanging onto the stem as you work it with spokeshave and block plane. I suggest clamping it into position on the mold and shaping just the lower (on the upside-down boat) portion of the stem to get the planking started. Installing the first four or five pairs of planks will anchor the stem and make it easier to shape. Another good reason for shaping the stem in stages is that it is easier to relate the bevel on the stem to the shape of the hull if the batten fol-

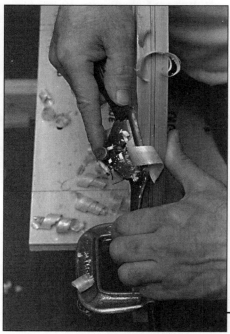

6-14

lows the plank line. This will be critical where the stern stem turns into the bottom, forcing the bevel to roll fast to keep up with the changing shape of the hull.

Keep at least 2" of prepared stem ahead of the planks so that the edges of the planks don't get damaged while shaping more stem. As the planking progresses, keep shaping the stem ahead of the planks, checking often with the batten so that you know exactly where you are. Remember to hold the batten parallel to the plank line, and don't force it to fit the

of the tool so that the only resistance you feel is the blade as it slices cleanly through the wood. Without the confusion of the friction between the sole and the wood, it is easier to concentrate on where the blade is and what it is doing.

Keep checking with the fairing batten to be sure you know where you are, and don't take too much off the inside edge. Watch for a crown that wants to develop in the middle; if you work the middle, the sides will take care of themselves (Photographs 6-15 and 6-16).

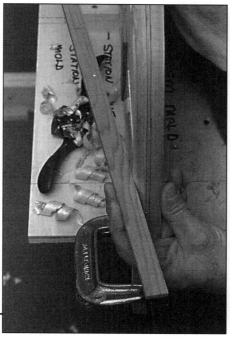

6-15

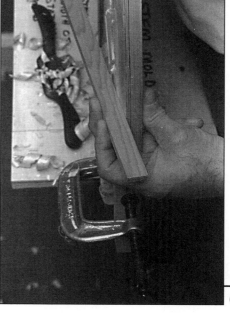

6-16

shape you have just cut. The batten's purpose is to give you information, not to be forced to say what you want to hear (Photograph 6-14).

To keep from cutting too deep with the wrong bevel, it helps to begin cutting the correct bevel from the beginning. This allows lots of time to adjust the angle before getting down to the line. If one side is first worked down to the line, there is a good chance of going past the line as the balance of the material is being removed. If the line is approached at the correct bevel, it is easy to stop cutting as the blade touches the line.

Keep your tools sharp. A sharp tool will be easier to control and safer to use than a dull one that fights you. A tool that does what you want it to do makes jobs like shaping stems a pleasure.

For ultimate control, wax the bottom

When you are sure that the stem won't have to be removed again, fasten the end of the stem to the station mold with a 1¼" × No. 6 screw and washer (Photograph 6-17). Keep in mind that this screw will have to come out before you remove the hull from

6-17

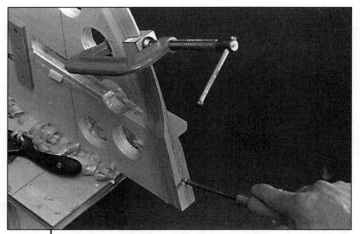

6-18

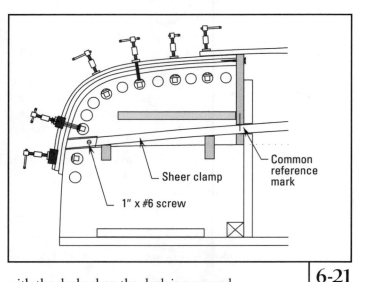

6-21

the mold. Note: Pilot holes are important to avoid splitting the stem and to draw the parts together.

If there is enough stem extending past the sheerline, a screw here will help keep the stem in position (Photograph 6-18). Use clamping pads that fit around the stem to keep the clamps from crushing the fragile edge of the stem after it has been shaped (Illustration 6-19).

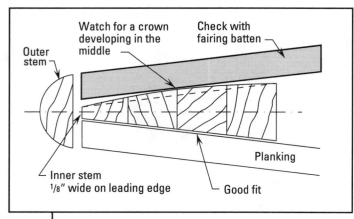

6-19

THE SHEER CLAMP

The purpose of the sheer clamp is to provide a graceful way of joining the deck to the hull (Illustrations 6-20, 6-21, and 6-22). During construction, the sheer clamp is glued to the deck and comes off

with the deck when the deck is removed from the hull and the mold. The hull is thus planked to fit the sheer clamp, so the sheer clamp will always fit perfectly inside the hull.

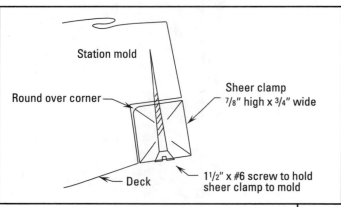

6-22

Cutting the sheer clamp to its exact length with a compound miter on both ends is easy only when you have accurate marks to go by. The trick is to measure carefully and mark accurately and, to back up one more step, find a common point from which to measure each end. It is virtually impossible to determine where the sheer clamp will end without springing it into position. We can overcome this by picking a point

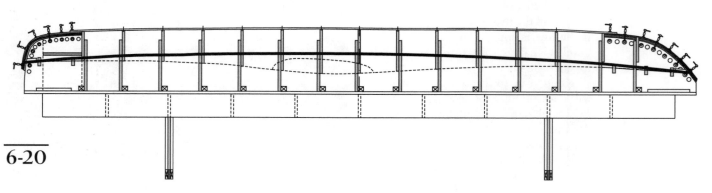

6-20

of reference on the building jig that is common to the sheer clamp and the mold. On our kayak, we measured from the first station mold (see Illustration 6-21).

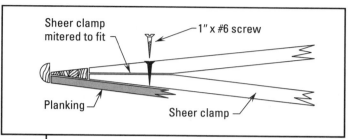

Sheer clamp mitered to fit

1" x #6 screw

Planking

Sheer clamp

6-23

The ends of the sheer clamps are mitered to fit each other and to fit snug to the inside faces of the stems (Illustration 6-23). A plank lying along the outside of the sheer clamp must fit to the beveled stem tightly enough to be glued (Photograph 6-31).

Installing the sheer clamp

Start by temporarily fitting the sheer clamps into position on the mold. Although the sheer clamps will eventually be screwed to the station molds, keep them mobile until the final cutting and fitting have been completed. Four or five ½" plywood fixtures, as shown in Photograph 6-24, for each side of the mold will effectively hold the sheer clamps in position for marking and fitting.

In areas where the sheer clamp runs over the strongback, prop it up to the sta-

tion mold with a stick (Photograph 6-25).

Mark the location of the middle station mold on the sheer clamp. When you reinstall the sheer clamp, this reference mark will be important to locating it precisely. Both ends of the sheer clamp now extend past the stem, ready to be measured, marked, cut, and fit.

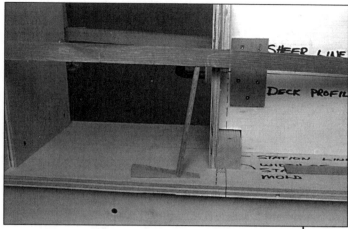

6-25

Establish a point to measure from. At one end of the boat, hold the sheer clamp into its notch in the last station mold and draw a reference mark across the station mold and sheer clamp. This will give you reference points common to both the sheer clamp and the station mold. So, now you can take a measurement from the building jig and transfer it precisely to the sheer clamp. Mark the stem to indicate where the sheer clamp will land on it. Measure from the mark on the station mold to the point on the stem where the top (longest) edge of the sheer clamp will meet the stem. Transfer this distance to the top edge of the sheer clamp, measuring from the station mold reference mark to locate the end of the sheer clamp.

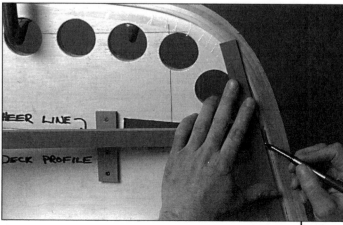

6-24

6-26

Now that we have a point to work from, it is a straightforward job to pick up and transfer the three bevels (Photograph 6-26).

Trim the sheer clamp just slightly longer than needed to make it easy to handle and afford the best visibility for measuring and marking.

To position the sheer clamp for marking, loosen the stem and press the sheer clamp into position in its slot in the stem mold. Pick up and transfer the angles from the back of the stem to the top and side of the sheer clamp. Do this by eye, or use the sliding bevel gauge.

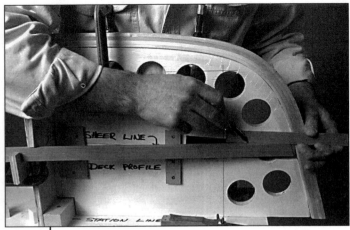

6-27

The miter runs along the centerline of the kayak. To **mark the miter,** hold one sheer clamp in position and lay a straightedge along the stem mold to project the side of the stem mold to the top (on the upside-down boat) of the sheer clamp. Draw this line on the top of the sheer clamp (Photograph 6-27).

The line will be slightly offset to one side of where we want it to be, but it will be parallel to the centerline of the kayak (Photograph 6-28). To find the actual cen-

terline, measure the width on the back of the stem and mark half this distance in from the edge of the sheer clamp.

Use the sliding bevel to pick up the angle from your line, and transfer it to the new mark. With the line drawn, an accurate cut is not hard to make (Photograph 6-29).

6-29

You may find it easier to take the sheer clamp off the form and **make the cut on the bench.** Cut outside the line and plan on doing a little hand work with the block plane for final fitting back on the mold.

Remember to use the reference mark when replacing the sheer clamp. If you don't keep going back to this anchor point, you could find yourself fitting something that is in a different place every time you try it. Also, make sure that the stem is centered and clamped to the stem mold before attempting to fit the sheer clamp up to it.

6-30

When you are happy with the way each of the ends fits together, drill pilot holes and dry-fit the ends of the sheer clamps together with 1" x No. 6 flathead bronze screws set flush. The screws will hold the

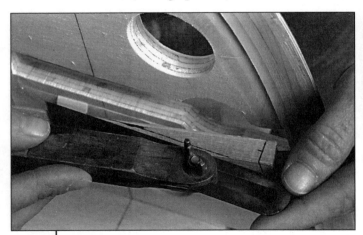

6-28

ends of the sheer clamp together for most of the final fitting to the mold and supply the clamping pressure when the ends are glued (Photograph 6-30).

Fit the outside faces of the sheer clamps to flow into the stem bevel. A plank lying on the face of the sheer clamp should lie close enough to the stem bevel to be glued (Photograph 6-31).

ultimately, the way the sheer clamp fits into the hull.

6-33

6-31

Check the fit between the sheer clamp and the station molds. Using a short straightedge, confirm that the sheer clamp lies flush with each station mold (Photograph 6-32). Here the sheer clamp simply fills up the piece we cut out of the mold, effectively restoring the original shape of the station mold. A good fit here is important, as it affects the way the first two planks on either side fit together and,

As the sides converge at the ends of the kayak, the sheer clamp will land on the corners of the molds, possibly causing the sheer clamps to sit proud of the molds. To correct this, pull the sheer clamp away from the mold, sneak in behind it with a rasp, and work the notch down until the clamp fits (Photograph 6-33). If you accidentally cut the notch too deep, fit and glue a shim behind the sheer clamp to bring it out flush.

When you are happy with the fit between the sheer clamp and the station molds, fasten the clamps from the bottom with 1½" x No. 6 screws. Pilot holes are important here to draw the parts together and avoid splitting the station mold.

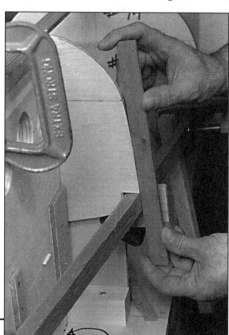

6-32

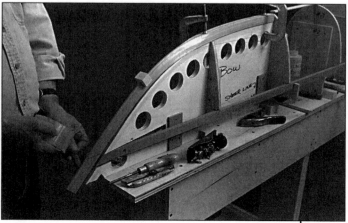

6-34

Glue and screw the ends of the sheer clamp together. If the only screws you have are steel, wax the screws just before gluing so they can be removed after the glue has cured. Plug the holes later (Photograph 6-34).

You don't want to glue the sheer clamps to the stems—yet. So, in preparation for gluing the sheer clamps together, protect the stem with plastic film or packaging tape.

6-36

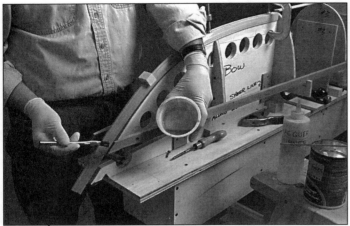

6-35

Because the miter cut has exposed the end grain, expect to apply two to four coats of catalyzed but unthickened epoxy resin before the wood has absorbed all it wants; this point of saturation will be indicated by the surface remaining shiny (Photograph 6-35). Thicken the remaining resin with whatever your epoxy manufacturer recommends, and coat both surfaces. If your joint is less than perfect, make the glue a little thicker. If very loose, make a dam on the bottom with masking tape and then fill the crack with epoxy glue.

Clamp the pieces together with a screw and clean up the excess glue (Photograph 6-36). Clamping the stem into position will allow the squeezed-out glue to make a perfect fit between the end of the sheer clamp and the stem.

There's one more detail to attend to before planking can begin. Since the sheer clamp is to become part of the deck, we must be sure it does not inadvertently become part of the hull at this time. As you did with the stems, **protect the sheer clamp** with plastic packaging tape (Photograph 6-37). This tape is very thin, glue won't stick to it, and it is easy to apply. (As the first plank is to be glued to the stem, trim the tape so that it does not extend over the stem.)

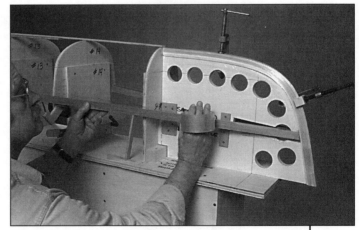

6-37

7 | The Skin: Planking

There is a good chance that your dream of building a kayak includes the process of planking the hull. In fact, it may have been the image of gluing carefully machined planks together over the mold, and seeing the kayak come alive, that first convinced you to build. Up to this point, things haven't been changing all that fast. If you squint hard enough, the kayak is there, but there are only four pieces in place now that will actually be in the kayak. The time has come to put skin on the dream and build a boat (Illustration 7-1).

Expect to spend about two full days planking if you take your time and do a good job. Building in the evening and putting on three or four planks per side each night will have it planked in about a week.

Once the first plank is hung, the other planks go on fast. A rhythm develops that will make you want to go faster and faster as more boat emerges. This is good, but don't get ahead of yourself. Take the time to wipe up the glue, and to check your work.

Savor the process. Make sure the boat is coming together the way you want it to. Feel good about the workmanship; it is hard to back up later if some detail bothers you. By building this kayak, you assume responsibility for it. It becomes a reflection of what is important to you.

THE PLANKING SEQUENCE
- Position and attach the first plank.
- Plank both sides of the hull to the centerline, and one side across the centerline.
- Cut the centerline and fill in the bottom.
- Fit and install the outer stems.

PLANKING TOOLS
Cutting and marking tools
(Photograph 7-2)
- Block plane and sharpening stone
- Dozuki razor saw (could also use a coping saw, fine back saw, or hacksaw with the blade set to cut on the pull stroke)
- Sharp 1″ or 1¼″ chisel

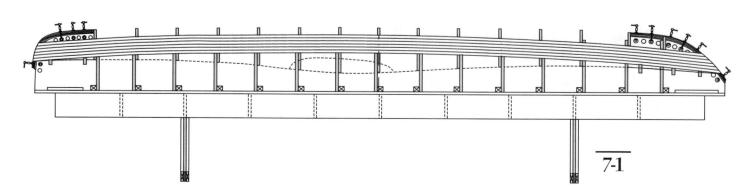

7-1

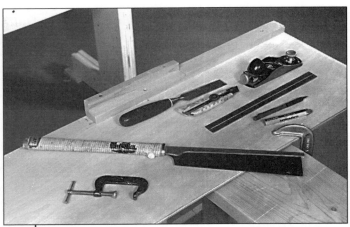

7-2

- Utility knife and sharp blades
- Straightedge (a 24″ metal straightedge is ideal)
- Sharp HB pencil or .05 technical pencil
- Red lumber marker (optional)
- Clamps (2″ "C" and small spring clamp)

Fastening and removing tools: some options and notes
(Photograph 7-3)
- Staple guns
- Arrow T-50 Tacker (*The standard, cheap and available, does the job.*)
- Black & Decker Powershot (*Great gun, easy to squeeze, good punch, but watch it. If you have been using an Arrow gun and pick this gun up without looking at it, the staple will exit from the rear of the gun. I have known several people who figured this out the hard way. If you are just firing off a shot to see if it works, it is quite natural to hold the bottom near the back of the gun with your left hand. You can guess where the staple goes. When choosing from other brands of staplers, look for one that takes a ⁹⁄₁₆″ staple with medium crown.*)

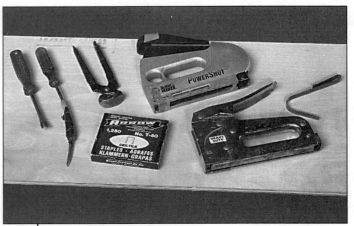

7-3

It may be necessary to modify the stapler if the crown of the staple is driven in so far that it bruises the wood. Build up the base of the stapler with masking tape just behind the place where the staple exits, varying the number of layers of tape to adjust the height. If there is a slight space between the crown and the wood, it will be easy to wiggle the staple puller under without damaging the wood.)
- Staples (⁹⁄₁₆″ or 14mm)
- Staple pullers (*Tack pullers, available at most hardware stores, will do the job. To make one from a long, flat screwdriver, bend the head to a slight angle and pad its underside with tape. Whatever you use, it should be able to be worked under the crown of the staple and pull the staple out without damaging the wood.*)
- Diagonal cutters (*Modify these by dulling the cutting edge. Sharp cutters will snip the crown off the staple, leaving the legs to be dug out of the wood. You can't leave them in; if they don't get your hand, they will get your plane.*)
- Stapler hook (*This handy little hook, which can be made of ³⁄₈″ brass stem band, fits on your belt to hold the stapler—handy when you run out of hands. You can also make one out of a doubled coat hanger wrapped with electrical tape.*)
- Planking glove (*This is a fingerless old work glove that fits the left hand. It will save your hand and the edge of the plank.*)
- Glue syringe

GLUE
Since the epoxy coating on both sides of the hull effectively stabilizes the moisture content of the planking, waterproof glue is not necessary between the planks. Look for a fast-drying, nontoxic glue that cleans up with water and blends with the color of planking being used (Photograph 7-4).

Lee Valley Cabinetmaker's Glue 202GF has good gap-filling properties, sands well, and cleans up with water. It dries to a mid-tone brown, highlights the glue line in light colored planking, and becomes inconspicuous in dark wood.

Yellow carpenter's glue is inexpensive, readily available, sands reasonably well, and cleans up with water. It dries fast to an opaque white or clear color, and looks fine with light-colored planking.

Titebond II, though promoted as a great boatbuilding glue, is not a good choice for edge-gluing the planking. It has very little body and takes forever to set up. The original Titebond is a better choice.

No large glue line will be attractive, so make the effort to fit the planks tightly together. Resist the urge to fill voids in the joints with glue; it looks awful and sands like bubble gum.

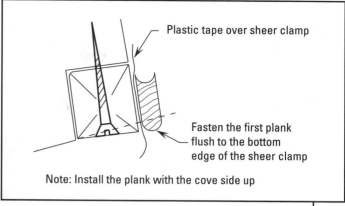

Plastic tape over sheer clamp

Fasten the first plank flush to the bottom edge of the sheer clamp

Note: Install the plank with the cove side up

7-5

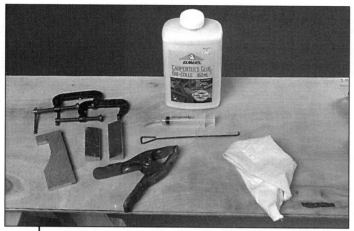

7-4

CONTROLLING THE COLOR AMONG THE STRIPS

This is your last chance to decide what your kayak will look like. If there is room, lay all the planks out and arrange them so that the color and texture on both sides balance and you are happy with the design. Lay out the deck at the same time as the hull. The deck will be the most visible part of the kayak, so you might want to lay it out first. Number the planks clearly in a conspicuous place; a random pencil mark will be hard to find. I like to number the planks with a red lumber crayon in a straight line across the middle station mold position. That way, the numbers are easy to find, and there is no question about which section of the plank to use.

If your planking is all close to the same color, or you want the color to take care of itself, choose the planks in pairs and attach one on each side of the hull or deck. Though subtle, this careful bookmatching will give a feeling of harmony to a random pattern.

THE FIRST PLANK

It is extremely important to install the first plank flush with the sheer clamp and in a fair curve. An unfair curve here will be repeated on each plank above it. If a contrasting plank is used as an accent, an unfair line will be highly visible.

The sheer clamp should be a good guide for lining up the bottom edge of the plank (Illustration 7-5). The time spent getting the sheer clamp to fit just right should make lining up the first plank a simple exercise. Begin installing the plank from the middle and work out to the ends, stapling the plank on every second station mold. The long space between staples gives the plank a chance to fair itself.

When you get to the stem, use a spring clamp to hold the plank in position so you can stand back and take a look at it. Try a lot of positions, looking for a fair curve at all angles. Don't hesitate to pull a staple and watch what the plank does when it is let loose. Sometimes you won't be able to decide whether there is a problem or not. When the staple is pulled, the plank might shift slightly and suddenly look right.

When you are happy with the position of the first plank, mark its position on the stem before removing the clamp. Apply a thin film of glue to the stem and staple the plank into place (Photograph 7-6). Controlling the amount of glue now will save a lot of work later when the hardened glue must be cleaned up from the inside of the hull. If the staple isn't enough to hold the plank up to the stem, put a spring clamp on it for a few minutes until the glue grabs.

Glue the other end and carefully trim the ends of the planks.

It is worth taking the time to trim the planks accurately, one plank at a time. The time saved by trimming in a haphazard manner is not worth the frustration of having to work the end grain of the planks down to a crisp curve.

Make the cut just a hair longer than the stem, and make sure it is at 90° to the centerline. Watch for tearout on the outside edge of the plank. If this is a problem, cut

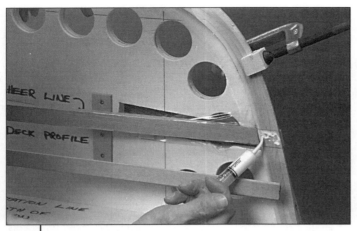

7-6

with the teeth pointing towards the stem. Any tearout will then be on the stem side of the plank and will be covered by the outer stem.

Finish stapling the plank to the sheer clamp, then install the plank on the opposite side in the same manner. Be sure that the ends of the planks are parallel to each other.

PLANKING THE REST OF THE HULL

Now the fun begins. Everything you have been doing up to this point has been preparation for this moment. It has taken awhile and been tedious at times, but if you have been patient and done everything right, planking will be easy.

Fill up the glue syringe. Begin by putting a thin film of glue on the stem, then run a bead of glue down the cove side of the sheer plank and coat the other stem. Make it a routine to always apply the glue to the stem, followed by the plank, and finish with the other stem. Not only will this save you from going back to check for voids, but it will also guarantee that all the planks are glued to the stem.

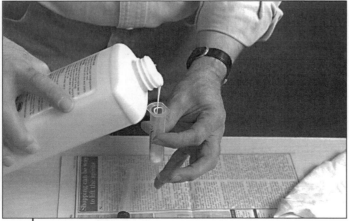

7-7

Use this little trick when filling the glue syringe to keep the glue from dripping all over your shoes: Place your little finger over the end of the syringe while pouring the glue in slowly. Stop pouring before it gets to the top, so that the plunger will fit in without making a mess. Start the plunger in with the tip over the glue container and squeeze out enough to lodge the plunger, then pull back enough to create a vacuum that will keep the glue from weeping out (Photograph 7-7).

If the hole in the end of the syringe is quite small, trim the tip back to a more functional size.

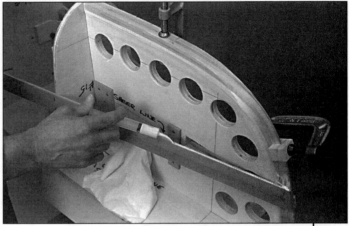

7-8

The amount of glue shown in photo (Photograph 7-8) is about right to fill the joint and leave just enough to squeeze out to ensure that the joint is full. Use the amount of glue consumed to make sure that the correct amount of glue is being applied. The size of syringe shown in the photo will glue about 20′ of planking. Obviously, if all the glue is gone and only 12′ have been covered, it is a little on the heavy side.

Begin installing the next plank at the middle station mold and work out to the stems. If you are working alone, it is awkward checking that both ends of the plank extend past the stems. To reduce the possibility of fastening the plank into position only to find one end short, find the middle of the plank by balancing it in your hand, and then place this point over the middle station mold. If you are working alone, put spring clamps on the end station molds to hold the ends of the planks until you can fasten them. As you fasten each plank to the stems, be careful that your staples are aligning in a neat, clean

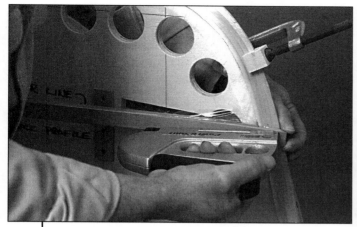

7-9 |

row parallel to the outline of the stems (Photograph 7-9).

Trim the ends of each plank perpendicular to the centerline after fastening (Photograph 7-10). A plank extending past the end of the stem is in danger of being caught and torn off by someone walking around the end of the building jig.

7-10 |

Wipe up the squeezed-out glue with a water-dampened rag. Try not to soak the wood around the staples, as this will often result in a permanent black stain around the staple hole.

A glue line will be unattractive, so make the effort to fit the planks tightly together. But if there are voids, fill them with a thickened epoxy-based filler tinted with sanding dust; this will be easy to sand and can be almost invisible.

The little tricks shown in Photograph 7-11, devised for our system of planking without staples (see page 124), come in handy when a staple is too much or not enough. Notice the clamping blocks holding the planks to the stem. The wedge-shaped blocks have sandpaper

glued to the bottom, effectively keeping them from sliding off when clamping pressure is applied.

| 7-11

The span from the stem to the station mold is about 15″, which is too long to expect the planks to stay together on their own. Rather than pepper the planks full of extra staple holes, two short pieces of planking are placed across the joint and the clamp tightened over the joint. This arrangement will hold the planks together until the glue gets tacky. Use this technique wherever you need to control the plank seams between the station molds.

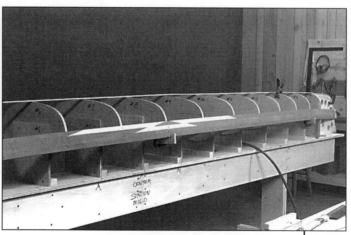

| 7-12

Now that you are off to a good start and know the routine, planking (Photograph 7-12) will go along with few surprises until you run out of shaped stem. Keep shaping the stem ahead of the planking. Plank on alternate sides to keep both sides coming up at the same speed. Getting too far ahead on one side could force the stem off center, and there is also the danger of losing control of the color balance.

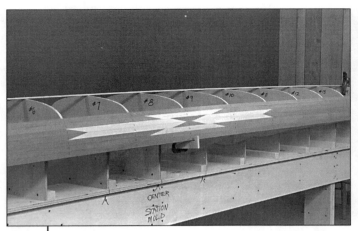

7-13

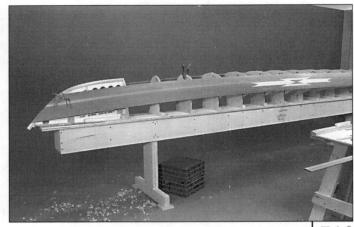

7-16

At the turn of the bilge where the sides begin to turn in to the bottom, it will take a little extra attention to get the bead to seat itself in the cove (Photograph 7-13 and Illustration 7-14). Try rocking the plank back and forth a few times to make sure it is seated before stapling.

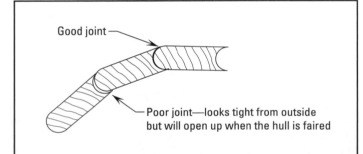

Good joint

Poor joint—looks tight from outside but will open up when the hull is faired

7-14

A staple that straddles the plank line is often enough to tie the planks together in this difficult area (Photograph 7-15). If this is not enough, consider the extra control available with the stapleless jigs. (See page 124.)

At the stage shown in Photograph 7-16, the stress in the middle has relaxed

somewhat but is about to get a bit fussy at the stems. This is a good time to take off the temporary stabilizing plank down the middle and finish shaping the stems. Pay special attention to keeping the fairing batten parallel to the plank line when checking the bevel; the bevel on the stem will roll quite quickly in places, and this is the only way to keep up with it. The area that is actually covered by the plank on this part of the stem is very deceiving (Photograph 7-17). To be sure the glue has been spread far enough, mark the area as a guide for applying the glue.

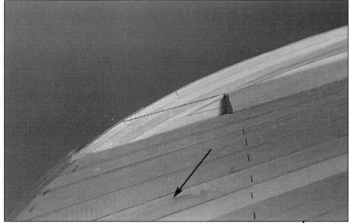

7-17

Rather than many staples to hold the plank to the stems, the two techniques shown in Photograph 7-18, from our stapleless bag of tricks, are good solutions.

When both sides are planked up almost to the end of the stem, stop planking one side and finish planking the other (Photograph 7-19). The length of the planks may be random, but must be long enough to cross the centerline. This is a good time to pay extra attention to bookmatching the planks; as the sides get closer together,

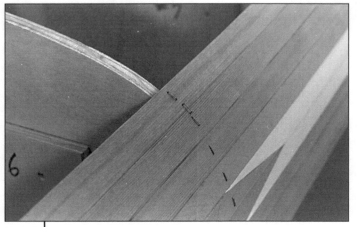

7-15

7-18

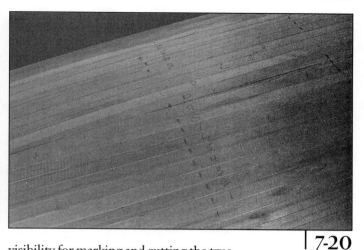

7-20

planks that are not a close mirror image of each other will become more obvious. (Photograph 7-20).

If you haven't already arranged and numbered the planks, at least plan the bottom. Choose the bottom planks in pairs, number them with a lumber crayon, use one of each pair now, and set the others aside to fill in the bottom later.

visibility for marking and cutting the true centerline.

Chisel off the bulk of the excess planking, still staying a safe distance from the centerline. Carve the planking away until you can see down the centerline on the building jig. Hold the chisel firmly with both hands, push it into the wood, and twist to split off the excess. If you have

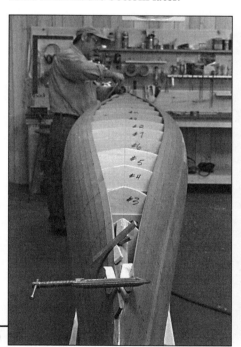

7-19

7-21

Cutting the centerline

The centerline will be ready for marking and cutting after one side of the bottom has been filled in and all glue has dried (Photograph 7-21). Begin by pulling enough staples to give you a clear path down the centerline. Mark a rough centerline that is a safe ½" to 1" over the finished line, and trim the excess planking back to this line. This will give you good

to use a mallet to sink the chisel, the edge may need touching up. Practice holding the chisel plumb now, as this angle will become important when you make the final cut (Photograph 7-22).

The utility knife works well for trimming the planking over the stem back to the centerline (Photograph 7-23). Holding the handle of the knife out near the end as you draw it towards yourself will

down the length of the building jig, transferring each of the centerline points to the outside of the hull. In theory, we should be able to join each of these points and have a straight line. In practice, slight variations could make the line less than straight.

7-24

help you steer in a straight line. Keep both hands on the knife, and it won't get away from you. Begin with light passes to get the cut started, gradually applying more pressure. Repeat on the other stem.

When we **mark and cut the true centerline,** it must, for obvious reasons, be in the intended place. To eliminate a few of the variables, we are going to use two different techniques for marking the centerline. When one method confirms the other, you can, with reasonable certainty, mark and cut to the line.

To prove this line, rig a string line from the centerline on one stem to the centerline on the other stem. Use 1" finishing nails driven at angles away from the middle of the boat to anchor the line. Lead the line around the nail (don't wrap) and down to the edge of the hull; pull tight and clamp. Place a small block under the line at both ends to raise most of the line off the hull (Photograph 7-25). Check that it is directly over the end station mold and that it is not hung up on anything. Sight down the line, and when you are sure it is straight, compare it to the set of marks on the planking. What you hope to see is a few marks that are off a bit to one side to balance the ones that are off on the other. If the line doesn't look like it is averaging the marks, find out why and correct it.

When you are ready to mark the line,

7-23

Begin by making a marking gauge that will transfer the centerline on the station mold around to the top of the planking. This simple jig, shown in Photograph 7-24, can be made from anything from a Corn Flakes box to thin plywood. Work

7-25

7-26

go by the string line, as it has the best chance of being a continuous fair line. Mark under the line at each station mold with a mark that is distinguishable from the first set of marks (Photograph 7-26). Remove the line and the nails.

7-27

Join the points with your best straightedge, using a ball-point pen to make a good, strong impression (Photograph 7-27). Avoid using a marker, as the ink could bleed into the wood. If you have a problem holding onto the straightedge while

you draw the line, try a spring clamp on one end of the straightedge.

Have a good look at the line to confirm that it is straight before you cut it. Position your eye at the end of the mold and just above the line. Squint to filter out the distracting images, allowing you to concentrate on the line. If it looks straight from both ends, trust your eye; it probably is.

7-28

Beginning the cut in the middle of the hull and working out to the ends will keep the chisel cutting across the grain and away from the line (Photograph 7-28). If the grain is approached from this direction, the blade will follow the angle of the grain and be led away from the centerline. As the chisel is twisted to break off the waste, the break will likewise be split away from the line. This should work as a rule with straight-grained wood, but watch for wild grain that doubles back across the centerline.

Develop a constant awareness of grain direction, and learn how to respond to it; it is a major component of all woodworking procedures, whether you use hand tools or power tools.

Stand on something to get your body into a comfortable, balanced position before beginning to cut with the chisel. Use your widest, sharpest chisel, with the flat back of the blade acting as a guide to follow the line just cut. Keep both hands on the chisel to guide it. This also keeps both of your hands behind the blade if it happens to jump out of the cut and go out of control. Use a pushing, splitting, paring action with the chisel to work up to the line. Holding the back of the chisel plum from the beginning of the cut will give you a better chance of ending up plumb when the line is reached.

The rabbet plane is the tool of choice to take the waves out, stopping as it just splits the line (Photograph 7-29). If you do not have a rabbet plane, the block plane will work. To do this, wedge the hull up enough to allow the edge of the plane body to clear the station mold. (Be aware that the plumb line we were after will be out of plumb, depending on the amount the hull has been wedged up.) When the cut is as good as you can make it without going past the line, staple the edge of the planking back down to the station mold.

Stand back and have a good look at the line from both ends. The accuracy of this line is not only to make a tidy joint between the sides, it also makes fitting planks up to it a simple process. The more predictable the edge, the easier it will be to mark the plank, cut a bevel, and have it fit.

7-29

Fitting the rest of the bottom

Fitting the balance of the planks into the bottom will require accurate measuring and precise joinery. Keep your pencil and your plane sharp, be patient, and take your time. If you are just getting familiar with your block plane, this is a good place to develop skill.

7-30

Lay the first plank into position with the end extending over the centerline, and mark the angle to be cut. A simple way to cut this bevel is to clamp the plank into a miter box, rough-trim it with the chisel, and finish up with the block plane. Expect to try it in place several times before it fits.

Don't try to force it to fit, as this will only distort the other side of the hull. Keep an eye also on the angle that will make the cut plumb when the plank is fitted to the centerline. This angle will change for each plank, becoming closer to 90° as you approach the middle of the kayak.

When you are happy with the fit of one end, hold the plank in place and draw a pencil line across the bead-and-cove joint, about 12″ from the end. Continue positioning the plank as you move down to the opposite end of the plank. When you get to the middle, draw another mark across the joint. This reference line will be used to position the plank when it is glued and fastened into position. Move down to the end and make another reference line a foot or so from the centerline. All final fitting of this end will be made to this reference line, so you won't have to fit the plank back into position each time the bevel is checked.

One end of the plank is now running past the centerline, and the plank itself lies parallel to the previous plank (Photograph 7-30). At the end that is not yet fitted, make small pencil marks on both edges of the plank to show where it crosses the centerline, add ⅝″ to these marks, and join these last two marks together. Cut to this line. The reason for the extra ⅝″ is that the plank must be longer than it now appears to compensate for its slipping back into the cove—plus a little extra for final fitting.

After making the marks, take the plank back to the bench to draw the line and cut the miter (Photograph 7-31). I find it less of a balancing act to draw the line with the plank on the bench. If you do this, make sure the marks are accurate and understandable when you get back to the bench.

an angle. Joints that look as tight on the outside as the one in Photograph 7-33 are sometimes too good to be true. A fit this seemingly precise could mean that the joint is undercut and is wide open on the inside. If you are curious, check from the bottom to see how you are doing. The voids from a less-than-perfect joint may be filled later with a color-matched epoxy filler, but try for an honest fit. The discipline is good for you.

7-33

7-31

When you take the plank back to the boat to try it, there is no need to fit the whole plank into position; the end of the plank is fragile and could get broken during repetitive fitting. Let the plank drape over the side at the most natural angle for working on the end. Try a spring clamp to keep the end under control if you don't have a helper.

When the plank is ready to go in, apply glue to the miter on the plank you are fitting, rather than trying to spread it along the centerline (Photograph 7-32). Spring the plank into position, line up the reference marks in the middle, and fasten.

Planks that do not come together flush along the centerline can be controlled with a staple that straddles the joint, driven at

Fitting the last plank

There is some advantage to installing the last two planks as one piece (Photograph 7-34). This trick is especially useful if the last plank is very narrow, fragile, and hard to handle. It helps to have these pieces glued together and molded into their approximate shape before marking and

7-34

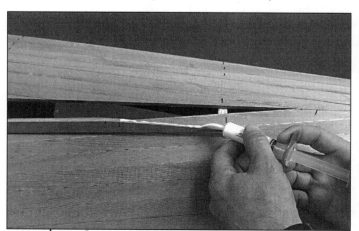

7-32

cutting. (The term "last plank" applies to both of these pieces in the following instructions.)

Glue them together some time after the planking has started to come across the bottom, when the edge of a fastened plank can be used as a mold. Rather than put an extra set of staple holes in the planks, consider stapling a short piece of sacrificial planking into position and gluing the pieces against that. (The bead edge, as will be described in the next paragraph, must be removed to fit to the second-to-last plank. Plane this edge off before bending. It will be awkward to hang onto the plank and shape accurately after it has been bent.)

The joint between the edges of the second-to-last and the last planks will be a simple, straight-sided edge joint to allow the last plank to slide straight down. So, before installing the second-to-last plank, plane the cove edge flat. Take your time to get a nice, straight square edge that will fit the square edge of the last plank.

7-36

7-35

average out the marks and smooth the curve. Trim almost to the line, but leave some wood for the final fit (Photograph 7-36).

Because the ends are going to be long, skinny, and hard to hang onto, try clamping the block plane in the vise and drawing the plank over the plane.

To do the final fitting, work each end to the middle reference mark. When the piece fits at the reference mark, the whole piece should fit. Resist the urge to dry-fit the whole piece more than you have to; it's hard to get out, and the ends could

By now, you are getting good at fitting the planks to the centerline, so the last plank will not be a problem. Lay the plank opposite the opening and put a reference mark in the middle. Use dividers to carefully pick up the width of the opening and transfer the measurement directly across to the plank; work out to the ends at 1"-to-2" increments (Photograph 7-35).

Bend a batten through these points to

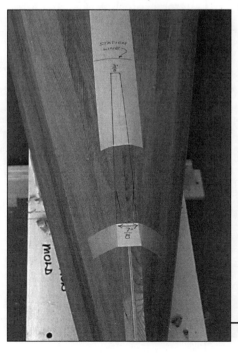

7-37

break off. You may have to reach underneath to support the planking as this last piece is glued into position.

Nice fit! Now isn't that a Kodak moment?

THE OUTER STEMS
Fitting the outer stems

The outer stems protect and seal the plank ends and create a traditional feeling and visual end to the planking, defining the profile of the kayak (Photograph 7-37 and Illustration 7-38). They must terminate about 1″ short of the heel of the inner stem; otherwise there will be a hole through the hull when the planking is cut out to receive the stems. The vertical portions of the the outer stems fit directly over the cut-off ends of the planking. As the stems become more horizontal where they turn in to the bottom, the outer stems are tapered and let into a slot cut in the planking (Photograph 7-39).

Since the inner and outer stems were glued up at the same time, in theory they should fit back together perfectly. Keep this in mind when you trim the ends of the planks. Be careful not to remove wood from the end of the stem; try to leave the centerline on the stem to show that you haven't gone too far.

Use a very sharp spokeshave to trim the ends of the planks. Finish up with a firm sanding block or fine rasp. If a crown begins to develop in the middle of the stem, you have gone too far. Keep the edges crisp.

As you shape the ends of the planking, keep in mind that you are working at 90° to the centerline of the kayak. If you don't keep this angle, the joint between the inner and outer stems will have a gap on one side. You won't get it perfect, but try to get as close as possible (Photograph 7-40).

To confirm the angle, lay a short straightedge across the stem to exagger-

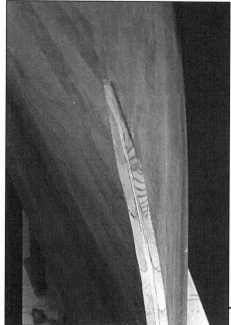

7-39

ate the angle. Choose a line that is at 90° to the centerline, such as the end of the strongback, to align visually with the straightedge. As you work the ends of the planking down to the stems, you will appreciate having carefully trimmed the planks to length.

The heel end of the outer stem (Photograph 7-39) should be tapered both to

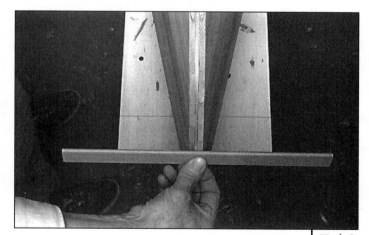

7-40

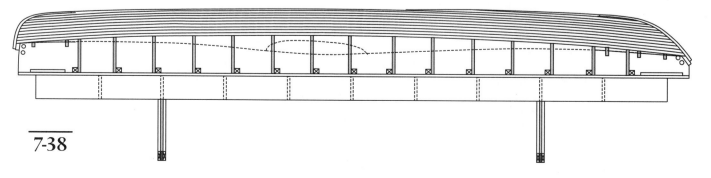

7-38

reduce its width for aesthetics and to allow more planking to bear on the stem. Start the taper just before the plank ends begin obscuring the inside stem, and taper down to about ³⁄₈″ wide.

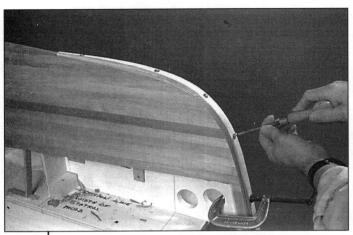

7-41

Shape the stem first, then use it as a pattern to trace the shape onto the planking. If this mark is accurate, it will be easy to cut the slot and have it fit.

Begin by tracing the shape of the stem onto the planking, then dress almost down to the line to remove the bulk of the excess. Put the stem back into position and mark the outline as precisely as possible. If you are working alone, duct-tape the stem into position. I have found that a blade, such as a pocket knife, will lie alongside the stem and project the shape of the stem to the irregular shape of the hull. Fill the line in with a sharp pencil to make it easy to follow.

Start the cut by scoring the outline. Use a sharp utility knife to make progressively firmer passes along the score line. Go down about ¹⁄₈″, then clean out the slot with a ³⁄₈″ or less chisel. If you work down to the stem in stages, there should be no problem stopping when the stem is reached.

Now that you are watching grain direction as a habit, note that, in most cases, the chisel will have to be worked from the middle of the boat out towards the ends.

Attaching the outer stems

When the slot has been cut and you are happy with the fit between the inner and outer stems, do a dry run with the screws in place (Photograph 7-41 and Illustration 7-42). The 1¼″ x No. 6 steel wood screws will temporarily clamp the stem

into position for checking the fit as well as the clamping pressure when it is glued into position. If the edges of the stem are overhanging the hull, mark the hull shape on the back of the stem and trim almost to the line before gluing. Avoid using drywall screws, as they are brittle and could break off when you try to remove them. Wax the screws (with paraffin wax) just before gluing to ease their removal, and plug the holes later.

Drill pilot holes around the perimeter of the outer stem on 6″ to 8″ centers. The hole should be just loose enough for the screw to slide in without binding. You will also need to drill smaller pilot holes into the inner stem as the screws are placed. Mark the length of the screw on the drill bit with a piece of masking tape so that the hole doesn't go all the way through the inside stem. Be careful not to overtighten the screws, as they have a marginal hold in the softwood inner stem.

Look for a decent fit over much of the area. If there is a gap on both sides and the stem is drawn down tight, there is most likely a crown in the middle. If it is open on one side and you are already down to the stem, leave it. Use your judgment. If you go past the original surface of the inside stem, stop. It is a big job to bring the whole surface of the stem down to meet the low spot. Don't expect the screw to have enough grab to distort the shape of the stem to fit a low spot. The glue/filler is going to be very thick and color-matched, so some sins will be hidden.

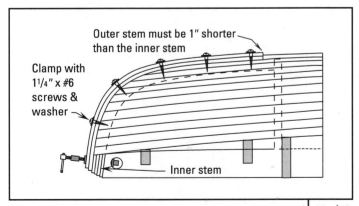

7-42

For a good bond when gluing to end grain, it is important that the end grain be completely filled with glue (Photograph 7-43). In cedar, the glue will migrate in as much as ¹⁄₈″, giving the joint a great mechanical bond. Apply catalyzed but

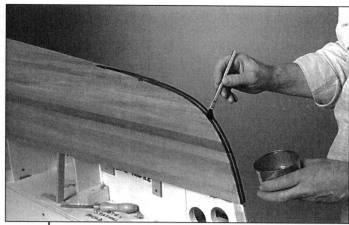

7-43

Pick up the excess with a putty knife and wipe the surface clean with lacquer thinner (Photograph 7-45). Check that the joint is full, and that the glue is flush with or slightly above the surface. If the joint is quite large and the glue is sagging out, mold it back into place and put masking tape over the joint; the tape will peel off clean after the epoxy has set.

unthickened epoxy resin to the end grain before adding filler to the glue. If this is not done, the glue will soak into the end grain, drawing the glue out of the joint. Expect to make three or four applications of glue and to wait five to ten minutes before the surface remains shiny, indicating that it has soaked up all the glue it needs. Thicken the final application of glue, and add sanding dust for color (Photograph 7-44). Keep in mind that the filler will be darker than the dust you began with; add the color slowly.

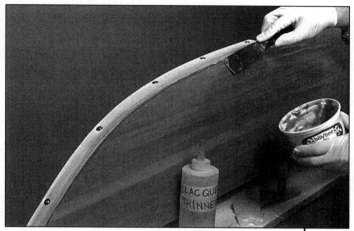

7-45

When the glue has set, carefully remove the screws. In spite of the wax, the epoxy will be gripping the screw tightly. Go easy with the screwdriver as you initially break the screw loose; apply pressure firmly, gradually building until it is free. If you feel the screw stretching but not breaking loose, try a percussion adjustment (hit the end of the screwdriver with a hammer while twisting the screwdriver)

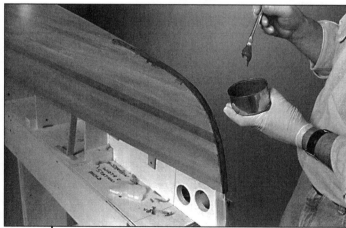

7-44

Make the mixture stiff enough to hold a point when the stir stick is removed. Apply a liberal amount to both surfaces—more if the fit is marginal—then screw the outer stem into place. (Are the screws waxed?) It is a good sign if the glue/filler squeezes out; you can be sure there are no voids. If for some reason the screws must be removed and replaced, use a fresh waxed screw; otherwise, there is a good chance that the screw will have lost its protection and will twist off when you try to remove it.

7-46

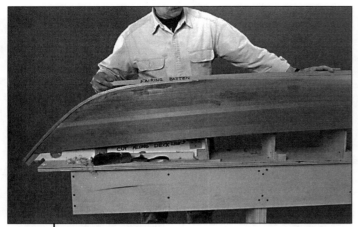

7-47

that the stem is coming down on the same line as the planking and not being over-cut. Resist the urge to finish shaping the stem with a power sander. The planking, being of a softer wood than the stem, will sand faster than the stem, creating a hollow in the planking before the stem is down to where you want it. Consider cutting the stem almost down to the planking, then finishing it with a scraper. The scraper, though aggressive, has better control for working around all the different grain directions. Complete the shaping with a firm sanding block, worked in the direction of the plank grain.

to help break it loose. When the screws have been removed, whittle and glue wooden plugs into the screw holes. It's not a bad idea to run a ⅛" bit into the holes to clean out the wax before gluing in the plugs (Photograph 7-46).

Begin by shaping the bottom portion of the stem so that it fairs into the bottom (Photograph 7-47). Stand back often and check by looking at the profile. This is one of those basic shaping techniques that may be applied to a variety of shaping situations. It is much easier to see a fair curve if the corner is crisp. Once the profile and face width are established, the radius of the edge should fall into place (Illustration 7-48).

7-49

Before beginning to round over the corners, draw a centerline around the stem as a reference. This line should remain on the wood until the end of the rough shaping step. When the radiused corner is as smooth as you can make it with the block plane/spokeshave, finish, using long strokes with a firm sanding block. Wrap a piece of sandpaper around the stem or use a soft sanding block to complete the shaping and smoothing.

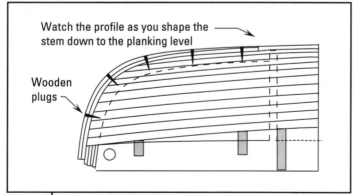

Watch the profile as you shape the stem down to the planking level

Wooden plugs

7-48

Shape the sides of the stem with a block plane and/or spokeshave as if it were an extension of the hull lines (Photograph 7-49). Be careful not to damage the planking while working the stem. If this is a problem, cover the planking with masking tape to protect it. Use a batten to check

PULLING STAPLES
Now it's time to pull out all of those staples. Whatever you find to use as a staple puller, remember that it should be able to wiggle under the crown of the staple and pull it out without damaging the wood. While it is possible to swell a bruise out with hot water, if the fiber is broken, the damage will remain visible.

8 | The Skin: Sanding

MORE THAN "SAND THE HULL"

At this point, I could simply say, "Sand the hull," and then move on to laying up the fiberglass. I have noticed that many how-to writers and casual builders assume that picking up the sander and sanding through a couple of grits is all it takes. Perhaps the reason many people find sanding frustrating and tedious is that they don't have a clear understanding of the tools, the steps, and what each step should look like. It was years before I sorted out the steps and looked at the chore of sanding as a simple system. After becoming aware of sanding as a series of steps, it was easy to tailor the system to get the appropriate results to suit the job. My sanding time has been reduced by at least 50% (Photograph 8-1).

Before you pick up the belt sander with the 60-grit sandpaper (definitely not recommended), be sure you know what you are trying to accomplish and the steps it will take to get you there. The order, the tool to use, and what each step of the process is expected to look like and result in are very important. Without this understanding, time could be spent using the right technique on the wrong step. Not only is this a waste of time and energy, but it also takes off more boat than is necessary to arrive at the desired surface. You won't know when you are finished until you get fed up with the dust and noise, your friends have all gone paddling, or the boat wears out.

With a good understanding of what to

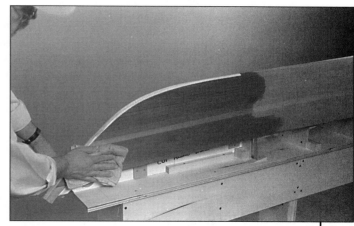

8-1

look for, the sequence of steps, and tools to use, you will feel in control and know that each step has a predictable end. Then, sanding can be quite pleasant and go quickly. When I sand a rough hull, I feel like a sculptor, liberating the boat I want out of a bunch of flat boards.

UNDERSTANDING AND CHOOSING SANDPAPER

Think of a sheet of sandpaper as a multitude of sharp cutting tools. On coarse-grit paper, the tools are large and far apart and cut deep, widely spaced grooves. A finer-grit paper has many smaller tools making many shallow cuts close together. Thus, the coarser grits are more suited to high-speed machine sanders, as it takes more passes before the cuts overlap. A finer grit, which cuts an even, though shallower, depth with each pass, is more effective for hand-sanding. Look for a balance between a coarse grit, making many fast, deep cuts to reach a determined depth but leaving deep scratches, and a finer grit, making more shallow cuts and arriving at the same depth with a smoother surface.

The surface you want left behind is an important part of deciding on the grit to begin with. While some sources suggest beginning with 60-grit, I don't think that is appropriate to the type of craftsmanship this kayak deserves. Once the shape is arrived at using the 60-grit, the scratches left behind are almost as deep as the original material that was intended to be removed. Considering that the planking is only 1/4″ thick to begin with and you have to do this again on the inside, you might want to preserve that extra thickness and save your time and energy for something else.

Consider the coating on the paper and how the particles were bonded to the backing. Sanding epoxy with 120-grit garnet paper would plug up very quickly while the same grit in a silicon carbide OC ("open coat") resin-bonded paper would stay clean and cut longer.

This brings up the backing that the grit is attached to and how it is attached. You will notice that the cheaper the backing and glue, the more the grit will fall off as the paper is bent. This is something to keep in mind when choosing paper—especially for hand-sanding curves. Cloth-backed resin-bonded sanding belts are excellent for hand-sanding.

The ideal is to have the right combination of the grit staying sharp and in place, not plugging up, and the backing not falling apart. In other words, all the systems should work together for as long as possible; eventually, everything should die at the same time.

It is economical to buy good sandpaper, but expect to pay a premium initial price for it. Aluminum oxide, resin-bonded to a good backing, is a good choice for sanding both wood and epoxy. Silicon carbide paper designated as "OC" is the first choice for sanding epoxy and varnish. Working on these hard plastic materials, the silicon carbide will stay sharp longer, without plugging up, than will cheap aluminum-oxide production paper.

I have noticed that with good resin-bonded discs, the finer grits are as aggressive as coarser cheap production paper

discs. They give a very controlled rate of material removal as well as ending up closer to the desired surface faster. If you are worried about going too fast, consider using good paper on a random-orbit sander to sand both the planking and the epoxy on the hull with 120-grit rather than starting with 80-grit. Doing all the sanding with 120-grit will use more sanding discs and will be a little slower going, but it will be aggressive enough to get the job done. If it is your first boat, you might appreciate the added control.

I don't suggest going finer than 120-grit on the epoxy surface. The varnish needs a good mechanical bond to the epoxy, and 120-grit gives it a good bite. When the varnish is applied, it will flow into the scratches and level the surface.

Sandpaper is like any other cutting tool: it's useful only if it's sharp. When the grit becomes dull, it stops cutting and simply burnishes the wood, compressing the surface fibers. When a finish or coating is applied to this burnished surface, the finish will be absorbed at an uneven rate. This inconsistent absorption of the coating material will give the surface a blotchy effect. So, when the paper stops cutting, change it.

Grits you will need for top-notch work
- 80-grit (rough-shaping the hull, rough-sanding epoxy)
- 120-grit (finish-sanding planking and epoxy, shaping hardwood trim)
- 220-grit (finish-sanding hardwood trim, sanding between varnish coats)

SANDING SCHEDULE
The following is a list of the steps needed to prepare the hull for the fiberglass covering. Each step has a variety of techniques and tools to choose from. Combine the choices to achieve the degree of finish you want.

Choices are listed from "A," the best, down to the least desirable. Choosing the underlined steps will produce an excellent-quality job. I can't think of many excuses for doing less than the suggested choices.

1. Shaping the hull initially
A. <u>Block plane and/or spokeshave</u>
B. Scraper
C. Sand with 60-grit sandpaper

2. Filling the voids in the hull
    A. <u>Color-matched epoxy-based filler</u>
    B. Plastic wood, natural color
    C. Voids not filled

3. Sanding with 80-grit sandpaper (the final shaping step)
    A. Hand-sand with a file board
    B. Power-sand with a ½-sheet orbital
    C. <u>Power-sand with a round random-orbit sander</u>
    D. Sand with dull paper
    E. Sand with a belt sander (not recommended)

4. Raising the grain
    A. <u>Dampen the surface with water</u>
    B. Go directly from 80-grit to 120-grit
    C. Stop sanding at 80-grit

5. Sanding with 120-grit paper (a smoothing step)
    A. Hand-sand with a file board
    B. <u>Power-sand with a round random-orbit sander</u>
    C. Power-sand with a ½-sheet orbital (it could leave swirls)
    D. Sand with dull paper

8-2

A NOTE ON SHAPING TOOLS
The **block plane** and **spokeshave** are indispensable for building a kayak. Used for shaping the outside of the hull, they will save a lot of sanding, and their use can be one of the most pleasant parts of the

project. When you look at the pile of shavings on the floor after you finish, picture them as dust everywhere; you'll be glad you didn't sand your way through shaping (Photograph 8-2).

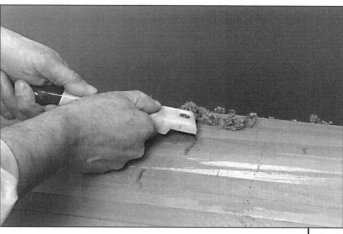

8-3

Don't underestimate the usefulness of a sharp **paint scraper** (Photograph 8-3). While ideal for hardwood, it will do a reasonable job on softwood if the blade is kept sharp. Not only will it take care of the excess glue, but it will also take a moderately aggressive bite of wood that is easy to control. Think of it as the low-budget profile sander kit; it gets into the corners, and you can file it into any shape you need. The cutting action of the scraper will be a combination of cutting and scraping. The edge is filed like a plane blade, and the steep angle of attack is controlled by you. Try different angles until you find the cleanest cut. If the tool is chattering, try holding the scraper diagonal to the grain. (While a traditional cabinet scraper will do the job, the paint scraper has the advantage of availability in any hardware store and a handle so you don't bash your

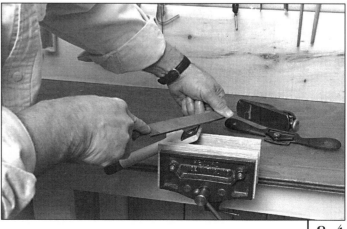

8-4

knuckles or burn your fingers.)

A paint scraper with the blade filed into an arch with a good edge will save hours of sanding on the inside of the hull (Photograph 8-4). The metal in these scrapers is quite soft, so, while sharpening is easy, the edge won't last long. When you stop getting a decent shave, stop and resharpen. Many paint scrapers have two edges on their replaceable blades. Keep one side straight for flat and outside curves, and shape the other side for inside curves.

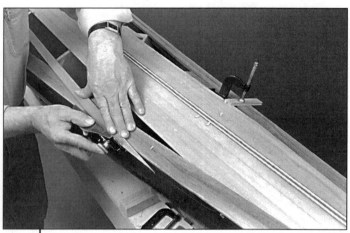

8-5

In the past the only **power sanders** available to the casual builder were the flat-, square-, or rectangular-shaped orbit or straight-line sanders (Photograph 8-5). While they were fine for flat and outside surfaces, there was no graceful way I know of to sand the inside of the hull without the corners of the pad digging in.

It is interesting to see the increasing number of professional-quality strip boats being built by first-time builders since the advent of cheap random-orbit sanders and safe, predictable epoxy resins. These two items have allowed the strip-plank/epoxy system to evolve to a higher stage.

Consider obtaining a round 5" or 6" random-orbit sander. It will do a lot of work, from 80-grit rough shaping to 220-grit scuffing between varnish coats. For a light-duty 5" random-orbit sander, expect to pay about $100 to $150. A heavy-duty 5" or 6" model with variable speed will cost between $200 and $250. Both machines are available with either a PSA (pressure-sensitive adhesive) or hook-and-loop pad system. Hook-and-loop is handy if you don't anticipate wearing out the disc before having to change to the next grit, but if you anticipate wearing each disc out,

they are not cost-effective.

The feature I like in the PSA system is its ability to make discs from any available sheet. Although we keep a supply of 80-grit and 120-grit discs, when a finer disc is needed, it is cut out of a sheet and the back coated with a spray adhesive such as 3M Super 77 or Sprayway Disc Adhesive 66. The disc will peel off the pad cleanly if it is removed while still hot from use.

The purpose of the **foam sanding pad** is to support the sandpaper and help it conform smoothly to the general contour of the shape being sanded. While the hard pad that comes with the sander is ideal for flat surfaces, a soft contour pad is superior for smoothing both inside and outside curves; as a rule, a soft pad will conform to a sharper curve than a firm pad will. There are exceptions and variables, such as the thickness and density of the pad, the type of paper, the speed of the machine, and whether a concave or convex shape is being sanded. A variety of pads are available for most 5" and 6" random-orbit sanders (Photograph 8-6).

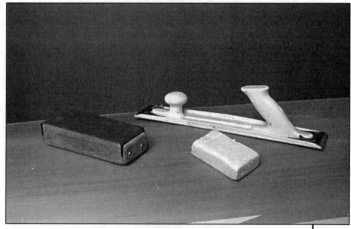

8-6

If you must sand your kayak by hand, consider the "Speed File," a commercially available **file board** that uses 2¾" × 14½" strips of sandpaper. This tool is used extensively for fairing in auto-body work. Although it will take more energy than using the machine, the file board will give you an incredibly fair hull or deck surface. Most of the outside of the kayak in this book was sanded with a file board. It wasn't as bad a job as I had imagined, and it took about three hours and a little sweat to go through the 80-grit and 120-grit on the hull.

A firm ¼- or ½-sheet **sanding block**

8-7

is handy for many shaping, smoothing, and sanding chores. It could be store-bought or cobbled up from foam or cork on a rigid or flexible backing block. The firm type of foam that electronic equipment is packed in makes a great sanding block. It's firm and easy to shape, and the price is right.

Cloth-backed resin-bonded sanding belts are excellent for shaping tight curves by hand and for getting into corners.

SAFETY CONSIDERATIONS FOR SANDING
(Photograph 8-7)
• Wear eye protection, especially when machine-sanding.
• Dress for it. Wear a dust mask and hat.
• Ensure good cross ventilation. Put a fan in the window and open the door,

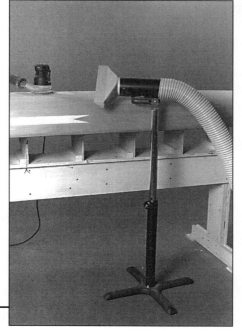

8-8

or sand outside.
• Provide good light.
• Have something solid to stand on when you need to get up higher.
• Wear ear protection when necessary. Machine sanding can get quite loud depending on the machine and what other machines are running at the same time.
• Control dust. A good shop vacuum or dust collector with the intake of the hose rigged up close to where you are sanding will do a lot to capture flying dust (Photograph 8-8). Watch the motor for overheating, as some shop vacuums are not made for contentious duty. Cover shelves and other hard-to-clean areas with plastic film to aid in cleanup. Sand outside when you can, but be cautious when moving the hull on the mold. Handle carefully and set up level in the new location.

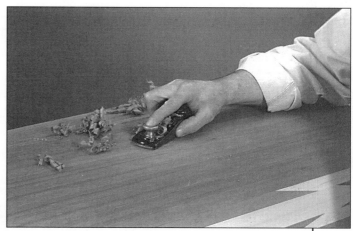

8-9

WHERE TO START
The surface on the outside of the kayak comprises the many flat surfaces of the individual planks plus any glue that was not cleaned up during planking. Have a good look at it now, because the block plane will take off most of what you see, leaving just a few low spots as a reference. You need to recognize this surface and keep an eye on it as you work it, stopping before it completely disappears.

The first step will be to go over the hull with the block plane and/or spokeshave and begin turning the flats into fluid curves (Photograph 8-9). Concentrate on dressing down the ridges between the planks first. This could be tricky if you are just getting the feel for your plane, but this is the place to practice. Watch the shaving as it exits the plane; it will show where the cut is being made under the plane sole. Try to balance the tool evenly on the ridge so that the low spots don't become too low. Work systematically, finishing one area before moving on to the next.

Edge grain will be much easier to work than flat grain. Flat grain must be worked in the right direction or the blade will tear out fragments of planking. Watch and listen for slivers of wood being ripped out rather than being cut off clean. If you see this happening, reverse the direction of the tool. This can be tricky on a strip-built boat, because the odds of all the planks having the same grain direction are slight. Working across the grain or on the diagonal is sometimes successful, as are scrapers. If your planking is tearing out miserably, scraping and then sanding with a firm pad and sharp paper is the only answer.

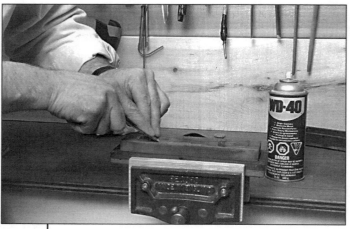

8-10

Learn how to sharpen the plane blade and keep it sharp (Photograph 8-10). Rub a little paraffin wax on its sole to reduce friction. The only resistance you should feel is the edge of the blade as it slices through the wood. Concentrate on where the blade is and what it is doing. When this becomes a habit, the tool will become an unconscious extension of your hands, allowing you to focus on the shape you are creating.

The major cracks between the planks should be filled before the epoxy-fiberglass sheathing is applied (Photograph 8-11). If these voids are not filled, there is a good possibility that air will be trapped under the 'glass, weakening the structure. To save an extra sanding step, fill after the surface has been faired with the plane and let the 80-grit sandpaper clean it up.

The ideal filler is a mixture of catalyzed epoxy and light fairing compound tinted with fine sanding dust. The color is easy to manipulate, and it sands at about the same rate as cedar. Keep in mind that the wood will be darker with a finish on it. Dampening the surface with lacquer thinner (water will work if you can wait until it dries before filling) will give you a preview of what the color will look like with the epoxy on it.

8-11

Mix up the epoxy and hardener, then add the lightweight fairing compound and sanding dust to make a thick paste of peanut butter consistency. You may end up mixing several batches of a different color to match your planking (Photograph 8-12). When you apply the filler, use a flexible putty knife, making sure that the filler is worked down to the bottom of each crack. If it is simply smeared over the top, then, when the hull is sanded, the crack will be opened, and you'll be back to where you started.

Use your judgment as to what should be filled, and don't use more filler than

8-12

is necessary; you do have to sand it off. Do not fill the staple holes. The epoxy will fill them when the 'glass is laid up. (See the next chapter.)

If the filler is excessive and is not sanding as fast as the wood, remove the bulk of it with a sharp scraper.

The first step with the machine will involve 80-grit paper (Photograph 8-13). This shaping step will reduce the remaining flats on the planks into fluid curves.

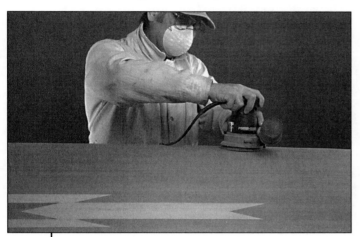

8-13

Let the sander do the work. Move in a relaxed yet firm oval, overlapping each pass. The motion should be slow enough so you can feel the cutting action. Each time you make a pass, the surface should look different. Pay attention to the surface that has just appeared behind the sander; it will tell you how much you are taking off and help you judge how much is left to go.

Use sufficient pressure to form the pad to at least part of the shape you are sanding. Not only will this give you a smoother curve, but it will keep the edge of the disc from digging into the planking. Listen to the sander: it should sound like it is working but not bogging down.

WHAT TO LOOK FOR

At the 80-grit step, leave a little of the original surface as a reference to be cleaned up with the 120-grit. When you lose this reference, be aware that you are working in the dark. The idea is to remove the least amount of wood necessary to give us the shape we want with the least amount of work.

Work systematically over one area at a time. Finish the work you are doing on one area before moving on, as this will

give you a feeling of accomplishment as well as save time in checking over later. When you get around to where you started, you should be finished. I generally work an area a comfortable arm's length (about 24″ to 32″) long, beginning at the keel line and working down to the sheer before moving to my left to begin the next section. (The clockwise motion of the sander seems to move the dust to the right.) If you have stapled the planks to the station molds, use these marks as a reference.

Be careful using the machine around edges and hard lines. Work up to the keel line or any edge, but don't let the machine pass over or the line will be rounded over. Finish up later with a long sanding block parallel to the line. Work both sides separately, and soften the edges last. Be especially careful around the stems when power-sanding with a foam pad. As the pad goes over the corner of the face and side, it wraps around the corner and takes a big bite. It's best to keep the machine back a bit and finish by hand.

Vacuum up the dust and check over the entire surface in preparation for raising the grain.

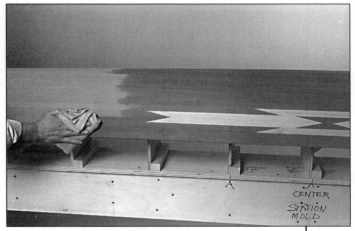

8-14

RAISING THE GRAIN

As part of the machining, fairing, and sanding steps, some of the soft part of the grain gets compressed below the surface. When a finish or coating is applied to this surface, the bruised, compressed fibers absorb a greater amount of material than the unbruised ones, and they expand. The bruised wood, because it absorbs more finish, will appear darker than the unbruised area. To raise this bruised grain before applying the epoxy, dampen the surface with warm water on a clean, lint-free cloth or sponge (Photograph 8-14). Leave no puddles. Wetting the surface will give you a preview of what the finish will look like when a coating is applied. After you have finished congratulating yourself on the beautiful craft you have created, look for spots of glue and filler that might have been missed in the sanding. Mark these so you can clean them up after the surface has dried.

The surface will be dry enough for the final sanding when the surface no longer looks wet. Sanding will heat up the surface and help to dry it further. The hull must be completely dry before applying a coating, so it is a good idea to allow the hull to dry overnight before laying up the fiberglass/epoxy. (If the surface appears extremely blotchy when wet, consider repeating the wetting and sanding step.)

Do this grain-raising step on all wood surfaces before applying a finish. It is, ultimately, the most efficient way.

SANDING WITH 120-GRIT PAPER

If the hull surface shows no rough spots or glue, the 120-grit step will be a fast, systematic pass to remove the 80-grit scratches and the raised grain. A surface that shows glue and unsanded spots will require a more aggressive pass.

After finishing up with the 120-grit, clean up and save some of the fine sanding dust for tinting the filler. Vacuum up the dust and check the hull over carefully. Make a real effort to remove all the glue, as it will become quite obvious when the epoxy is applied. The glue will be more of a problem to get off the inside than the outside; learn to recognize what it looks like. Pay particular attention on the inside along the plank seams in the turn of the bilge.

With the sanding complete, take a breather and pat yourself on the back for a job well done. This is a good time to clean up the shop and start thinking about the fiberglass.

9 | Fiberglassing the Hull

UNDERSTANDING THE SYSTEM

The secret to an epoxy clear coating is to control the film thickness of each layer as it is applied. Building up the epoxy-fiberglass sheathing over the wood may be compared to making a mirror; the prepared surface of the wood is the back reflective coating, and the epoxy-'glass surface is the glass or lens. In order to reflect the clearest image of the planking, the lens must be clean, smooth, and of a consistent thickness (Photograph 9-1).

It is impossible to apply the epoxy resin in a haphazard manner and then sand it back to a consistent thickness. Also, when the epoxy builds up thick all at once, air is trapped inside and will appear as a white blemish or streak. If it is in the first coat, there is a good chance it will be in or below the surface of the cloth. Sanding will not remove these blemishes without cutting into the glass fiber, thus weakening the structure.

I have heard of a variety of ways of applying resin to get a clear coat with epoxy and fiberglass. The system I recommend is a result of continual experimenting and refining of the system to get consistently good results. So far, this system is the only way I know of to get such excellent results consistently.

Since I started building boats in 1972, the materials have evolved and become safer and easier to work with—and of course, I may have gotten fussier. If you follow these steps in order, the system will work for you.

9-1

Building the layers up evenly will involve a different technique for each layer. Each layer accomplishes a specific function and is dictated by specific objectives.

On the outside of the hull, where durability and clarity are prime considerations, three layers of epoxy resin and one layer of fiberglass fabric are used. The 'glass cloth is always laid up in the first coat of epoxy, the second coat fills the weave and levels the surface, and the third buries the cloth, giving enough depth of resin to sand smooth without hitting the fiberglass.

On the inside of the hull, consider omitting the third coat of epoxy. This surface will be less slippery, yet it will look good. Also, this eliminates about 95% of the epoxy sanding on the inside—a step that could be expected to take about one day to complete. The trick here is to be extremely careful squeegeeing the first and second coats; the texture of the weave must be consistent in order for it to look good. Think about this when you are squeegeeing the outside; it is a good place to practice getting an even texture.

SAFETY CONCERNS

- Read and understand the safety information for the epoxy system you are using. Building this kayak should be good for your health.
- Allow good cross ventilation.
- Wear gloves. Try cornstarch in the gloves to absorb sweat. Talcum power or baby powder will work, but the smell might be too cute for the boat shop. Disposable sleeves are great for protecting your arms and clothing, especially when you are working on the inside of the hull.
- Before discarding thinner-soaked rags, drape them over something—preferably outside—to allow the solvent to evaporate.
- Don't smoke or eat.
- Lay cardboard on the floor around the perimeter to catch drips. (Plastic is slippery, and newspapers stick to the floor.)
- To reduce your exposure to toxic, uncured epoxy, allow the epoxy to reach a full cure (up to two weeks) before sanding.
- Protective skin cream, used on your bare arms above the gloves, will offer some protection when working into the ends of the hull.

MORE ON SAFETY: OVEREXPOSURE

If you are working with epoxy, hardener, and the associated solvents, exposure and the results of overexposure should be understood and respected. Gougeon Brothers, Inc., the manufacturers of WEST SYSTEM epoxy products, has studied epoxy safety in great detail. Their *WEST SYSTEM Epoxy Safety Manual* contains important information on epoxy exposure and the results of overexposure, and I recommend you read it thoroughly. (You can reach Gougeon Brothers at 517-684-7286; see Sources, page 173, for more information.)

According to that book, the dangers of overexposure include dermatitis, allergic dermatitis, chemical burns, and respiratory irritation; the danger is greatest when handling epoxy in its liquid form, and when sanding partially cured solid epoxy.

By understanding and taking appropriate precautions, you won't be troubled by the thought that this kayak might be bad for your health.

9-2

TOOLS AND MATERIALS
(Photograph 9-2)
Fiberglass cloth
It is important that the finish on the fiberglass cloth be compatible with the resin you are using. After the glass fibers have been woven into cloth, the cloth is fired to remove all residual wax and oil and then finished with a coupling agent. The coupling agent is the interface between the glass fibers and the resin. Sticking well to both glass and resin, it keeps the bond from deteriorating. There are many different finishes available, but few are compatible with epoxy for our purpose. To be sure, buy your cloth from your epoxy dealer and ask if the finish is compatible with the epoxy.

When you buy cloth, insist that it be carefully rolled. If it is folded, the creases will not come out. On the outside, there is a chance to sand them flat with the possibility of hitting the 'glass and having to patch it. On the inside, if only two coats of resin are used, the wrinkle will remain visible.

Using 6-oz. cloth will result in a strong boat, but if you can give the kayak reasonable care, consider using 4-oz cloth to save some weight. I would guess at a saving of 3 to 4 lbs. on the 17' kayak.

Determine the width of cloth by measuring the girth of the hull and the width of the deck at the widest station mold. With careful cutting, we were able to get both hull and deck out of 60" cloth. The widest cloth you are likely to find is 60", so if your kayak requires wider cloth than this, look for a narrow width that gives the least amount of waste.

To calculate the length, add 12″ to the overall length of the kayak for the outside. On the inside, the length of the kayak is long enough.

Epoxy

The epoxy and fiberglass cloth are a major component of the kayak structure; these take the place of the ribs in a traditional boat. Not only should the epoxy-fiberglass coating begin life looking like twelve coats of varnish, but it should also age gracefully. Of the hundreds of epoxy formulations available, few are suitable for a strong clear coating on wood.

The best epoxy systems seem to have been developed by boatbuilders for their own use. We have not used all of the brands of epoxy listed in the Sources, but have seen or heard of excellent results from all of them.

We began using WEST SYSTEM in 1976 after a bad experience with an epoxy that turned spruce an ugly green. Over the years, Gougeon Brothers, Inc., have continually improved their product, making it safer and more user friendly. The company's technical support is excellent, with much emphasis put on the safe handling of products.

The instructions given here relate directly to using WEST SYSTEM 105/207 epoxy, but most resin systems will handle in a similar manner. Even thin epoxies such as MAS will benefit from a finishing pass with the squeegee.

Read and understand the instructions and safety information for the resin system you are using. If you are considering a resin system not listed in the Sources, talk to someone who has used it. Ask about workability, cure time, smell, technical support, sandability, color, and how well it ages. Don't take a chance on your health or your kayak to save a few bucks.

Solvents for use with epoxy resin

Solvents are as much of a chemical safety concern as is epoxy. They are highly volatile and flammable. There is a variety of ways to minimize the health risks when handling solvents. (One manufacturer of a reputable epoxy system recommends not using conventional solvents at all.

Brushes, rollers, and gloves should be disposed of after use, and excess glue should be scraped and sanded after it has cured.)

Tools should be sanded clean after the epoxy has set, or uncured glue should be wiped off with a dry disposable cloth.

Biodegradable cleaning solvents are available, as are blended solvents that are less volatile than lacquer thinner.

Vinegar is reasonably effective for removing uncured epoxy, but it can cause more problems than it solves. It appears so harmless (it does taste good on chips) that it seems to lull some people into working without gloves and then washing up with vinegar. The problem is that the vinegar will remove more of the natural oil from the skin than will conventional thinners, and it leaves the skin unprotected for the next application of misdirected epoxy. (If you use any of the "safe" solvents, handle them the same as you would lacquer thinner or acetone.)

Lacquer thinner, though a nasty chemical and a fire hazard, has been my thinner of choice. It evaporates at a moderate rate, does not leave a harmful residue, and the smell is not too bad. Buy a low-grade lacquer thinner made for cleanup. Cross ventilation with a continuous supply of fresh air is imperative. Gloves should be worn, but do not expect vinyl and latex disposable gloves to last long in lacquer thinner. When the glove lets go, change into a fresh glove. Because lacquer thinner evaporates quickly, the fumes are not a long-term problem.

Acetone works much the same as lacquer thinner, but it evaporates faster and the smell is more objectionable. It is also more expensive and harder to find.

Use a plastic squeeze bottle such as a clean shampoo container to dispense solvents. It will make it easier to control the amount of solvent used for cleaning.

Resin/hardener dispensing pumps

It is worth having a set of dispensing pumps that will give the correct ratio of resin and hardener with one stroke of each pump. Most manufacturers of epoxy supply these pumps. The WEST SYSTEM mini-pumps come with a volume/ratio tester. Use it. If there is a problem later, the question of the pump's reliability will have been eliminated.

Brushes

Look for an inexpensive natural bristle brush, 2½" or 3" wide. A brush with short bristles that are not too thick works best; a good varnish brush would not be a good choice, as it will hold a great deal of material. Not only is a thick brush wasteful of epoxy, but it is also hard to clean. Old epoxy will collect inside the brush and harden before the project is complete. Because of its greater viscosity, epoxy resin should not be expected to flow out of the brush as freely as paint or varnish.

Avoid using ultra-cheap "Chip" brushes with blonde "natural" bristles. They shed like a dog with the mange, and the bristles are almost impossible to see on light-colored cedar. All brushes are going to shed some when they are new, but a dark bristle will be easier to see. Shake out as many bristles as you can before using the brush for the first time.

Take care of the brush. It will get better the more it is used. When you are finished using the brush or you feel it beginning to get stiff, scrape as much of the excess resin as possible out of the brush into a grunge can, and then rinse it in lacquer thinner. Shake the brush completely dry before using it again. Store the brush in clean lacquer thinner between coats, then wash it with soap and water or a water-soluble brush cleaner. When the brush is soaking in the thinner, cover the brush and can with a plastic bag to slow down evaporation and contain the fumes.

Rollers

Foam rollers sound like a good idea, and they almost work. But, when used for applying epoxy to dry cloth, there are several problems. First, it is tricky to get enough resin on to wet out the surface of the wood and the fabric. Second, as the resin is squeezed out of the roller, air comes with it; this could get trapped in the weave of the cloth. Finally, the cloth has a tendency to stick to the roller and roll up as the roller passes over it. On the second coat of epoxy, the roller is useless as the weave is very coarse and will cause the resin to foam up; this foam could be trapped in the bottom of the weave.

On the third coat, the roller will work. After rolling the epoxy out evenly over a 2' or 3' section, work the surface gently in a fore-and-aft direction with the tip of a dry brush to break the bubbles. If you do use the roller for the third coat, consider applying a fourth coat, as the roller does not build up the coating thickness as fast as a brush will.

Squeegee

Squeegees are available from most epoxy dealers and some automotive supply stores. Treat this 3" x 5" piece of flexible plastic as a precision tool; it is the key to a finish that looks like 12 coats of varnish. Check the edge for nicks; repair and soften the edge with 400-grit wet sandpaper.

Rags

White, lint-free cotton tee shirts or white cotton bed sheets make the ideal wiper. Avoid colored fabrics, as the dye could be dissolved by the lacquer thinner and transferred to the hull surface. Synthetic cloths are not very absorbent, and they could react with the solvents.

9-3

Grunge can

If I am ever to become famous, it will be for my grunge can idea (Photograph 9-3). One of the problems encountered using the squeegee is what to do with the waste resin (grunge) after it is picked up with the squeegee. If the waste is not removed from the squeegee after each pass, it is transferred to the beginning of the next pass. This leaves a line of waste resin where it should be clean.

The can of choice is the rigid cardboard frozen juice can, although the hot drink-type paper cup or cardboard milk container will do. Cut a slit ¾" down from the top edge, and use this slit to draw the squeegee through. Both sides of the squeegee will be scraped perfectly clean and the grunge will run into the can. The depth of the slit is important. If it is too deep, the sides of the can will spread, and you won't get a clean scraping action. Apparently, the brand of juice is not all that important. Ron Frenette of Canadian Canoe Company swears by "Five Alive"; personally, I have had unfailing results with "Old South" orange juice. You can also use this can trick to clean the putty knife when picking up waste glue, etc.

The next problem is what to do with the grunge that is in the grunge can. As the volume of old resin builds up in the can, it will begin to heat up quite rapidly. At some point it will boil out over the top and run down the side. Not only could this cause a painful burn, but the fumes are very toxic.

When you begin to feel the heat building up through the side of the can, dispose of the waste resin in a large container with 2" or 3" of water in the bottom. The water will dissipate the heat. A large two-quart disposable soft drink container with the top cut off will work well, and you can watch the resin harden into some interesting shapes in the water.

APPLYING THE EPOXY AND FIBERGLASS CLOTH

The optimum working temperature is room temperature, or about 70° F. If you are comfortable in a tee shirt, it should be about right. At about 80° F, the epoxy's pot life drops dramatically. When it gets this hot, watch the time between applying the resin and removing the excess.

Never work in direct sunlight, as the rapid heating will cause the air in the hull to expand, resulting in a condition called outgassing, which causes bubbles. If possible, begin lowering the temperature as soon as the layup is complete.

To begin the layup, pick a time of day that will give you the most controllable working temperature. The second and third coats are affected less by the temperature and will be controllable in less-than-ideal conditions.

Assemble all materials and supplies and set aside a block of time when you will not have to deal with distractions. This is a one-shot deal, and it deserves your undivided attention.

Clean the surface of the hull with a rag dampened with lacquer thinner to pick up the dust. This is not a washing step; use only enough thinner to dampen the rag sufficiently to hold the dust on the cloth. Run a clean, dry hand over the surface to check for dust particles. The small particles and fine dust will build up around the edge of your hand. Resist the urge to handle the surface between sanding and the layup any more than necessary, as oil from your hand could be transferred to the surface and compromise the bond between the epoxy and the wood. Wash your hands before handling the sanded surface.

Roll the cloth out over the hull, leaving about 6" extra at each end. With a person at each end holding the cloth in the middle, tug the cloth back and forth in a gentle seesaw motion to center the cloth on the hull. While holding the cloth at the middle with one hand, use the other hand to work down to the edge, tugging against your partner every 4" or 5". This exercise will shape the cloth perfectly around the hull. You should be able to manipulate the entire piece of cloth from the end.

Use this technique if wrinkles develop in the cloth during the layup. Trying to brush them out with your hand could put a permanent crease in the cloth. Do not trim the 'glass around the edge yet, as the excess will keep a lot of the epoxy runs from dripping onto the floor.

MIXING EPOXY

Note: These instructions are given for using WEST SYSTEM 105/207 epoxy resin. If you are using another system, refer to the product's technical information regarding ratios, quantities dispensed by pumps, working time, etc. Most resin handles best at room temperature. If you are working in cold conditions, keep in mind that the resin in the can will not heat up as fast as the air in the room.

Designate a mixer. This is a good part of the project to have some help on. Break the duties down to mixer and applicator. Both are critical, although if this is your boat, you may want to be the one in direct control of the visual aspects by applying and squeegeeing the resin.

Mixing requires complete concentration. There is no graceful solution to having left one shot of hardener out of a batch that is being applied to the cloth. On the second coat, the resin could be washed off, but when it is in the cloth and the wood, more drastic solutions must be considered. Don't let anybody distract the mixer.

Get into the habit of dispensing the resin first, followed by the hardener, and always stopping after the hardener. Count to yourself or out loud if it helps: one (resin) one (hardener), two (resin) two (hardener), etc. If you stop pumping after the shot of hardener, the ratio will be correct (Photograph 9-4). Keeping to a system will reduce the odds of getting lost. If for some reason you have doubts about the accuracy of the ratio, discard the mix rather than take a chance on spoiling the layup.

When choosing the number of shots per batch, there are several things to consider. Once the resin and hardener are combined, a chemical reaction begins that produces heat, and this heat produces more heat. The larger the batch, the faster the heat will be generated. As the heat builds, the epoxy, after thinning briefly, begins to thicken. This thicker resin will not soak into the surface of the wood or the glass fibers as freely as the thinner, fresh resin will. You will see this thick resin as a lighter shade on the planking, and the glass fibers could be visible. If you feel the resin beginning to heat up, discard it immediately. Always use fresh resin, and tell the mixer just before you run out so that there will be a fresh batch of resin ready as soon as you run out. Adjust the batch size to the speed of application. Try to get the resin out of the can in 10 minutes or less; 15 minutes is the maximum.

9-4

Suggested batch sizes:
- First coat on dry fabric: four shots or ½ cup
- Second coat (filling the weave): two shots

- Third coat (brush or roller): three to four shots

Stir the resin/hardener mixture for at least 45 seconds, more if the resin is cool and thick (Photograph 9-5). Scrape the sides and bottom corners often and reverse the stirring direction from time to time.

9-5

WEST SYSTEM 105/207 has a usable pot life of about 15 minutes and a working time of about 40 minutes at 70°F, less as the temperature goes up, more as it goes down. For other systems, refer to the product's technical information. If, during the layup, you notice that the brush is getting stiff up around the ferrule, take the time to scrape out the old resin and rinse the brush in thinner. Shake the brush completely dry before reusing.

It is a good idea to scrape the excess resin out of the brush every three or four batches if the resin is thick or when you see a lot of foamy resin in the brush. This will help to keep all the resin in the brush closer to the same age.

Applying epoxy

Eye protection is a very good idea when brushing epoxy because of the possibility of resin splattering off the brush. Be particularly conscious of this when working around other people. Do not try to wipe epoxy off plastic eyeglass lenses with lacquer thinner; wipe with a clean, dry cloth and wear goggles to protect your glasses.

Applying the epoxy resin to the hull surface will require a different brush technique for each coat. The function of the brush on the first coat is to transfer the resin from the can and spread it gently over the dry cloth. Make no attempt to work the resin into the cloth, as this will introduce air bubbles into the resin that may or may not come out when it is squeegeed. The speed that the resin soaks in will depend on the viscosity of the resin. The viscosity or thickness of the resin is affected by the temperature and the brand of epoxy being used. Keep an eye on the thinner epoxies, like MAS. Because they soak in fast, there is a danger that the wood will keep on absorbing resin and starve the cloth.

Load the brush and spread the epoxy with controlled but bold strokes (Photograph 9-6). As you work aggressively ahead, keep an eye on the area that has just been covered. Watch for places where the cloth looks dry or starved and add fresh resin rather than pulling a sag of questionable age over to it. (Don't fuss over the sags; they will be removed later with the squeegee. This is one place where working aggressively without regard for neatness is the most appropriate thing to do.) The fresher you can keep the resin at the working edge, the more consistent the color will be. When you dip the brush, there will be resin on both sides of the brush. Turn the brush over to transfer the resin from both sides to the surface.

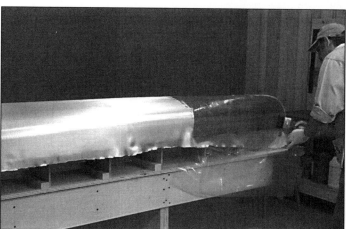

9-6

As the resin soaks in, you will notice that the weave of the cloth has become visible first around cracks and staple holes. The cloth works as a wick, effectively feeding resin into the voids. (If the epoxy resin were applied to the raw wood without the fiberglass cloth, this void-filling action would not happen. Rather, the surface tension of the resin would break at the void and the resin would pull back and pile up around the void like the rim around a crater.) If an even film thickness is to be

maintained, this now-irregular surface must be made consistent before proceeding with the layup; apply fresh resin to the starved areas.

The surface of each plank will absorb the epoxy resin at different rates. It is important to supply enough resin to give each plank as much as it wants. Watch for dark heartwood planks, as they seem to absorb more than light-colored planks.

If you have not worked with epoxy and fiberglass and are hesitant to begin, do a test first. Using a piece of excess cloth and a scrap of planking, mix a small batch of epoxy and apply to the sample as if it were the boat. Note the time it takes the resin to soak in and the time you have to work with it. When the elapsed time is right, practice with the squeegee to get an even texture. Check this test in three or four hours to be sure it is setting up the way it should. If there is a problem with the mix, it will be obvious at this time.

9-7

Where to begin

When deciding where to begin applying resin, the main consideration is keeping the edge of the resin fresh as you proceed down the hull, wetting out the cloth (Photograph 9-7). This will depend on the size of the hull and the number of people helping.

If you are working alone, begin at the keel line about 3' back from one end. Work down to the sheer and out to the end. This will tighten up the cloth and move the excess cloth out to the end of the hull. Repeat this on the opposite side of the hull, then move back to the side you began on for the third section. Change sides every 3' as you work down the hull.

By the time you get to about the

halfway point, or when 20 to 30 minutes have elapsed, the area first wet out will be ready for squeegeeing. It is important to squeegee only the first area as the section beside it will be five to seven minutes behind.

Keep track of the time. Try Ron Frenette's "Time Tapes" trick: Stick a piece of masking tape, marked with the time the section was finished, plus 20 minutes, on the strongback below the edge of the section. A good job for the mixer could be placing and monitoring these "Time Tapes." When the first section reaches 20 minutes, the routine will change. You will now alternate between wetting out one section and squeegeeing one section. If the mixer has a good idea of how you are applying the resin, he or she could fill in for you until you catch up.

9-8

Using the squeegee

This step—one of the trickiest in the whole building process—dictates what your boat will look like. It is one of those steps that is difficult to reverse. You must do it right the first time. I say this not to scare you, but rather to inspire you to give it your full attention.

The purpose of the squeegee is to even out the film thickness by scraping off the excess resin (Photograph 9-8). The planks have now accepted all the resin they want, and the cloth is saturated but floating in places. Squeegeeing will remove all the excess resin and leave the cloth evenly saturated and lying flat on the hull. The surface should appear almost dull, with no shiny puddles or lines. Throwing this excess resin away will keep your kayak as light as possible and eliminate a lot of sanding. Check the weight of the grunge

can when you finish; its contents could have been excess kayak, or dust.

As most plastic squeegees have a slight curve from end to end, hold yours so that the corners turn up. Turned over, the corners will dig in and scrape too much resin out of the cloth. Hold it so that your thumb is on the bottom side and your fingers are spread out to control the pressure along the edge.

The angle at which the squeegee is presented to the hull is most critical. The angle should be quite flat, with your thumb almost dragging on the hull. A steeper angle will put too much direct pressure on the edge with the danger of squeezing the cloth dry. Be conscious of keeping this low angle as you go around the turn of the bilge. There is a tendency to allow the angle to get steeper as you move around the bilge to the vertical surface.

If too much pressure is applied, much of the resin will be squeezed out of the cloth. This is undesirable, as, after the resin sets up, the fibers of the cloth will be coated and sealed but not filled. The second coat will not be able to penetrate the fibers any further, and the glass fibers will remain visible. This will be most noticeable in bright sunlight or on dark wood.

If you don't press hard enough, the surface will remain shiny and the cloth will float. In practice, it is a good idea to work a section down in stages rather than try to get it all in one pass.

Begin at the centerline (keel line) of the hull and draw the squeegee down to the sheer with overlapping strokes. The rate should be slow enough to allow the resin to roll up in front of the squeegee.

The amount that the successive passes overlap will depend on how much resin is being removed. If there is a lot of resin, pick up only as much as you can hold on the squeegee and transfer it to the grunge can. As you get closer to the desired saturation, use the full width of the squeegee.

Work gently over the section until the vertical shiny tracks are removed. You won't get all of them, but try to get as even a texture as possible without wasting too much time. Keep in mind that this is practice for getting an even texture on the inside, where it will be more visible.

As you work these last tracks out, be very conscious of not taking too much and starving the cloth. If too much resin is squeezed out, the cloth will have a subtle, white glitter rather than a saturated, dull shine. Should this happen, add fresh resin rather than dragging old resin over to it.

Check that the cloth is lying down flat to the surface around the edge of the hull.

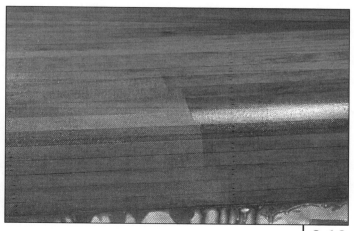

9-9

Finishing the cloth at the stems

Assuming that you have gone to the trouble of installing outer stems, wrapping 'glass around the end of the stem is unnecessary. This is one of the bonuses of using outer stems: they effectively tie the sides of the hull together. Wrapping a 'glass patch around the end is not only difficult but frustrating, because there is no way of doing it gracefully. The double layer of 'glass at the stem will always appear a different color and density than the single layer on the rest of the hull.

Wet the cloth out on both sides, then trim it to about 1″ past the end of the stem with the scissors. After the resin has firmed up (about three hours) trim it off clean with a sharp knife (Photograph 9-9) and soften the edges with 120-grit sandpaper. Leave the excess at the sheer to catch the inevitable runs; trim this when the layup is complete.

Scrape as much excess resin as possible out of the brush, then soak it in clean lacquer thinner until the next coat. Clean the squeegee and scissors with a thinner-dampened rag, then take a break.

THE SECOND COAT OF EPOXY

The purpose of the second coat is to fill the weave and level the surface of the cloth (Photograph 9-10). No attempt should be made at this point to build up the resin thickness. Remember: the surface is too coarse to brush or roll onto without the

9-10

resin foaming up and becoming trapped at the bottom of the weave.

The minimum time between coats is about three hours, or when you are able to trim the cloth without the resin sticking to the knife. The three coats should go on as close together as possible. Applying a successive coat before the previous coat has fully cured will result in a chemical bond as well as a mechanical one.

If you can time it right (about four to five hours), a quick hand-sanding with 120-grit paper will make the surface easier to work on. Since the depth of the weave is reduced by this, slightly less resin will be required to level the weave.

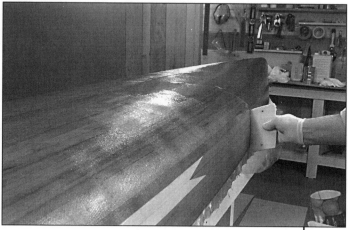

9-11

If it has been more than eight hours since the last coat was applied, the surface should *definitely* be sanded. This is important, because the integrity of the bond between the layers now depends on the layers being mechanically stuck together.

On a horizontal surface or on the inside, it is possible to pour a small puddle of resin onto the hull, then spread it around with the squeegee (Photograph 9-11). The

9-12

9-13

technique that works for me on the outside is to use the brush to transfer the resin from the container to the hull. Because the brush deposits more resin than is necessary to fill the weave, spread the resin only about one-third of the way down from the centerline. This should be just enough resin, when spread, to fill the weave all the way to the sheerline.

The first time over, concentrate more on filling the weave than on making it look good. Work the resin aggressively enough to force the trapped air out of the weave. After roughly spreading each batch, go back over the section systematically, scraping off and disposing of the excess resin.

Use a steeper angle and slightly more pressure on the squeegee than before to force the air out and level the surface.

The part you are most likely to miss is the vertical surface along the sheerline. Check for dull patches that indicate an area that has been missed. It is hard to sight along the vertical surface, so move around until you find the best angle. Listen to the squeegee. As it passes over a dry patch, it will make a harsher sound.

If there is a problem getting the vertical tracks out, try finishing up in a fore-and-aft direction. On the inside, where you want to remove all the tracks, go over the surface with a dry brush. This may require aggressive motion in a fore-and-aft direction.

Finally, check that the ends of the stems have been coated evenly.

THE THIRD COAT

The purpose of the third coat is to bury the fiberglass cloth with enough epoxy resin that the surface may be sanded smooth without hitting the cloth (Photograph 9-12 and 9-13). Even though the surface has been squeegeed and the cloth is buried, expect to see some of the weave after the third coat.

This coat will be applied with a familiar painting motion. Since we are now working on a reasonably smooth substrate, a more aggressive motion may be used without introducing air into the resin. If you do see bubbles forming excessively, lighten up.

The idea is to apply as much resin as

9-14

you can get on in an even film thickness without it sagging excessively. You will have to use your judgment to find the balance between just right and too much. Too much will give the brush a mushy, skidding feel, while too little will produce noticeably more resistance. Controlling the film thickness by feel is often more reliable than doing it visually, especially in marginal light. In practice, you will use a combination of both vision and feel.

Load the brush and apply epoxy to a section about 3' long, or as long a section as you can comfortably work. Spread with a long, vigorous, but controlled back-and-forth motion to work the resin out into an even film thickness. Check for consistency by brushing up and down and diagonally, feeling for consistent resistance in the brush.

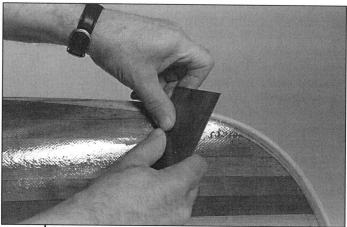

9-15

After spreading the resin over the section being worked, go back to where you started and finish off with long, flowing fore-and-aft strokes (Photograph 9-14).

To help the resin blend in evenly with the adjoining section, brush with a motion similar to an airplane landing and taking off gently. When applying the resin beside a completed section, brush into the completed section to keep from building up a double density of resin at the overlap. Hold the brush at a low angle with the handle pointed forward and lightly draw the resin over the surface. A high angle would push the material along and pile

it up at the end of the stroke. Try this brushing technique for applying paint or varnish, too. It works.

There is a limit to how long you can work the runs out. At some point, the resin will begin to firm up, pile up, and not flow out. This is the time to quit, because from this point on, working it will only make it worse. A good resin will most likely have some self-leveling properties. While this is a desirable feature for taking care of brush marks, it is also what allows the resin to run on vertical surfaces. Don't take a few runs on this coat too personally, as they happen to all of us. Remove the runs with a sharp cabinet scraper after the resin has cured (Photograph 9-15).

Trim the 'glass at the sheer after the third coat has hardened. Notice how many runs have been captured by the excess cloth (Photograph 9-16).

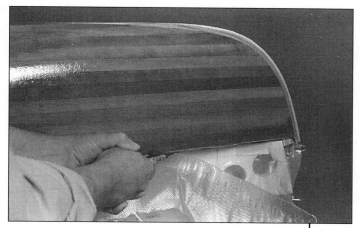

9-16

10 | The Deck and Hull Interior

Now that the hull is complete, the kayak should feel like it is yours, and you have no doubt that you can finish it. You will most likely feel more comfortable and confident working from now on. If this is your first boat, most of the things to learn will have been learned. All of the basic techniques and tools used from now on will be familiar.

The deck might be more fun to build than the hull; it is not very big, it is at an ideal working height, and the surface is generally horizontal (Illustration 10-1). If you are into showing off, a few cheap tricks will make the deck come alive. Prepare to be dazzled.

THE STEPS IN BUILDING THE DECK
- Prepare the cradle molds.
- Temporarily fasten the hull to the sheer clamps and stabilize the station molds.
- Remove hull and mold from the strongback.
- Set up the hull in the cradle molds.
- Remove the mold extensions.
- Shape the sheer clamps to the deck molds and trim the stems.
- Look at planking patterns.
- Consider planking without staples.
- Plank the deck.
- Sand the deck and fiberglass it.

Making cradle forms
Before you remove the hull and mold from the strongback, prepare a set of four cradle forms (Illustration 10-2). Make these from ½" or ¾" plywood or particle board.

Use the plans to pick up the shapes and the heights of the cradle forms. Measure from the 4" waterline, and add enough to clear the mold blocks. Add ⅜" to the station mold line to accommodate the planking thickness plus some padding. After cutting the forms to shape, round the edges over and pad them with something soft and not too slippery.

Turning the hull over
When the hull is removed from the strongback, there is a good possibility that the

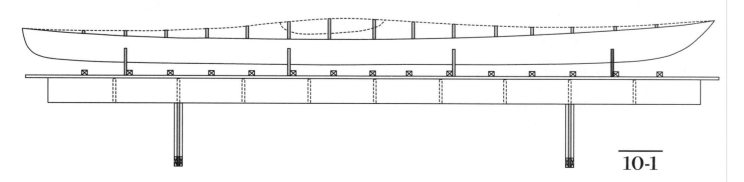

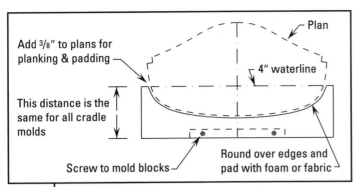

Add ³⁄₈" to plans for planking & padding

Plan

4" waterline

This distance is the same for all cradle molds

Screw to mold blocks

Round over edges and pad with foam or fabric

10-2

unsupported weight of the molds will cause the middle of the hull to sag and the sides to spread. While this may not harm the hull, it will loosen some of the molds. It is to your advantage to have the molds remain stuck to the hull in the set-up position for planking the deck. The molds will be lightly held in place by the squeezed-out glue on the inside of the hull and the screws through the sheer clamp into the molds.

Tie everything together for the move with a few clamps around the sheer to anchor the hull to the sheer clamp. Put something around the middle of the hull to keep the sides from spreading (e.g., rope or duct tape).

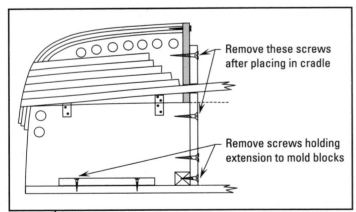

Remove these screws after placing in cradle

Remove screws holding extension to mold blocks

10-3

Unfastening the molds from the strongback

Remove all the screws holding the stem molds and extensions to the mold blocks (Illustration 10-3). It will take two people to lift the hull and molds off the strong-back and set the whole affair upright on padded horses or on the floor.

Attach the cradle forms to their appropriate mold blocks and set up the hull in them. Check that the hull is fitting comfortably in all the cradle forms (Photograph 10-4).

The screws that are holding the sheer

clamps to the station molds will now have to be moved to the sides of the hull. Move the 1½" x No. 6 screws one at a time, so

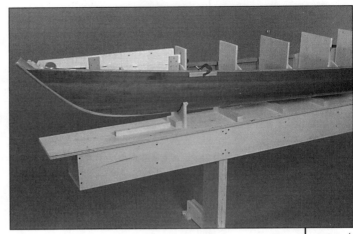

10-4

nothing gets out of control. When you drill the pilot holes, anticipate where the edge of the hull will be after the sheer clamp is shaped to follow the deck; keep the head set flush and below this line (Photograph 10-5).

Carefully remove the mold extensions so as not to dislodge the station molds. To remove the extension portions of the stem molds, remove the screws in the cleats that you can reach, and split around the ones you can't get at.

It is a good idea to tack a couple pieces of scrap planking across the tops of the molds to help stabilize them while getting ready to plank the deck.

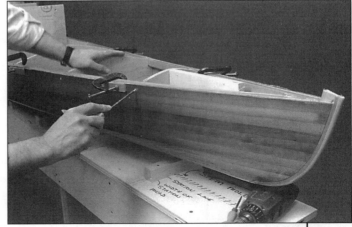

10-5

When all of the sheer clamp screws have been replaced, remove the temporary C-clamps and trim the stems (Photograph 10-6). I would suggest trimming the inner-stem flush with the sheer clamps so that it supports the planking, and leave the outer

10-6

stem longer for now. Trimmed flush with the top of the planking, the hardwood outer stem will offer some protection to the end of the softwood deck.

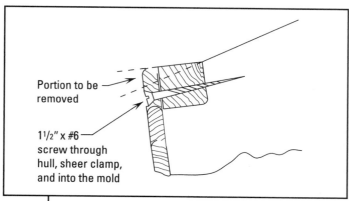

Portion to be removed

1½" x #6 screw through hull, sheer clamp, and into the mold

10-7

Shaping the sheer clamp
(Illustration 10-7)
Plane the edge of the hull and top of the sheer clamp down so it becomes an extension of the deck lines (Photograph 10-8). Cutting through the fiberglass on the hull is going to be hard on the plane blade, so expect to stop and sharpen a few times. Forget the belt sander, as this step requires

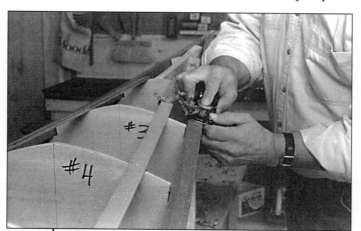

10-8

more control than can be expected from the machine. Keep checking the bevel with a flexible straightedge, looking for a smooth curve extending from the deck mold across the sheer clamp (Photograph 10-9).

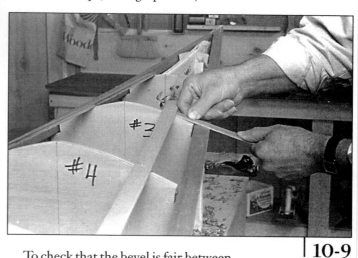

10-9

To check that the bevel is fair between the station molds, find a position where you can see along the edge of the hull. Look for a long, smooth curve (Photograph 10-10).

10-10

The last thing to do before planking the deck is to make sure that the deck does not stick to anything that won't be deck. Cover the deck portion of the station molds with plastic tape. While wax will work, there is the danger of contaminating the sheer clamp with wax.

It is very important that the deck does

not get bonded to the top edge of the hull; once the deck is glassed, there won't be any access to the interior. Carefully cover the edge of the hull with plastic packaging tape and rub the tape down firmly. Fold the excess over and press down to protect the hull (Illustration 10-11). The inside edge of the sheer clamp is already protected with tape; if this wasn't disturbed during shaping, it should be enough protection. If you are worried about it, back out the screws and slide a piece of plastic film down between the hull and sheer clamp, and tape down the excess plastic to protect the outside of the hull.

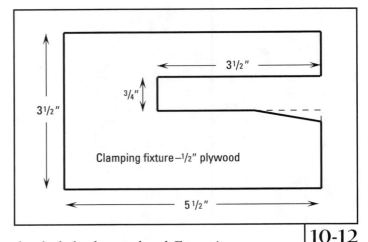

10-12

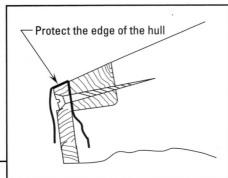

10-11

Planking without staples

It had been my intention to demonstrate some of the tricks we use to eliminate staples while planking the deck. As it turned out, the tricks we came up with were so simple and fast that the jigs we would normally use on the hull were unnecessary. Decks are the essence of simplicity, and there is no reason to put holes in their planks. In case you are interested in building the hull without staples, I will demonstrate a variety of the simple techniques that I use for planking the hull. (These might be overkill on the deck.)

Why build without staples? From up close, the staple holes are inoffensive if lined up neatly. It is true that from 10' away you may not notice the staple holes at all, so why the fascination with trying to eliminate them? The difference is magic. Which question would you rather answer: "What are all the little holes for?" or "How did you hold all those pieces together?"

On the engineering side, the planks are held together much more tightly and consistently with the jig than can be expected from the leg of a staple. In theory, this should result in a stronger structure because the possibility of voids between

the planks has been reduced. Expect it to take longer to build without staples than to staple the planks to the mold. Some compensation for this extra effort is provided by the time saved by not having to pull staples and then deal with the holes.

If you are working a few hours each evening and can do one setup of three planks each side per evening, the hull will be planked in about ten days.

If you are playing with your own idea of a clamping jig or looking at some other system, keep the following general principles in mind.

- The point of the exercise is to control the plank in two directions. Most systems address holding the plank to the mold, but few offer controllable pressure between the planks.
- Keep it simple. Look for low or no tooling cost to make a jig that is simple to prepare, set up, and reposition.
- The jig should be versatile enough to be easily moved to another mold without modification.
- The jig should accommodate more than one plank per setup. A complicated jig that only handles one plank at a time will be slow going. Three planks at a time seems to be a good balance between getting on with the job and having time to position the planks before the glue sets.

Coming up with new ways of clamping the planks together while the glue sets will continue to tease strip-plank builders as long as there are strippers.

We began playing with the stapleless system we are using here in the early 1980s. This was about the time we built a canoe for Pierre Elliott Trudeau, then prime minister of Canada, as his personal wedding gift to His Royal Highness, Prince Charles, and Lady Diana, Princess of Wales. Since then, we have planked all of our recreational canoes without staples. The system evolves every time I use it, as I hope it will for you, if you decide to try it.

The foundation of our system is the 3½ × 5½″ C-shaped piece of ½″ plywood. (Illustration 10-12). Clamped or screwed to the station mold, it provides two sides from which we can apply controlled clamping pressure with softwood wedges. The opening in the "C" is deep enough to accommodate three planks, plus it provides enough room for part of the wedge.

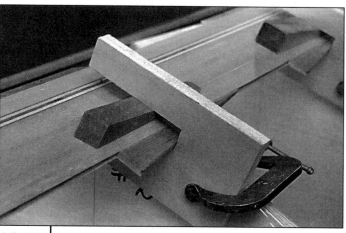

10-13

The jig handles three planks best when the ends of the planks do not have to be fitted and the curve of the bilge is not extreme (Photograph 10-13). It is ideal for planking the hull sides and bottom, and for some deck patterns. When you start planking around the bilge, or if fitting to the stems is slowing things down, cut back to one or two planks. Adjust the number of planks you install per setup to the time it takes to get the plank into place and settled before the glue grabs. If there is any doubt about the planks fitting together gracefully, do a dry run before adding glue.

To get started, the first plank must be firmly anchored to the mold to provide something for the wedge to push against. On the hull, the plank would be secured to the station molds at the sheerline and glued to the stem. The first plank on the deck is either the covering board or the kingplank. The kingplank would be handled similarly to the hull, while the covering board is glued to the sheer clamp.

There will be considerable pressure from the wedges, and we want to be sure the plank is not pushed into an unfair curve. Along the sheer, where the holes will be covered by a gunwale or guard, I use a 1¼″ nail. If the ends of the hull will be built up, making the first plank visible, fasten an L-shaped cleat to the side of the station mold to support the plank and hold it up to the mold.

In Photograph 10-13, we are using a C-clamp to hold the jig to the station mold. If you do not have enough clamps for this, screw the jigs to the mold or drill and fasten them with a carriage bolt and wing nut.

It is most efficient to install three planks at a time. Since the top plank of each gang of three will not have glue applied to it, put this one on the mold and wedge it out of the way for now.

Prepare a few simple fixtures that will hold two planks together on edge, at the bench, to facilitate applying glue to both edges. Apply the third bead of glue to the edge of the last plank on the mold. This can be awkward, as you must start and stop the glue between each station mold; pull back on the plunger at the end of the pass to keep the glue from making a mess.

Beginning in the middle of the building jig, slide the two planks up into the plywood clamping devices, fit these planks together, then bring the top plank down into position. Press a couple of softwood wedges in just enough to hold the three planks to the mold. The wedge on top, made from scrap planking with the bead on one edge, will be pressed in more firmly. I would suggest working quickly out to both ends from the middle, clamping at the stems, then going systematically

10-14

over the whole setup, fine tuning the wedges where necessary.

As planking progresses, there will be situations where this jig will be too bulky and must be supplemented with something more compact. Use your ingenuity, but remember: any device must have adjustable control over the plank in both directions.

This planking system can be adapted to a variety of situations. The simple setup in Photograph 10-14 gives excellent control, clamps one plank at a time, and will fit into a confined space. The anchor block is fastened to the mold with a 1″ × No. 4 screw that allows the block to swivel to match the angle of the wedge. Notice that the wedge, a piece of planking with the bead edge preserved, fits into the cove of the plank and holds it down to the mold.

10-16

10-15

The same style of jig is used in Photograph 10-15 to hold the plank up to the stem and press it into the plank below. Note the spacer between the jig and the stem to keep the jig level and the wedge working between the screw and the plank. The beveled clamping pads on the end have sandpaper glued to the inside face to keep them from sliding off.

Working on the same bridging principle that we used on the stem, the jig in Photograph 10-16 is holding the planks into a concave section of the deck mold as well as applying controlled pressure to the edge of the plank.

There will be some stages of construction during which pressure from overhead will be needed to hold the partially planked hull to the mold. After tiring of long sticks secured against the ceiling falling on my head, I arrived at the

simple and versatile setup in Photograph 10-17. Once the frame is built, levers may be located at any point along it to direct pressure in the required direction. Clamp the lever so that it almost touches the surface, then use a wedge to apply the correct amount of pressure.

Since the joints of the frame are temporarily clamped together, it may be necessary to locate a lever on the hull opposite the lever applying force to keep from wracking the frame.

Another trick that has been successful in holding the planking to the mold is an occasional spot of glue in a strategic place. If the edge of the mold has been protected with plastic tape, place a piece of masking tape over the plastic. When you position the plank, put a spot of glue on the tape, then wedge the plank into

10-17

position. When the wedges are removed, the plank should stay down on the mold. The glue will stick to the masking tape, but the strength of the bond will be marginal. When the mold is removed, this bond between the glue and masking tape should let go before the wood is damaged. If the mold has been waxed, you will have to scrape off the wax before the masking tape will stick.

Note: Use this trick sparingly on the kayak deck, because it could complicate removing the deck.

10-19

10-18

pensive to make, and easy to set up and adapt to other molds and applications. Even if you decide to build with staples, keep these little tricks in mind. There may be places where they could save using an unsightly bunch of staples or nails.

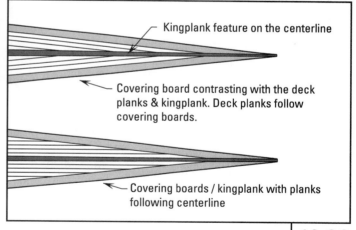

— Kingplank feature on the centerline

— Covering board contrasting with the deck planks & kingplank. Deck planks follow covering boards.

— Covering boards / kingplank with planks following centerline

10-20

Photograph 10-18 shows a good example of applying the principle of control in two directions, using whatever is available. At this point, we have run out of stem to fasten a fixture to, so we are using two thin pieces of wood to apply the pressure. The long piece that is being bent over the stem and held in place with the rope is applying pressure between the plank and the stem. The shorter piece is clamped at both ends to draw and hold the plank edges together.

Plastic packaging tape (Photograph 10-19) is excellent for many awkward clamping duties. Here we are using the tape to draw the planks together at the centerline and hold them while the glue sets. Stretch the tape as it is being applied to create the clamping pressure.

These are the basic tricks we use, and they work for us. They are easy and inex-

Suggested planking pattern for the deck

The direction in which you decide to plank the deck has most to do with the number of joints you want to cut vs. the pattern you have in mind. The deck planks will most likely follow either the centerline of the deck or be sprung to the curve of the edge of the hull (Illustration 10-20). Some interesting patterns have been made by positioning the planks on a diagonal, but make sure the pattern you come up with can be planked in a fair curve. The

10-21

direction you use and the way you combine the directions is up to you and what you have to work with. The technique we used earlier on the hull plank feature also offers a lot of design possibilities for the deck, and is worth consideration.

Regardless of the plank direction, I like the traditional feel of covering boards. They define the shape of the deck and make a logical conclusion to the plank lines. Use a wood of contrasting color to increase the definition.

The planking sequence we are using on our kayak will show the covering boards being attached first, followed by the kingplank (center feature plank). The deck is then planked out from the kingplank and the ends individually fitted to the covering boards. If the planks had been installed following the edge of the hull and fit to a kingplank, the amount of fitting would be about the same as our deck. But if one side had been planked across the centerline at random, as we did with the hull bottom, the individual fitting would be cut in half.

Individually fitting each plank to the covering boards could be eliminated if you have a router and are comfortable using it. Plank the deck fore and aft from the centerline, letting the planks run out at random past the line of the covering board. Then, trim to make space for the covering board using the router and a straight bit. You'll need a jig to follow the outside of the hull so the deck planking is trimmed a consistent distance in from the edge. The base of the router will ride on the deck to control the rolling bevel. (Be sure the deck is fastened securely to the mold before trimming.)

Installing covering boards

Install the first plank with the bead extending over the edge of the hull enough to be trimmed completely off later. This will make a crisp joint between the edge of the deck and the guard.

Begin by drawing a line on the top of the sheer clamp to show the area covered by the first plank. Make up a simple marking gauge that will follow the edge of the hull and guide the pen (Photograph 10-21). It will be easier to see this distinct line from the top than to try to feel the bead overhanging the hull. Use this line to show the area to be covered with the glue.

To find the miter on the ends of the plank, clamp the plank into position. Lay a straightedge along the centerline of a few station molds and center it on the stem. The straightedge will lay on top of the plank and show exactly where to make the cut; expect to do some final fitting when the two complementary planks are fitted together. Draw a few reference marks to locate the plank fore and aft before removing the clamps.

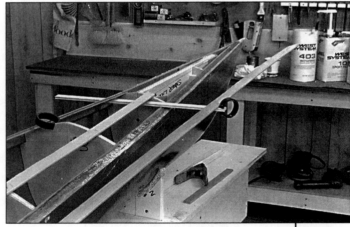

10-22

Some thought should be given to the type of glue used to attach the plank to the sheer clamp. Look for a glue that has sufficient working time to allow you to apply it, position the plank, and clamp before it begins to set up. If the plank was stapled, you could most likely keep up with regular carpenter's glue. But it would be pushing it to use carpenter's glue and expect to get all the clamps on before the glue began to skin over. As the joint is well sealed from both sides, delamination shouldn't be a problem with a slow-setting, water-resistant glue.

Besides being the ultimate waterproof

10-23

10-25

bond, epoxy glue has the advantage of having a good open time for positioning the clamps. Apply the glue in a thin, even film, using an acid brush. Be as neat as possible, as the excess glue squeezed out on the edge of the hull could make it hard to remove the deck. Assuming you have a good fit between the plank and the sheer clamp, a thick layer of glue is not necessary.

Support the ends of the plank as you begin clamping at the middle reference mark (Photograph 10-22). Work out to the ends, clamping at each station mold, then go back and fill in between with more clamps. The clamps we are using in Photograph 10-23 are ¾" slices of 2" plastic drain pipe. They are an economical solution to needing many clamps occasionally. The clamping pressure is adjusted by the diameter of pipe and the width of the slice.

Use plastic packaging tape to clamp the ends. Clean up the squeezed-out glue and check the fit of the plank to the reference line (Photograph 10-24).

Use the technique we used to fit the hull bottom at the centerline to mark and cut the miter. It is a good idea to do a dry

fit with both planks before mixing the glue.

We have removed the cove edge on the second pair of covering board planks before installing; the fore-and-aft deck planks will be mitered to fit this edge. If possible, make this cut on the table saw, as the more consistent the cut, the easier it will be to fit up to it. If the deck planks are laid following the covering boards, the cove, of course, would not be removed.

Notice the clamping block that straddles both planks in Photograph 10-25; try to make these two planks appear as one piece.

Do what you must to get the planks to meet flush at the miter. The tape on the clamp in Photograph 10-26 is holding the handle of the clamp down to direct the pressure forward, even though the

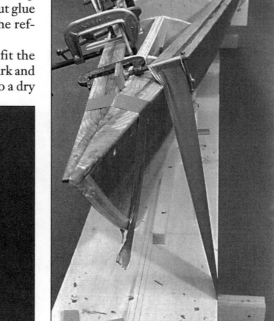

10-26

10-24

clamp is above the surface.

Photograph 10-27 shows a situation in which planking without staples is as simple as it is likely to get. The glue is applied and the plank is pulled into position with short pieces of scrap planking. Instead of driving the staple through the plank, drive it through the scrap. While lacking the sophisticated control of the wedge, the pressure and control are similar to a staple through the plank. There are still the same number of staples to pull, but the holes are disposable.

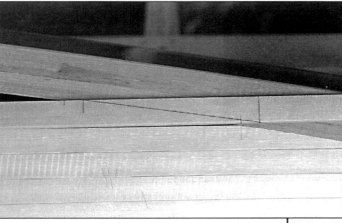

10-29

staples out of and when. I have never planked a hull using this technique, but see no reason why much of a long, skinny kayak hull could not be planked this way. It would be a very relaxed pace, but not ridiculously so, if the glue were fast.

10-27

If each plank is being fitted to the covering board, there will be lots of time for the glue to grab while the other side is being fitted and installed. Looking at it this way, the only difference between holes or no holes is what you decide to pull the

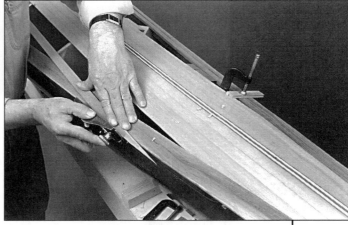

10-30

The kingplank we are using in Photograph 10-28 is laminated basswood and dark cedar. The single plank must be balanced on the centerline and requires extra attention to recreate the subtle ridge along the middle of the deck. If the design you are building has a ridge on the centerline, consider using two planks to make this feature. The joint between the planks will make it easy to establish the detail and maintain it during shaping and sanding. Install both planks at the same time with temporary clamping blocks on either side. Check from the end to be sure it is straight before committing to the ¾" finishing nails. Leave enough of the nail head above the plank to pull out later.

Fit the deck planks to the covering board using the same procedure we used for marking and cutting the bottom of the

10-28

hull (Photograph 10-29). Remember to add the extra ⅝″ when marking for the second cut and keep an eye on the secondary bevel.

After cutting to the line on the bench, do the final fitting on the boat (Photograph 10-30). As before, work to the reference mark rather than replacing the whole plank for each trial fit.

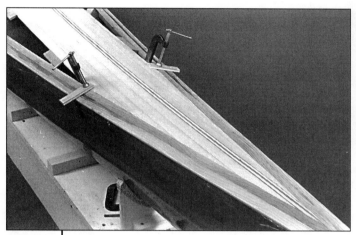

10-31

Pay attention to the fit between the plank and the covering board (Photograph 10-31). The joint must be flush on top as well as a fair curve that fits the shape of the deck. To be sure things are aligned, clamp a short block across both planks until the glue sets. When you get to the second-to-last plank, remove the machined edge to make a simple edge joint with the last plank.

Photograph 10-32 shows another way to pick up the shape of the last plank. Paper is taped over the opening and the pencil is stroked rapidly back and forth. As the pencil hits the edges of the opening, it makes a darker mark. When all of the lines are looked at together, we have

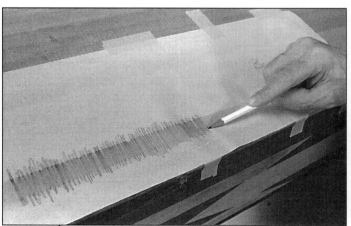

10-32

an accurate picture of the opening. The paper trick works here because one side of the plank is straight. If there is much of a curve on both edges, picking up the shape with dividers will be more accurate.

10-33

Carefully cut the pattern to shape, trace the shape onto the plank, and trim the plank to the line (Photograph 10-33). Do the final fitting on the boat, working to the middle bench mark.

Photograph 10-34 shows the piece we have been looking for!

Sanding the deck

Because the deck is what you will see the most of, pay particular attention to keeping it as fair as possible (Illustration 10-35). The places to watch especially are the details along the centerline and around

10-34

the edges. Waves along the edges of the hull will become obvious when the guard is installed.

Use the same shaping and sanding routine as we used on the hull. If you do the first sanding and shaping step with the file board, your effort will be rewarded with an extremely fair deck. For maximum clarity of the wood grain, consider again wetting the wood to raise the grain.

Fiberglassing the deck

Assuming that doing the layup on the hull was a good experience, you should find 'glassing the deck quite straightforward (Photograph 10-36). It will be a simpler layup than the hull, because there is the better visibility and less area to cover. But don't relax yet—this is the one that counts.

As with the hull, put off trimming the excess cloth until after the third coat of epoxy has been applied. (Photograph 10-37). The epoxy resin will run, and the cloth seems to do a good job of keeping it off the hull. If there are places where the cloth must be trimmed close, protect the hull with plastic film.

After the last coat of epoxy has set, trim the cloth to the edge of the hull and remove the sharp edge with a sanding block. It is glass, and it will cut.

Removing the deck

Removing the deck will be, I hope, as simple as removing the screws that go through the hull and sheer clamp into the station mold (Photograph 10-38). After removing the screws, break the deck loose by picking up one end of the hull and giving it a few up-and-down jerks. The weight of the mold inside will help to spring the bottom down and spread the sides. If this doesn't pop the deck up, first check for forgotten screws, then try carefully working a stiff putty knife along the seam between the deck and hull.

Go easy here; don't try to pry up too hard, or the edge of the deck could break.

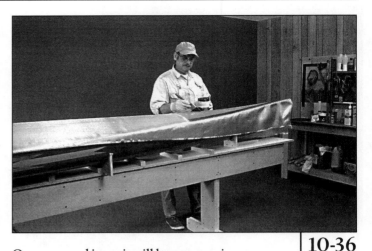

10-36

Once one end is up, it will be easy to wiggle the rest loose. If it appears to be stuck somewhere, try to determine the cause before something gets broken.

Set the deck out of the way and remove

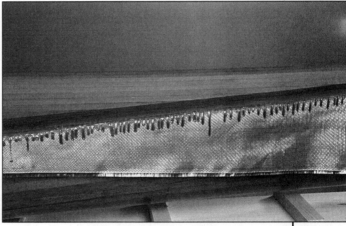

10-37

the station molds. Remember the screws that go through the station mold into the end of the stem.

SANDING AND FIBERGLASSING THE INSIDE OF THE HULL
Shaping and sanding inside

Preparing the inside of the hull will lack some of the joy of shaping with the block plane. While some of the flatter areas may be worked on a diagonal with the spokeshave, most of the roughing out will be

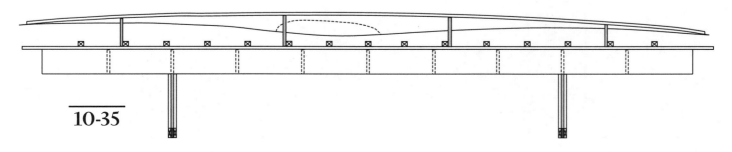

10-35

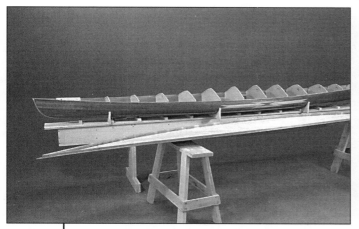

10-38 |

| 10-40

with the scraper (Photograph 10-39).

File the edge of the scraper blade into a curve that will fit most of the inside shape of the hull. In tighter curves, hold the blade on the diagonal to reduce the width and keep the corners from digging in.

Try to do most of the shaping step with the scraper (Photograph 10-40). There will be a temptation to get a machine in your hands and let it do the work, but trust me, the scraper is best.

10-39 |

If you are looking to skip a few of the sanding steps, some sins may be hidden with the deck. Although some parts of the interior will be out of sight after the deck is installed, it is important at least to sand out the steps between the planks. If you must cut a few corners, at least completely sand the area that will be visible through the cockpit opening and the hatches.

Here is a cheap trick that will take out the waves left by the random-orbit sander in the hollow of the bilge (Photograph 10-41). This is a smooth-sided plastic soft drink bottle that has been filled with water

to keep the sides firm and add weight. Wrap sandpaper of the appropriate grit around the bottle and fasten it on with masking tape. When the sanding is complete, clean up and prepare to 'glass the inside of the hull.

| 10-41

Fiberglassing inside the hull

While 'glassing the inside of the hull should not be more difficult than 'glassing the outside, there are several additional tricks worth looking at (Photograph 10-42).

Roll the cloth out on the hull and cut both ends about 4″ to 6″ short on both ends. There is no advantage in taking the 'glass all the way to the stem, and it does get progressively more difficult to work in these areas as the space is reduced. Some conscientious builders have tried to take the 'glass all the way to the stem and overlap the ends. If you try this, two things are going to happen. First, a lot of time will be wasted that might be better spent keeping the part that makes a difference under control. Second, the cloth will not fold around the sharp corner and will leave air

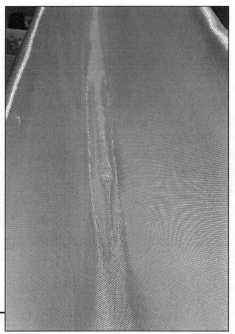
10-42

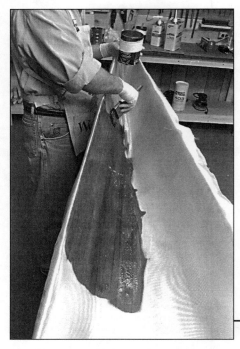
10-43

settled as possible before mixing the resin. Begin by fitting the cloth around the sides of the stem, then smooth up to the sheer and out to the end. Notice that the cloth is floating over the hull at the ends; leave it for now.

bubbles that are going to be miserable to repair. If this is your first layup and you run the 'glass out to the ends, cleaning up the mess will take some of the fun out of the project.

With someone on each end of the cloth, bring the corners together, folding the cloth in half. Carefully lower the cloth along the centerline of the hull and drape it over the sides. If there is not enough excess 'glass hanging over the edge to hold it in place, try a few clothespins to anchor it until the resin is applied.

Beginning in the middle of the hull, anchor the cloth with one hand and smooth up to the sheer and out to the ends with the other. Try to control the amount of cloth in the hull by lifting up the cloth and repositioning it. If there is too little cloth in one area, and the cloth is tugged only locally, this will either pull it away somewhere else or drag the cloth over the edge of the hull, with the danger of snagging the cloth. Likewise, don't expect to move excess cloth by pushing or pulling with your hand. The cloth won't slide, and you will simply fold the surplus cloth over, making wrinkles that may or may not come out. Hold the cloth clear of the edges of the hull with one hand as you smooth the cloth down to the hull with the other.

Repositioning the cloth around the stem and up in the ends when the cloth is wet will be difficult, so try to get it as

Applying the epoxy

Begin applying the resin along the centerline, about 3' from one end (Photograph 10-43). Apply gently and spread from the wet to the dry. Bring each section up to the sheer before advancing. When you begin working around a stem, it is time to add another technique to your repertoire of brushing tricks.

Used like a sponge, the brush is laid on its side and the resin is squeezed out of the bristles. This is very effective for applying the resin without disturbing the cloth. It also means that the brush is lying almost flat and fits the narrow end of the kayak. Control the amount of resin deposited by how hard the brush is squeezed. A common problem for the first-time builder is applying too much resin in the ends of the hull, right where it is the hardest to clean up.

One of the problems with working up in the bow is that the edges of the 'glass unravel as you brush over it; the strings get caught on the brush, and things get crazy. To avoid this, stop applying the resin about 2" from the end of the cloth. Fold the cloth back enough to expose the bare

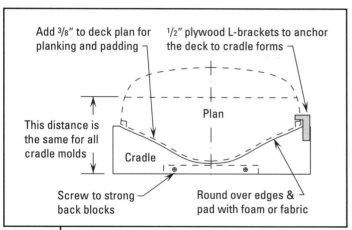

10-44

wood. Brush resin over the stem and planking, then fold the cloth back into place. Some resin will soak through from the back, but if you must add more resin, apply it with a controlled, downward sponging motion.

After squeegeeing, cut the cloth along the centerline of the stem, beginning a couple of inches before the end of the stem. Then make a short cut across the end of the stem. Push the cloth down alongside the stem and allow it to extend above the stem. After the epoxy sets up, slice the excess cloth off with a sharp chisel and finish it with sandpaper.

The second coat of epoxy
Before applying the second coat, trim the 'glass around the stems and sand the edges smooth. If it is firm enough, feather the cut edge at the end of the cloth. Make a fast pass over the hull interior with 120-grit sandpaper to cut the tooth, then clean up. Apply the resin in the same manner as outside, with extra care given to squeegeeing and dry brushing.

When the last coat of resin has set up, carefully trim the cloth at the sheer and clean up the edge. Do not disturb the shape of the edge on the hull, as it must remain intact to fit the deck and sheer clamp.

Finishing the bottom side of the deck
When the hull layup is complete, it is time to set up for 'glassing the deck's underside. Prepare a set of cradle forms to fit the deck and fasten to the appropriate mold blocks on the strongback (Illustration 10-44). Place the deck in the cradles and anchor with plywood L-brackets.

Scrape and sand the underside of the deck in preparation for the 'glass and

epoxy. While a less-than-perfect sanding job is probably appropriate here, remember that the hatch covers, made from deck cutouts, will come off and be seen. Do a tidy job of sanding in these areas (Photograph 10-45).

10-45

The screw holes in the sheer clamp left over from clamping to the mold should be filled to keep the moisture out. If you find whittling plugs to fit the holes too tedious, at least fill them with the epoxy filler while filling the cracks in the deck. The filler should not be expected to fill the hole completely because of the air pressure that will build up inside as the glue is pressed in. Use masking tape over the hole on the side to mold the filler and keep it from sagging out.

The fillet joint between the deck and the sheer clamp
There is a way to get the 'glass to go around a sharp corner gracefully, but the sharp corner must be modified first (Illustration 10-46). A fillet, or cove, is molded into the joint between the deck and the

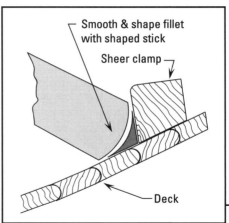

10-46

10-47

sheer clamp. This reinforces the joint and allows the cloth to fold up the side of the sheer clamp and tie everything together.

Make the filleting compound by thickening catalyzed epoxy with a lightweight filler. Add filler to the resin to make a mixture of peanut butter consistency, or thick enough to hold its shape without sagging.

Shape and smooth the filler with a tongue depressor–shaped stick. After the fillet cures, sand any rough edges before doing the layup.

One of the problems with making a fillet is how to get the bulk of the filler out of the can and positioned along the joint before it can be smoothed with the shaped stick. Try the cake-decorating trick of using a strong plastic bag (i.e., freezer bag) to deposit a controlled amount of filler along the joint. To load the bag, hold a corner of it and fold it back over your left hand, then pile the filler onto the bag. Turn the bag right-side out, work the filler into the corner, and twist up the open end. To apply the filler, cut the corner off and squeeze (Photograph 10-47).

Protect the outside edge of the sheer clamp with masking tape; it will save having to file off the runs later (Illustration 10-48). Encourage the 'glass cloth to follow the fillet up the side of the sheer clamp. Check that there is no air between the cloth and the fillet.

Trim the excess cloth after the first coat of epoxy has firmed up, and smooth the edge with sandpaper. Two coats of epoxy on the underside of the deck should be

sufficient; the second coat should cover the entire sheer clamp.

Fitting the deck to the hull and fastening

Well, here comes another one of those Kodak moments. Since the deck was planked to fit the hull, it should fit like a lid on a cookie jar.

Set up the hull cradle forms on the strongback and place the hull in it. If necessary, place a few duct tape tabs at the middle of the hull to spread it. It is also a good idea to soften the inside edge of the sheer clamp so it doesn't catch on the edge of the hull and splinter. Carefully fit the deck into the hull and appreciate the perfect fit. Go easy handling the ends of the deck; because the 'glass is only on the outside of the deck here, the ends are fragile.

The next step is to fasten the deck to the hull. The fastenings you use will hold the parts together as one convenient unit for working on the deck now, as well as provide clamping pressure when the hull and deck are glued together later.

Use ½″ to ¾″ x No. 4 or No. 5 brass or bronze flathead screws on about 6″ centers. Brass or bronze is preferred to steel, as there will be less damage to the plane blade if you happen to hit a screw head while trimming the deck. Drill pilot holes and countersink the heads slightly. It is important that the screwheads be flush or slightly below the surface when the edge of the deck is being trimmed. Be sure the parts fit tightly together before fastening.

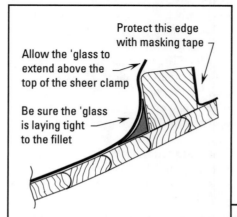

10-48

11 | The Cockpit and Hatches

Finishing up the 'glass work is the end of a major portion of this building project. I hope that building to this stage has been everything you wanted it to be and that you are happy with your work. The pace will slow down now, with less grunt work and more contemplation. As you begin the finishing touches, take the time to do good work and enjoy the satisfaction that comes with giving it your best shot.

When the hull and deck are fitted together, we'll have a structure that will float. But, unless it is going to be used for a final trip to Valhalla, openings must be cut for the cockpit and hatches (Photograph 11-1).

Part of the attraction of building your own kayak is choosing among the many options available to customize the craft to suit your needs. Before you start cutting holes in the deck, have a good idea about how the kayak will be used and where. Think about long-term as well as short-term use; adding some equipment later could be simplified by planning ahead now. While the rudder is best installed before the deck is permanently attached, hatches and all of the deck fittings may be added as the need arises. If options that require backing blocks are to be added later, anticipate the need and install the blocks before gluing the deck into place.

CUTTING AND TRIMMING THE OPENINGS

The cockpit coaming and hatch trim play a significant role in the function and struc-

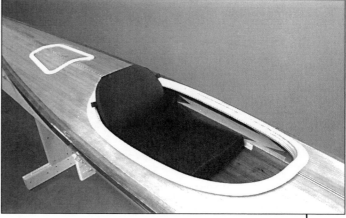

11-1

tural integrity of the kayak. It can also make a distinctive visual statement.

The function of the cockpit coaming is to finish the edge of the opening and raise the edge to help keep the water out. The overhanging rim makes a lip to anchor a spray skirt and, if the cockpit is sized to fit you, will help to anchor your body to the kayak. The hatch trim covers the joint and provides a ledge for the sealing gasket.

Give some thought to the size and shape of the coaming in terms of function and comfort. Deciding on the cockpit size and shape might best be done by purchasing the skirt first and making the opening to fit. If knee support is important, the keyhole-shaped cockpit opening used by whitewater paddlers provides excellent knee support while keeping the opening size to a minimum.

The framing of the opening is important to the structural integrity of the deck. Being a monocoque structure, the deck is strong when it functions as an unbroken unit, similar to an egg. Once the continuity of the structure is broken, the strength is greatly compromised unless the structure is reinforced and tied back together with a frame.

The style, shape, and materials used will determine what the coaming will look like and how it will function. The possibilities are endless, and range from a simple stacked plywood affair, to complex laminated shapes. If you begin by considering the materials and tools that are available and the time you have to spend on the project, the possibilities will be narrowed down. (See Sources for coaming styles other than what we are using here.)

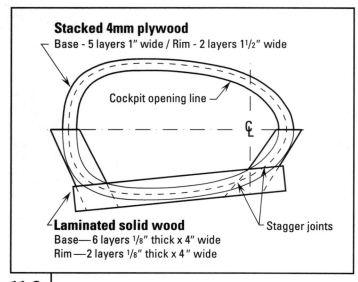

Stacked 4mm plywood
Base - 5 layers 1" wide / Rim - 2 layers 1½" wide

Cockpit opening line

CL

Laminated solid wood
Base—6 layers ⅛" thick x 4" wide
Rim—2 layers ⅛" thick x 4" wide

Stagger joints

11-2

Tools and materials

The style of cockpit coaming we are using may be built up from layers of 4mm (³⁄₁₆″) plywood or from thin pieces of solid wood (Illustration 11-2). Although this coaming style is about as basic as it can get, it will make a structurally sound frame and, if care is taken, it can be beautiful, too. Whatever the material chosen, it must be flexible enough to follow the compound curve without distorting the deck.

Plywood is the simplest and most common material for constructing the coaming and hatch trim. Look for marine-grade lauan for a good-looking rim; exterior-grade waterproof plywood of any species will work, but watch the weight. With careful planning, the parts of the cockpit coaming and hatch can be cut from one

sheet of 4mm plywood. Pre-cut plywood parts are also available (see Sources). The parts could be a continuous piece if the deck has a smooth crown, or divided down the middle into two parts if there is a ridge along the centerline of the deck. Dividing the segments along the centerline will allow the parts to be nested on the plywood sheet, thus saving a considerable amount of material. Save the pieces with the best grain orientation for the top layer.

Solid wood is a good choice if you have the facilities to resaw and dress thin pieces of wood. When choosing a wood species, consider strength, flexibility, weight, and color. We have used white pine for the frame on our cockpit coaming and ash for the rim. The pine is light, easy to work, and came from some thin off-cuts I had moved too many times.

Although we have chosen one of the simplest methods of building the coaming, gluing everything together will require about 16 **clamps** if only one side is glued at a time. This may sound like a lot of clamps, but any style of coaming will require a lot of them for a short time. If yard sales don't supply enough cheap clamps, beg, borrow, or watch for sales at Wal-Mart.

Lay out the deck openings

While there is some flexibility in the size and shape of the cockpit, I would suggest not moving the position of the paddler unless there is a good reason and you understand what it is that you are trying to correct. Assuming the designer has arrived at the seat position by calculation and experience, the position will be based on the distribution of the volume along the length of the kayak and will not necessarily be in the same position as on another kayak of the same length but different style.

If you are contemplating changing the size of the cockpit opening, keep in mind that spray skirts come in standard sizes and shapes. Planning ahead could save having to have a skirt custom made.

As there will be considerable stress on the rim when the skirt is pulled off, we have chosen a hardwood (ash), for its strength, rather than use a greater mass of a softer wood or 'glass cloth to achieve the same objective.

The strength of a single-layer 4mm

11-3

Cutting the openings

To start the cut for the cockpit opening, drill a hole inside the line a little larger than the saw blade (Photograph 11-3). Use a sharp, hollow-ground 10-tpi blade that cuts on the upstroke. The up-cutting blade will put any tear out on the top of the deck where it will be buried under the coaming. (Between the masking tape and a good blade, little tearout should be expected.) Look for a clean cut with no delamination or tearout on the bottom edge.

Notice in Photograph 11-3 the duct tape that has been placed across the line after cutting to support the cutout and keep it from sagging down, binding the blade, or breaking off.

plywood rim must be increased by 'glassing both sides of the rim. 'Glass and sand the underside of the rim before gluing the parts together. Cover the outside after the coaming has been installed, shaped, and sanded. Some people are bothered by the plywood and have tarted-up the plywood with a layer of fancy veneer glued to the rim. I have also seen it painted, and it didn't look bad.

All the information you need to lay out the openings will be found in most plans. The size, shape, and position shown for the hatches in the plans are offered as suggestions. Consider what you will put in the compartment, and estimate the minimum size opening you can live with. When laying out the deck openings, it is important to work from the centerline on the deck and double-check that the pattern has equal space on both sides. Unless there is a distinct line on the deck that you trust, lay masking tape along the centerline and draw a crisp line on the tape.

To help visualize the openings and to double-check their size and position, make poster-board templates and tape them in position. This can be most helpful if you are still deciding on size and placement of the hatches. Make the templates as accurate as possible so that they can be used to mark the openings as well as the trim parts.

If the surface of the deck has been sanded, a pencil mark will show up and may be washed off later with lacquer thinner. On unsanded epoxy, or for the most distinct line, lay masking tape over the approximate position, then draw lines on the tape with a ball-point pen.

11-4

As the cutout for the hatch opening will be used to make the cover, this cut must be started without damaging the edge of the deck or the cover. To provide access for the blade, make a slit along the line by drilling overlapping holes with a 1/16" drill bit (Photograph 11-4).

Take your time making this cut, as cleaning up the shape later will result in

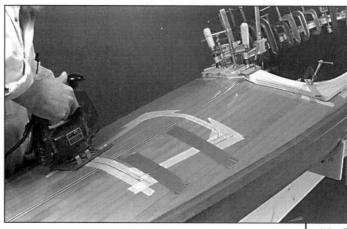

11-5

11-6

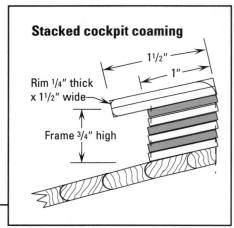

11-7

be tricky but not impossible, as the pieces will want to slide around when the clamps are tightened. If all else fails, try the clamping trick we used on the stem to keep the laminations in line.

If you are cutting the parts out of a plywood sheet, I would suggest cutting the pieces oversize (about ½" on all sides) and trimming to the pattern after gluing. Trim the ends to the line and draw reference lines across the end of the plywood. Use these marks as a guide to line up the layers.

The exact dimension of the solid-wood stock will depend on what you have to work with and how well it will bend to fit the shape of the deck. The stock we are using is ⅛" thick and 3¾" wide. These off-cuts that had been cluttering up the shop for too long worked out just right to make each side of one lamination in three pieces. The joints of each layer were alternated to tie everything together. After being glued up and trimmed to shape, this overlapping joint will look like a deep finger joint.

a sloppy-fitting cover. For the best possible control, you might need to stand on something to get your body into a comfortable, safe working position with good visibility. As the cut progresses, try a couple of duct tape tabs across the cut; this will keep the cutout from sagging down and binding the saw; it will also reduce the danger of the cutout breaking off at the end of the cut (Photograph 11-5).

Use the duct tape tabs to remove the cutout (Photograph 11-6).

Stacked cockpit coaming

1½"

1"

Rim ¼" thick
x 1½" wide

Frame ¾" high

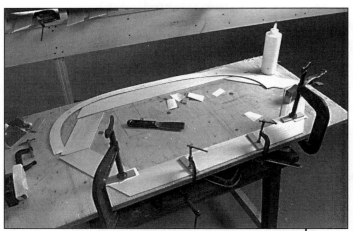

11-8

Preparing the coaming parts

Laminating the coaming is the same for both plywood and solid wood (Illustration 11-7). If you are using plywood and making the coaming in halves, lay the pieces out on the material for the best cut. Make one pair of parts with the grain running fore and aft, and use this for the top layer of the rim.

Precut coaming kits or plywood parts cut to the finished size will require care to keep the pieces stacked up in line; if they are not, you will lose a lot of coaming cleaning up the edges. Expect this to

On our boat, to simplify gluing the stacked-up pieces together, the three segments that make up one layer of one side were butt-glued together with carpenter's glue beforehand (Photograph 11-8). This was a simple alternative to juggling 18 slippery pieces of wood, keeping the joints tight, and positioning the clamps at the same time.

The butt-glued joint will be strong enough to hold the pieces together for gluing but will not stand up to much twisting as the piece is clamped to follow the curve of the deck. Notice that we have positioned the first set of clamps to stabilize the joint before clamping the ends down at the centerline (Photograph 11-9).

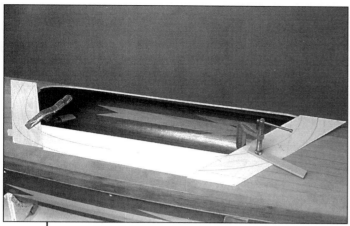

11-9

Because there will be a lot of clamping activity around the edge of the cockpit, it is important to protect the underside of the deck from damage by the clamps. To facilitate this, we used two-sided carpet tape to stick softwood clamping pads to the underside of the deck (Photograph 11-10). Leave the pads in place until the gluing is complete. There will be enough to keep your hands busy without having to deal with the clamping blocks at the same time.

Cover the deck around the opening with plastic packaging tape to protect the deck until the coaming is ready to be glued into place.

11-10

Building the coaming

The system and order that you use to glue the pieces together is worth some thought. Everything considered, it all comes down to the time you want to spend and the quality of the results you expect.

On the fast end of the scale, it is possible to stack and glue all the precut parts together plus glue it to the deck, all in one session. This would not be my first choice,

as there are so many pieces and clamps to handle that the possibility of it getting out of control is quite real. Also, the edges are going to be hard to clean up, especially under the overhanging rim.

I have broken this one big step into a series of manageable steps that will eliminate some of the variables and give us control over the finished product.

The first step will be to laminate the parts for the frame (Photograph 11-11). In theory, we could glue both the frame and the rim at the same time, but drawing so many layers down will put a lot of stress on the deck. The frame and the rim will be shaped independently, as they would not be glued together at this point anyway.

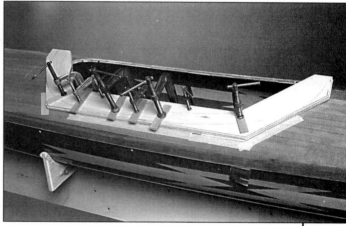

11-11

Use reference marks on the parts to ensure that they align correctly so the intended shape may be cut from the entire stack after the glue sets. Project the lines to the ends of the pieces so they are still visible after the pieces are stacked. The two inside lines will be positioned at the edge of the opening on the centerline. Notice that we have done a dry run with

11-12

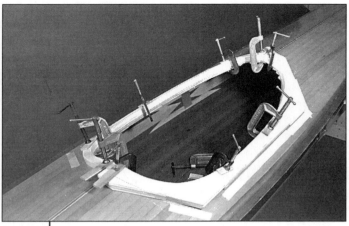

11-13

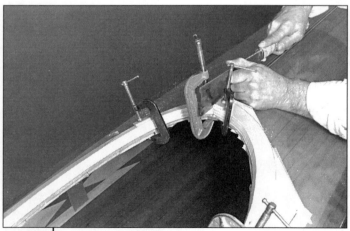

11-14

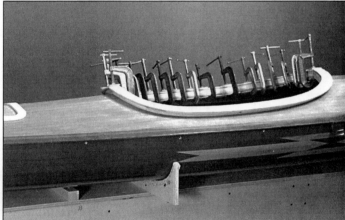

11-15

the first layer and marked its position on the deck with masking tape.

Apply thickened epoxy to all mating surfaces. Be sure that both surfaces are evenly coated. Begin clamping at the corners to protect the butt joints. There is a tendency for the thin layers to curl up at the edges, so we are using clamping pads long enough to hold them down.

When many thin layers are glued together at the same time, there is the danger of waves developing between the clamps. To avoid this, use lots of clamps with substantial pads, and don't over-tighten the clamps (Photograph 11-12).

Laminate the rim over the deck using the same routine as we used for the frame.

After gluing up both sides of the frame, clean up the ends so they fit together well at the centerline. Loosely clamp the frame to the deck and scribe the shape of the opening on its bottom. Trim the frame to this line, but leave the outside alone until after the final fitting at the centerline. Notice the space between the masking tape on the deck and the edge of the frame

in Photograph 11-13. This is how much we lost during our final fitting.

To make the final fit, clamp the two parts of the frame in position and run a fine saw through the joint until the ends fit to your satisfaction. If you are worried about cutting into the deck, a couple of layers of masking tape on the deck might help (Photograph 11-14).

Check the fit around the inside between the frame and the opening. There is a possibility that the frame is now extending over the edge of the opening. Scribe the new shape onto the bottom of the frame and dress to the line at the bench.

With the centerline joint fit and the inside edges under control, you can now mark a 1″ parallel outside line, using the inside shape as the guide. After cutting the outside shape, clean up and finish-sand this edge, as it will never be easier to get at than it is now.

Gluing the frame to the deck

If the deck has not been sanded yet, at least sand around the opening before gluing. This will ensure a good bond to the deck, and you won't have to worry about hitting and damaging the frame with the sander when you do get around to sanding.

When the frame has been glued to the deck, the rim may be shaped and installed (Photograph 11-15). Work through the same routine as used on the frame to mark and fit the rim. Watch for squeezed-out glue on the underside of the rim, and clean it up well before it sets.

It might be a good idea to tie the joint together at the centerline before installing the rim. Picking the kayak up by the coaming at the centerline will put considerable tension on this butt joint if the boat is

11-16

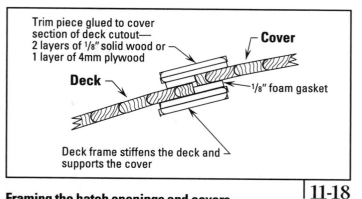

Trim piece glued to cover
section of deck cutout—
2 layers of 1/8" solid wood or
1 layer of 4mm plywood

Cover

Deck

1/8" foam gasket

Deck frame stiffens the deck and
supports the cover

11-18

heavily loaded. For insurance, we have
bridged the joint with a bit of carbon fiber
(Photograph 11-16). Glass fibers taken
from a scrap of fiberglass cloth would
work, as would inlaying a piece of wood
with the grain running across the joint.
When the rim is glued on, the inlaid piece
will turn the butt joint into a spline joint.

Because the parts have been put together
in a logical order and with care, cleaning
up and shaping the coaming should be quite
straightforward. Use a sanding block to
round over the outside edge. The inside
edge should be rounded over, too, for comfort and safety. We have used the router
with a 1/2"-radius roundover bit on the
inside, but this shape could be developed
just as well with a spokeshave and sanding block (Photograph 11-17).

Framing the hatch openings and covers

As with the cockpit coaming, there is more
than one technique for framing the opening and making the cover (see Sources).
The system we have come up with has a
low profile and uses the cutout from the
deck to make the cover (Illustration 11-18).

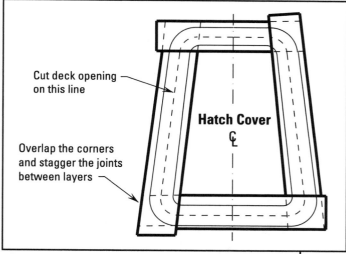

Cut deck opening
on this line

Hatch Cover
C̸L

Overlap the corners
and stagger the joints
between layers

11-19

It makes a beautiful, functional cover that
continues the subtle compound curves of
the surrounding deck. The frame on the
bottom of the deck will support the cover
and will also be fitted with a gasket.

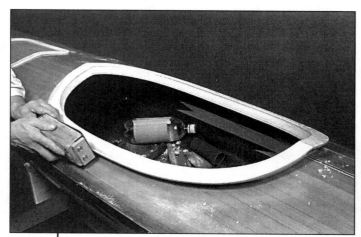

11-17

The plastic-pop-bottle-with-the-sand-
paper trick worked great for sanding the
inside of the cockpit coaming and for
putting a 1/4" radius on the inside bottom
corner. Sand up to the 120-grit stage; save
the 220-grit step for just before applying a sealer.

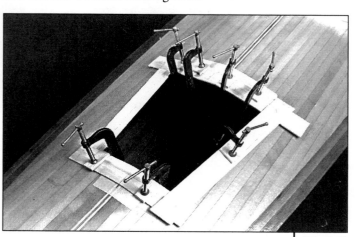

11-20

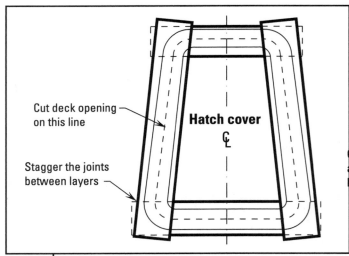

Cut deck opening on this line

Hatch cover
CL

Stagger the joints between layers

11-21

The trim piece for the cover is the same shape as the deck frame; both will be glued up and shaped before being glued into position. Two layers of ⅛ x 1¾″ ash will make a strong frame that will match the style of the cockpit. Glued up as illustrated, only one end of each piece will have to be cut and fit (Illustration 11-19).

In Photograph 11-20, we are using the top surface of the deck as the mold for both parts. It would be awkward to try to assemble and clamp the pieces of the frame from underneath the deck. Also, laminating the frame in place on the cover could distort the cover, making it fit badly.

try to use a continuous piece, as it will be stronger.

Our deck has a slight but distinct ridge down the centerline. Trying to bend the ⅛″ ash to this shape dry seemed to push the wood close to the breaking point. There was a good chance that this much tension would distort the deck, even after gluing the layers together. To ease the pressure, the pieces were steamed by setting them on edge over the kettle spout for about ten minutes. The pieces were then bent by eye over the edge of the bench and held until cool. This took all of the downward pressure off the centerline of the deck and allowed the frame to assume the true, relaxed shape of the deck and cover.

11-23

Although the deck frame employs a simple-to-make and structurally sound lap joint, the glue joints are not symmetrical (Illustration 11-21). Since the joints on the cover are not as structurally significant as those of the deck frame, we are going for good looks first. In keeping with and reinforcing the lines of the kayak, all the

11-22

If you are using solid wood, glue up the deck frame with the joints staggered to make a lap joint at each corner. Take your time fitting the pieces at the corners. Place reference marks across the joints when you are happy with the dry fit.

If it can be avoided, I think it is a good idea not to make a joint on the centerline. Unless the deck is a sharp inverted "V,"

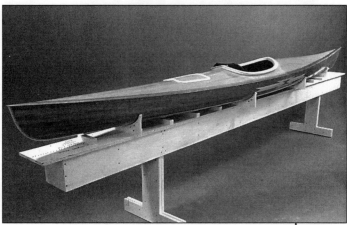

11-24

grain on the top layer runs fore-and-aft. Hold the short pieces on the ends together with masking tape. When you apply the glue, be sure to apply it to the edges of the segments (Photograph 11-22).

Using the template, cut the frames to shape and finish the edges (Photograph 11-23). Cutting the inside shape will be a little tricky in the corners. If you have a Forstner-style bit of the appropriate diameter, use it to drill out the corners for a consistent radius.

Glue the frames in place and clean up the glue; it will be hard to sand out later (Photograph 11-24).

12 | Form to Function

SANDING THE EPOXY

Even though sanding the epoxy surface gives a flawlessly smooth surface, it may not turn out to be your favorite part of the building process. With this in mind, there are ways of getting it over with quickly, safely, and in relative comfort. Because the sanding may be done at any time after the epoxy has cured and before the varnish is applied, look for an opportunity to move hull and deck outside before you start. The part that bothers me the most about sanding epoxy is cleaning up all that fine dust afterwards. Even after cleaning up the shop several times, there will be little pockets of epoxy dust that keep being uncovered.

Safety

Refer to the section on epoxy safety for detailed information on safe handling.

Sand the epoxy outside if possible, but if this is out of the question, use a fan in the window to create a cross draft. Try to keep your back to the draft, so the dust is drawn away from you. Cover machines, shelves, and other hard-to-clean areas with plastic film. Use sweeping compound to keep the dust down while sweeping the floor. Vacuum the dust off the surface rather than brushing, which will make the dust airborne again. Wear protective clothing and a dust mask or respirator.

Don't eat or smoke in the shop while sanding. Wash all exposed body parts with soap and water when you are finished sanding and cleaning up.

Tools and sandpaper

See Chapter 8 for detailed information on sanders, sandpaper, and sanding.

The **random-orbit sander** is the tool of choice for sanding epoxy; expect to finish edges and details with a hand-sanding block.

Using a good **silicon carbide paper designated "OC"** will result in the best finish in the least amount of time.

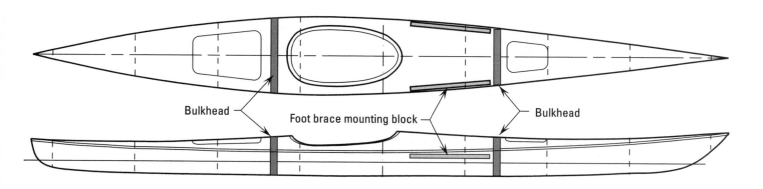

Bulkhead — Foot brace mounting block — Bulkhead

What to look for

Beginning with the shiny but wavy, raw, cured epoxy, the surface will go through several visual steps before it is ready for varnish. Recognizing what each step looks like will tell us where we are, what steps remain, and precisely when to stop. With this understanding, you will have control over what you are doing as well as a predictable end to each step (Photograph 12-1).

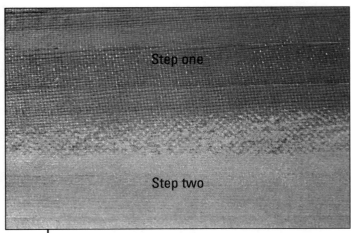

Step one

Step two

12-1

Step 1 will begin with the shiny epoxy surface; the profile of the weave is visible, as are a few runs. In this step, you'll use 80-grit paper to take the surface to a roughed-out stage with some shiny spots remaining. It is important at this stage to leave a few shiny spots as a reference. Once the gloss is gone, you will be getting close to the 'glass, so it would be wise to switch to 120-grit paper. When all the gloss is gone, the surface will not change until the glass fiber becomes exposed.

Use a sharp cabinet scraper to shave the sags and runs down flush with the surface. A sander with a foam pad will have a tendency to follow the profile of the sag, leaving a good possibility of hitting the 'glass on the surrounding surface before the run is leveled.

When you begin to sand, the first thing you will see will be white scratches on the high points of the surface, where one strand of fiberglass runs over another. Expect the pattern of the weave to become more distinct as the sandpaper cuts its way down to the bottom of the shiny craters. If the layup has gone well, there should be enough epoxy built up over the cloth that all the shiny spots will disappear without hitting the glass fibers.

(Note: If you are not using 80-grit

sandpaper for the first step, steps one and two will be combined using 120-grit.)

Step 2 will begin as an even, flat, white surface with a few shiny low spots, and will finish with all the gloss and most of the 80-grit scratches removed. The moment this surface appears, stop. The surface is now prepared for varnish; going past this point will expose the glass fibers.

This step is a fine balance between just enough and going too far. Again: when all the gloss has disappeared, move on and leave this area alone. If you have been using 80-grit paper up to this stage, a quick once-over with 120-grit will finish it up. If you have been using 120-grit exclusively, check the surface over and remove any remaining gloss.

Step 3 is the one you don't want to see, and it happens when the sander has gone past the point of removing the gloss and the weave becomes visible again.

The pattern we have been looking at and trying to eliminate is the shiny space between the fibers. Now we see the fibers themselves. Cutting into the 'glass a bit could make the glass fibers visible in bright sunlight even after varnishing. If more of the fiber is removed, the integrity of the structure is compromised. Try to avoid this condition, because even though applying more resin to the oversanded area will correct the problem, it will be tricky feathering it into the surrounding area without hitting the 'glass again.

Sanding the inside of the hull and deck

If the inside of the hull and deck have been finished with two coats of epoxy, preparing the inside will be quick and easy. Sand the inside by hand, using 120-grit paper. The object is to knock off the rough points without flattening the surface or cutting all of the gloss.

Some brands of epoxy, particularly when they cure at cool temperatures, leave behind an amine blush. The amine blush is a byproduct of the hardener and comes to the surface during the curing process. This residue, if not removed, will compromise the bond between the varnish and the epoxy surface. Remove the blush by washing with water fortified with ammonia, and rinse well with fresh water.

MAKING THE BOAT FUNCTIONAL

With the hull and deck sanded, the two major components are ready for varnish. This is a pivotal point in the construction sequence, as the way the kayak is to be fitted out decides what will happen next. The form of the kayak is complete, so the next step is to decide what accessories will complement the form to best fulfill our intended function.

One of the unique features of the kayak and of building your own is the direction the boat can take from here. It can be as Spartan as a canoe or as self-sufficient as a cruising sailboat. And it can be outfitted on a large or small budget. In this chapter, we'll explore features and components that fall into two basic categories: those driven by safety, and those driven by propulsion.

SAFETY-DRIVEN FEATURES

Keeping the kayak buoyant can happen on a number of levels. The number of these levels you choose to address should be appropriate to the boat's anticipated use.

The least you can get away with is having some way of occupying the space under the deck that is not being used by the paddler. This is very important, as a kayak hull filled with water becomes a submarine and is about as useful as a cast-iron lifejacket. The flooded hull will be extremely heavy and awkward to empty, even in the most ideal conditions. You must have sufficient positive flotation within the craft to float you sitting in the flooded cockpit, while maintaining enough freeboard around the cockpit to pump or bail the cockpit dry.

The most basic way of achieving positive flotation is with the use of **inflatable air bags** or **dry storage bags**. Inuit paddlers had great success with inflated seal-intestine bladders, but, fortunately for the seals, we have other options. Bulkheads are a common solution and, when fitted with a hatch, become a sheltered space for cargo.

A second, and not so common, line of defense is the **sea sock** used by some bluewater paddlers. It is simply a waterproof sock that encloses the lower body with the opening drawn tight around the cockpit opening. Sea socks do limit the amount of water that can enter the hull, but some paddlers find them uncomfortable.

The final and major line of defense is the **spray skirt.** With the space between the paddler and the cockpit opening sealed up, the boat and paddler are as buoyant as a duck.

Safety-driven features include:
- Air bags, dry bags, or dual bags (an air bag with provision for dry storage)
- Bulkheads
- Spray skirts
- Hatch and seal
- Grab handles and loops
- Deck tiedowns/paddle float
- Bilge pump, bailer, and sponge
- Nonskid on bottom

Inflatable air bags

Air bags are available in a variety of shapes and sizes from outdoor equipment and paddling retailers. The uninflated bag is placed under the deck and inflated via a long plastic tube. Try the bag in place before deciding whether it needs to be strapped into place. Make sure there are no sharp edges or points within the cavity that could abrade or puncture the bag. I like the idea of an uninterrupted foredeck on our classy day tripper. Fitted with an air bag forward and bulkhead aft, a good seat, and foot braces, we will have a simple yet fast and elegant way to spend the day cruising. By replacing the forward air bag with a dry bag for storage, our simple day tripper becomes a serious expedition craft.

Dry bags and dual bags address the problem of occupying the space in the cavity as well as provide dry storage for gear.

Bulkheads

Bulkheads are fixed, watertight partitions that divide the hull into sections in much the same way as in a ship. Access to the enclosed space for inspection and ventilation is important. The minimum acceptable opening would be a 4″ or 6″ plastic inspection cover on a rigid bulkhead. Deck hatches provide this access as well as create functionally dry and usable storage space.

A bulkhead aft of the cockpit will also function to support the deck. This area will bear the weight of the paddle if it is placed here for boarding; in this case, the weight is transferred directly to the bottom of the hull. Rigid bulkheads may be constructed from 4mm to 6mm marine plywood or scrap planking laid up with fiberglass and epoxy. The flexible bulkhead uses $1^1/_2$" to 3" closed-cell foam bonded to the cavity with a flexible bedding compound. Commonly used is Ethafoam, a dense, moderately flexible, closed-cell foam that is easy to cut and shape.

For structural reasons, my preference is the foam bulkhead. As a monocoque structure, the hull is strongest when an impact is allowed to be transmitted over the whole surface. A rigid bulkhead will interrupt this even distribution of force and concentrate the load at the bulkhead line. Ethafoam, being flexible, will allow the hull to function as designed and to absorb and distribute the shock evenly.

To fit a bulkhead, do all measuring and fitting with the deck in position. If the bulkhead were fastened to the hull with the deck off, there would be a good possibility that hull and deck would no longer fit together.

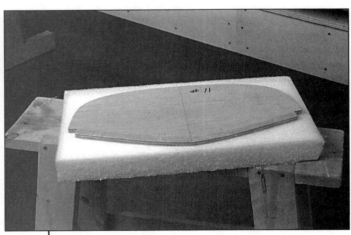

12-2

Begin by making up a pattern from illustration board or thin plywood (Photograph 12-2). Pick up the shape from the closest station mold and trim enough to fit into the cavity. Wedge or tape the pattern into position and scribe around the edge to pick up the exact shape of the hull and deck. Use a small block of wood against the hull to transfer the shape to the pattern. Naturally, the same block would be used to transfer the line back to the bulkhead material.

Another simple but accurate method of picking up the shape is to hot-glue small pieces of card around the pattern to establish a number of points that define an exact shape. Two-sided tape will work in place

of the hot glue. Before removing the pattern from the kayak, mark the position of the pattern on the hull with masking tape. All future fitting and installation will be made to the reference marks.

The time to begin **installing a rigid bulkhead,** or any type of bulkhead, is before the interior is varnished and the deck glued into place. There are quite a number of steps in fitting and attaching the rigid bulkhead that must be performed in awkward positions with poor visibility. Broken into steps, much of the work can be done in relative comfort with the deck off.

The order of assembly is as follows, beginning with the deck screwed temporarily to the hull.

- Make a pattern and transfer the shape to the bulkhead material.
- Cut the bulkhead to shape and make final adjustments. Coat the sides and edges of the bulkhead (if wooden) with epoxy and sand it before installing.
- Stabilize the bulkhead in position with wedges or duct tape.
- Apply a partial fillet to tack the bulkhead to the hull.
- When the fillet has set, remove the deck and complete the fillet, stopping short of the sheer clamp.
- Reinforce the fillet with fiberglass cloth or tape.
- Sand and feather the edges of the 'glass before brushing on the second coat of epoxy resin.
- Complete the bond between the top of the bulkhead and the deck after the deck has been glued into position.

The bulkhead will be bonded to the hull and deck with fiberglass cloth or tape over a low-density fillet. Use the same materials and procedure as we used to reinforce the sheer clamp. If the color is important to you, the filler may be tinted with sanding dust. Don't expect it to go very dark by your adding homemade sanding dust. (As the ratio of dust to filler increases, the filler will become hard to smooth.) To achieve a darker color, try using a commercial mahogany wood flour or a dark filler such as WEST SYSTEM #407 low-density filleting compound or microballoons.

While it is possible to fillet and 'glass the bulkhead to the hull and deck all in one step, it will be less frustrating if you do it in stages. Begin by putting the bulkhead into position and stabilizing it with wedges. If inserting the wedges is pushing the bulkhead out of position, try a pair of wedges inserted from opposing sides to keep things balanced. Use duct tape if your fit is so good that there is no room for the wedges.

Working between the wedges, tack the bulkhead to the hull with part of the fillet. One side is enough for now; if the hull is sitting in the cradle forms, there should be very little stress on the joint if the deck is carefully removed. After the fillet sets, you can remove the deck to complete the fillet on both sides and then reinforce everything with fiberglass.

Use a strip of 6-oz. fiberglass cloth or 4"-wide tape to reinforce the joint. Working the flat fabric into two curves at the same time will be more difficult with the tape than with the cloth. The selvage or woven edge of the tape will have little give and may have to have darts cut in it in order for it to lie down. Don't make these cuts until after the tape has been wetted out to avoid having to deal with the cut edge falling apart.

Tape that has been cut from fiberglass cloth will be easiest to work with if it is cut on the bias or with the fibers running at 45° to the edge of the tape. This will minimize the amount the fibers are expected to bend and allow the woven fibers to shift to follow the compound curves of the hull and bulkhead.

Try the following trick to save fighting with the edge of the cloth. Cut the cloth oversize, then wet out only the area you want covered. Using a sponging motion with the brush, keep the epoxy back from the cut edge. When the first coat of epoxy has cured, slice off the excess 'glass cloth with a sharp chisel or knife. Hold the blade flat to the surface and slide it along the edge of the wet-out cloth. Feather the edge of the 'glass with 80-grit sandpaper and brush on a second coat of epoxy.

The joint between the bulkhead and the deck will be made after hull and deck have been joined. When varnishing the underside of the deck, protect the sanded epoxy surface where the bulkhead will join the deck; epoxy will not bond to the varnish. (Just before gluing the hull and deck together, you might also want to mask off the varnish.)

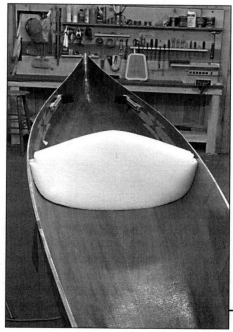

12-3

The foam bulkhead will be bonded to the hull and deck with a flexible adhesive-sealant such as Sikaflex 241 or 3M Fast Cure 5200. Look for a compound that remains flexible, sets up in a reasonable time, and is available in an appropriate color. These bedding compounds will stick to both sanded epoxy and varnish, so in Photograph 12-3 we are doing the final installation after the interior has been varnished. The interior hull surface will have the best protection, and this will save having to varnish around the foam.

Cut the foam to shape with a jigsaw, bandsaw, or serrated bread knife. Look for a snug but not wedged-in fit. There should be some space for the bedding, but try for a decent fit.

There are a couple of options as to how or when the foam bulkheads are installed. At Canadian Canoes, where they have lots of hands available and like to keep things moving, they install the bulkhead at the same time the deck is being glued to the hull. If you have enough hands to keep both jobs going at once, give it a try. It will make a good joint and get the job over with quickly.

After dry-fitting the foam bulkhead with the deck in place, mask off the hull and deck to mark the location and protect the varnish. As the epoxy glue is being applied to the sheer clamp, run two healthy beads of bedding compound around the hull-facing edges of the foam and press it into place. Apply more bedding to the top edge of the foam and fasten the deck in place. If the amount and placement of the bedding are just right, the compound will fill the cavity and squeeze out to the edge without much waste. Smooth the compound flush with the face of the foam and remove the tape. An alternative would be to spread the excess around the joint to shape it into a neat cove. Shape the joint by running your finger (in a glove) around the joint. Spit on your finger or dip it in soapy water to keep the compound from sticking.

These bedding compounds are sticky and have a tendency to spread. Work clean, wear gloves, and use masking tape. Clean up stray bedding compound with a rag dampened with mineral spirits. If there is a wide glue joint that you don't want to disturb with the rag, wait until the compound has just skinned over before cleaning up. The compound will rub off the varnish and foam without messing up the fillet, but don't wait too long to clean up.

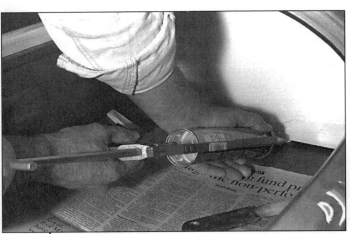

12-4

If you are working alone or are not in a hurry, try the method in Photograph 12-4.

The advantage of the former method is that you can apply the adhesive-sealant along the edge of the foam, giving the bond a good surface area. I don't think the bond is necessarily better if the bedding fills the entire joint, but the corners should be tight on both sides. (If the fit between the bulkhead and hull is loose, it could mean a lot of heavy material will fill the joint, and that will make the joint stiffer than it should be.)

You can finish the adhesive flush with the surface of the foam. This can be

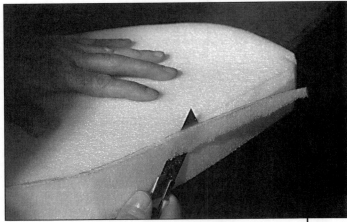

12-5

achieved by relieving the edge of the foam to increase the surface area and by forcing the bedding back into the joint with the thin nozzle of the caulking gun. A bedding surface of about 1″ on each side of the foam should be plenty (Photograph 12-5). If the joint is too tight to take the bedding and you don't want to relieve the edge of the foam, a fillet on both sides will also work. The fillet is not my first choice in terms of neatness, as the joint will lack the clean lines that our kayak deserves. In the photos, we have made the bond within the joint and finished the bedding flush with the surface of the foam. The bedding is the same color as the foam (white, but black is also available), giving the bulkhead a crisp outline where it meets the hull (Photograph 12-6).

12-6

Spray skirts

A spray skirt has two components—the tunnel and the deck—that must fit the paddler and the cockpit coaming to be comfortable and dry. The tunnel (or chimney) should fit comfortably up under your arms, effectively keeping the water out without restricting movement. The material on the deck should be stretched enough to be flat and make a watertight seal at the cockpit rim.

The most effective, durable, and expensive skirts are made of neoprene. The deck can be stretched flat to shed water, and the tunnel makes a tight seal to the body. Neoprene is a must with a whitewater kayak, but the fairweather sea kayaker may find it hot, with too much restriction of upper-body movement.

Skirts entirely of coated nylon are lighter and cooler than neoprene and have the least restriction of movement. They seem to be favored by the recreational paddler who does not anticipate heavy going or having to roll. The deck will not be as firm and flat as neoprene, nor should it be expected to be as durable.

A compromise is the neoprene deck with a coated nylon tunnel. The deck on this skirt will stay flat to shed the water, without the restriction of a neoprene tunnel.

Skirt sizes are based on your waist size for the tunnel and the cockpit opening for the deck. The deck should stretch enough to make a good seal but not so tight that you have to fight to get it on and off. Some skirts have an adjustable bungee cord around the deck that will allow the skirt to be used on a variety of sizes and shapes of openings. The unstretched neoprene tunnel should be about 85% of your waist size, but, as it also fits above the waist, try it on to be sure.

Hatch seal

Deck hatches come in two types: the ones that don't leak, and the ones that do an excellent job of keeping most of the water out. The most reliable covers are the British VCP rubber hatches or plastic marine inspection plates. While watertight, neither of these covers will look great on the deck of our kayak (although the inspection cover is quite appropriate for access through a rigid bulkhead).

The other type of cover is more common and is identified by the straps and buckles or bungee cord that hold the cover in place. Several factors contribute to the quality of the seal on this style of cover:

- If the shape of the cover does not match the shape of the deck, a thicker foam gasket must be used to compensate. To make this work, greater downward pressure must be created, which is hard to do with the straps.
- Too much pressure or too few straps on a flimsy cover will distort the shape, causing the corners to curl up.
- Dirt and grime on the gasket could hinder the seal between the foam and the deck.
- Insufficient triangulation to create downward pressure with straps becomes more of a problem on a flatter deck. Unless there is a substantial arch in the middle of the deck and cover, there will be a problem creating downward pressure with straps that are fastened at the sheer. If the crown of the deck is low, increasing the tension of the strap will not increase the downward pressure by much.

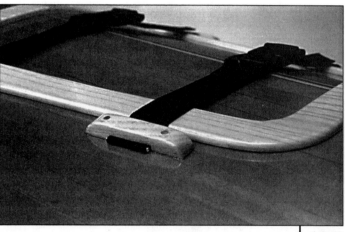

12-7

To address this potential problem, in Photograph 12-7 we are anchoring the strap close to the edge of the cover to direct the pressure from the tightened strap straight down the side of the cover to the deck. This is more effective than the shallow angle of a strap fastened at the edge of the deck.

The anchor blocks are $3/8'' \times 1/2'' \times 2^{1}/2''$ hardwood with a slot in the bottom sufficiently large to take a double thickness of the strap. The nylon strap is folded back on the end about $3/4''$ and is sewn or welded (melted with a soldering iron or hot knife) together to form a flat loop. The loop is pushed through the slot and a small brass pin or dowel is inserted into the loop to secure the strap. If the tension on the strap and friction in the slot are not enough to secure the pin, try a spot of hot-melt glue. Don't get carried away with the glue, as the pin will have to be removed in order

12-8

have a good bite inside the strap anchor block. The block is also glued to the deck to seal the joint (Photograph 12-9).

Install the foam gasket after all the varnish has been completed; the wood will have the best protection, and you won't have to varnish around the foam (Photograph 12-10). On our style of cover, use a gasket on both the cover trim and the deck frame. Since these surfaces fit together dry, when a gasket material is applied to both surfaces, the perfect fit is maintained. With a good fit, the controlled downward pressure of the straps, and the great surface area of the double gasket, a reliable, watertight seal may be expected.

to remove the straps for revarnishing.

When I began thinking about this idea, the main problem was how to gracefully fasten the strap anchor block so that the upward load was distributed into a large portion of the deck surface. Being at the edge of the opening, there was a danger of the joint failing in the wood from the direct upward pull if the block were simply glued to the deck (Photograph 12-8).

12-10

12-9

Pressure-sensitive neoprene foam gasket material is available in a variety of sizes and densities from automotive, marine, and building-supply retailers (Photograph 12-11). Choose the thickness of the gasket material to match the quality of the dry fit. A good fit will work best with a thin (1/8") foam; increase the thickness of the foam for a less-than-perfect fit, but also plan on increasing the downward

I thought a screw or dowel through the anchor block into a backing block would work, but to be effective, the fastener would have been out of proportion to the block and the boat. The method I decided on uses a No. 8 brass or bronze screw going through a backing block on the underside of the deck and coming out the top of the strap anchor block. After gluing, the end of the screw is cut off and filed down flush, leaving what looks like the end of a 1/8" brass pin. Aside from being attractive and easy to make, it is a structurally sound solution. The head of the No. 8 screw has a good hold on the backing block, and the threads of the screw

12-11

pressure to help everything come together.

Take the time to miter and fit the gasket around the corners rather than trying to bend the foam to follow the curve. Forcing the foam to follow the corner will result in a greater density of material in the corners—enough to unbalance the watertight fit we have been trying to achieve.

You can hope for, but not count on, any covers being 100% watertight. But they must be tight and secure enough to accomplish their primary function, which is positive flotation in an emergency. To be safe, assume that they will leak, and pack accordingly. Packing in waterproof bags will not only keep your stuff dry but will add another level of positive flotation.

Lifting toggles, grab handles, and loops

Reliable anchor points at bow and stern are useful in a variety of ways and situations (Photograph 12-12). As a safety feature, the handle, loop, or bow/stern line is something for a person in the water to hang on to. In practice, it will be most useful for lifting and moving the kayak by two people. When installing the anchor point, keep in mind the load it is expected to carry.

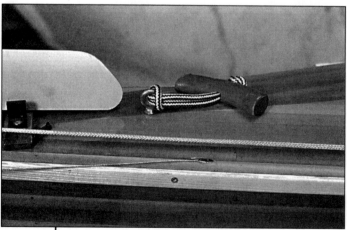

12-12

Some ways of attaching loops and handles are:
- Eyebolt fastened through a backing block under the deck
- Eyepad screwed or bolted to a backing block
- Loop of nylon webbing or tube screwed to the sheer clamp or to backing blocks on the centerline
- Hole drilled through the stem with copper pipe bushing

Since our kayak is to be a simple, yet classy, uncluttered day tripper, inconspicuous holes through the inner stem are used to anchor a bow/stern line or lifting toggles. A short piece of copper pipe is used to seal the hole and protect the edge of the hole. Choose the diameter of the pipe to fit the size of line you would like to use.

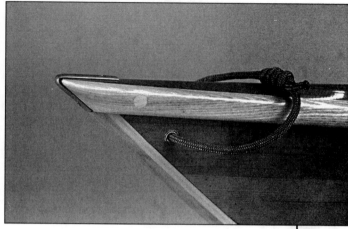

12-13

We are using ¼″ (inside diameter) copper tubing, but plastic pipe will also work (Photograph 12-13). Note that epoxy glue will not bond with the plastic pipe; install it using the same flexible bedding we used for installing the foam bulkhead (e.g., 3M 5200 fast or Sikaflex 241).

To make sure the hole is where you want it to be, cover the area with masking tape and mark the hole on both sides. To increase your chances of coming out in the right place, drill halfway through from each side. Saturate the inside of the hole with unthickened epoxy, feeding the end grain as much as it will take. Sand the outside of the pipe to clean and roughen the surface, add thickened epoxy to the hole, and insert the pipe. It is a good idea to plug the ends of the pipe so it doesn't get filled with glue when it is inserted. When the glue has set, file the pipe flush to the hull surface. To soften the inside edge, flare it by putting an awl part way through the hole and rotating the tool around the hole. This will roll the soft metal over, making a smooth radius that won't cut the bow or stern line.

Deck tiedowns

The purpose of deck tiedowns is to make the cambered deck of the kayak into a portable shelf and wet-cargo space (Photograph 12-14). Used as part of the paddle-

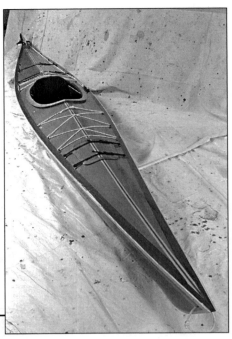

12-14

caulking or bathroom-grade silicone sealer. The bedding compound/adhesive used on the foam bulkhead will bond the pad to the deck; removing it will break something.

A simple, low-profile alternative to the rigid fitting is a loop of 1″ nylon webbing fastened with a No. 6 × ¾″ oval head screw and cup washer (stainless steel, brass, or silicon bronze). Cut a piece of 1″ webbing about 4 ½″ long. Fold it in half to make the loop, then turn about ¾″ of each end inside to finish and reinforce the ends; the hole for the screw will go through all four layers. If you don't like the look of the cup washer, there is no reason why a thin hardwood block could not be used in its place.

Other than the tiedowns aft of the cockpit being used with a paddle-float/self-rescue setup, the size and position and way they are rigged are up to you. If you are undecided on what you will use, screw-in-place fittings may be added at any time in the future. Knowing what backing blocks will be under the tiedowns will decide the positions of the fittings and the tension on the cord.

The important part of the **self-rescue setup** (Illustration 12-15) is the cords running parallel to the edge of the deck. They will do most of the holding when the paddle is slid under to be used as a float. Secure the ends of the cord with a blood knot or metal swages. If swages are used, consider covering them with heat-shrink tubing.

float/wet-entry setup, the paddle blade will be secured by the elastic cords behind the cockpit. Rigged up farther aft and on the foredeck, tiedowns will secure maps in cases, spare paddles, water bottle, foul-weather gear, or any cargo you might need in a hurry or that is too long to fit into the hatch.

If the anchors are screw fastened, install them after the varnish. Glued anchors should be installed before varnishing.

Materials
- ¼″ or ⅜″ elastic cord (bungee cord)
- Eye pads (padeyes, eye straps) in plastic or metal, purchased from marine hardware suppliers or kayak dealers. Hardwood eye pads are easy to make and don't have to be out of proportion to be strong enough. The wooden eye pad may be glued to the deck if evidence of metal fastenings and plastic fittings bothers you. The only downside is that they will complicate varnishing, and since the glue makes them part of the kayak structure, they must be kept well maintained. An alternative would be to mount the wooden pad with screws, as if they were the manufactured type.
- Bedding compound. A spot of bedding compound around the screw is a good idea to keep moisture from entering the deck. If you expect to remove the fittings for revarnishing, use a soft

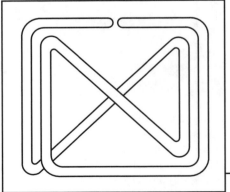

12-15

Bailers, sponges, and pumps
Although we have taken all the steps to keep the water from entering the kayak, there will be times when water will have to be removed from the interior. Small amounts of water from a leaking skirt or drips from the paddle are best removed

with a sponge. A large, thirsty sponge on a tether should be considered basic equipment even for the most leisurely paddle.

To remove large quantities of water, use a cut-down one-gallon plastic jug or handheld bilge pump. This piece of equipment would be useful if you were swimming alongside your swamped kayak and wanted to get back in.

Of interest to the builder is the deck-mounted bilge pump that requires fitting and installation. These pumps are popular with serious bluewater sea kayakers because they may be operated with one hand without removing the spray skirt. This could be a real advantage if there are seas coming over the deck.

If this kayak is going to become your yacht, you may want to consider an electric bilge pump. They are available, but the idea does sound a little out of harmony with the kayak's functional simplicity.

Nonskid bottom

The area in front of the seat is a potential safety hazard on a varnished kayak. Stepping onto this slick surface with wet feet will feel less than secure.

Nonskid compounds are available as a power to be mixed with paint or varnish. Mask off the desired area, then brush on a liberal coat. This should be done after the varnish has been completed, as varnishing over the nonskid will soften the texture.

We are using a nonskid film with a PSA backing on our kayak. This industrial material is sold for use on steps and walkways in factories, so we can expect it to age well on our kayak.

PROPULSION-DRIVEN FEATURES

These features concern paddler comfort and effective transmission of energy into forward motion. The degree to which these are developed will be guided by the intended safe use of the boat and the performance expected. While all of the components are available off the shelf, making some or all of the pieces from available material is quite feasible (see Sources for accessories you can make).

These features include:
• Seat
• Foot brace
• Rudder
• Hip, thigh, knee, and heel pads

Seat

Think of the seat as two components, for the back and bottom function separately and serve different purposes. The seat bottom should sit as low as is functional for your kayak, yet raise your butt enough to keep it out of the water. There should be enough shape to provide good lateral support and keep you from sliding forward. There should also be some fore-and-aft adjustment for trimming the boat to your weight distribution and paddling conditions. Make the seat comfortable. Give some thought to a surface that will breathe (Photograph 12-16). A varnished wooden seat of molded veneer would look beautiful and keep you in one place, but the blisters would be on more than just your hands.

12-16

When the body is pressed aft as you apply pressure on the foot braces, the lower back should be supported at the waist. Position the back support low enough that it does not dig into your lower back and hinder movement. It should be comfortable as you relax and listen to the beads of water roll off your impeccably varnished deck.

The back supports are functional in a number of forms or styles, whether homemade or store bought. Some examples of these are:
• An adjustable padded back strap, which could be manufactured or homemade
• A molded plywood back covered with Ensolite (from that old sleeping pad) supported by straps to the cockpit coaming
• Part of a manufactured seat-and-back unit. Our seat has a molded plastic back support within the fabric frame. It is

fitted with elastic cord to keep the back from falling forward, and there are sewn-in loops on top for the lines that will anchor to it.

An effective seat bottom can be made from thin plywood supported by a low frame that has been shaped and glued to the hull bottom. This platform may be covered with Ensolite or an inflatable pad (the pad is inflated; you sit on it and release the air until the optimum fit is achieved). Fasten the pad with Velcro or straps to keep it from sliding. With the forward edge of the platform raised for comfort and leg support, this could be a good seat even if it lacks fore-and-aft adjustment. This could be overcome by mounting the seat on rails, but this is starting to get complicated.

You can save money by making all these parts, but to make them well will be time consuming. If solving problems with simple solutions is the object of this exercise, you will enjoy making these components. If you are pressed for time, hesitate before gluing anything to the boat that is not up to the standards of the rest of the craft. A better solution might be to purchase ready-to-install components, and take your time installing them with care.

Our seat bottom is sculpted Ethafoam in a coated nylon mesh cover. We have adapted our mounting system to the attachment points on the seat. Commercially available seats will have their own style of attachment. Using the techniques shown here and some ingenuity, any seat should be mountable in a wooden kayak.

In Photograph 12-17 we are using hardwood cleats, $3/8'' \times 5/8'' \times 3''$, as anchor points for the straps. Since these parts are glued to the hull, install them before var-

nishing the interior. Cut the slot in the bottom just deep enough to take the strap and round off the edges. When gluing the cleat to the hull, coat the inside of the slot with epoxy, as this may be the last finish it will see. We are using sticks from overhead to supply the downward clamping pressure. This setup worked well, as it gave complete control of the pressure and allowed access for cleaning up the excess glue.

Hook-and-loop fastening (Velcro) is used to secure the soft seat bottom to the hull. Used in conjunction with the straps, the hook-and-loop fastening will stabilize the seat from side to side. Our seat has the loop component sewn to the bottom of the cover; the hook component is applied to the hull as a pressure-sensitive patch installed after the varnish.

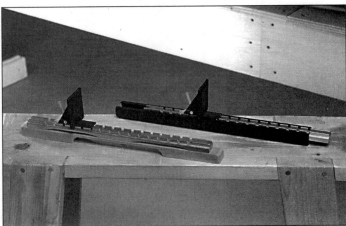

12-18

Foot braces (foot pedals, foot pegs)

Foot braces of some kind are important pieces of basic equipment for your kayak (Photograph 12-18). The braces complement the seat and provide the other major anchor points for your body. They should be sturdy enough to sustain panic loads in an emergency. For comfort and balance, they should allow the feet to be spread as far apart as possible. Their height is important. Look for a height that will support the toes with your foot angled comfortably forward.

Fore-and-aft adjustment of the braces is a much-appreciated feature. It allows the leg position to be adjusted for comfort, changing paddling conditions, and other paddlers. The simplest of these adjustment systems can be homemade using a series of holes and wing nuts, but most simple systems will be difficult to adjust while sitting in the cockpit. Design-

12-17

ing and building a homemade setup that is easy to adjust will take you from the realm of simple solutions into an engineering exercise.

A simple, effective solution is the adjustable foot brace unit used in popular synthetic kayaks. In addition to being adjustable fore and aft, the unit slides in a track that is fastened to the hull, providing steering control for a rudder.

Since our kayak is not fitted with a rudder, we have eliminated the track and are using just the foot pedal and the rail it is fastened to. The position and method of attaching the mounting blocks will be the same for a foot-controlled rudder setup.

The block that the track is mounted on does not have to be massive or heavy. It should be thick enough to take a $^3/_4$″ × No. 8 screw, which would make $^5/_8$″ about right. Make the length and width to fit the track, but keep a gluing surface to the hull of about 1″ wide. If a track is being used to control the rudder, make the mounting block 3″ longer than the track. This is to accommodate an elastic cord (bungee) that puts tension on the slider and keeps the pedals under control. Use a moderately dense hardwood such as mahogany for a balance of workability, fastener holding ability, and light weight.

We have cut away part of the inside face of the block for several reasons. As there is very little stress on the joint other than a forward sheering action, the whole surface is not necessary for the glue. Removing wood reduces weight and makes less of a hard spot in the side of the hull. Less surface area also makes it easier to fit accurately to the hull.

As the foot-brace position relates to leg length, find the position by measuring out from the seat back. The pedal has about 12″ of adjustment, so it does not have to be positioned with rocket-science accuracy. Sit on the floor with your lower back against something firm. With the pedal in the farthest extended position on the rail and your leg outstretched, have someone hold the pedal and rail against your foot and pick up the measurement to the seat back. This will allow a full 12″ of adjustment for a person your size, but compromises for other-sized paddlers may be worked out. While you are sitting down with your feet and legs at a relaxed and comfortable angle, have someone mea-

sure the height of the track from the floor. Use this as a guide but also take the shape of the bottom of the kayak into consideration. The top of the mounting block on our Endeavour 17 is located 1$^3/_4$″ down from the top edge of the hull.

Clamp the blocks into position and double-check the distance from the seat. It is also a good idea to measure both sides from the bow to confirm that the mounting blocks are parallel. When you are happy with the positions of the blocks, mark their outlines on the hull with masking tape (Photograph 12-19).

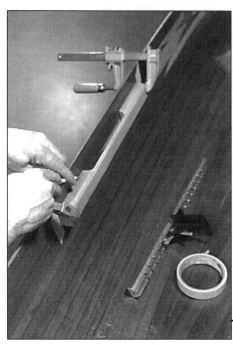

12-19

The mating surface of the mounting block needs to be shaped slightly to follow the curve of the hull. Pick up the shape with the block clamped lightly into position. It will not take much pressure to distort the hull to fit the blocks, but that is not what we are after. Thicken the glue to suit the quality of the joint, and be careful not to distort the hull with the clamps.

Fit the track to the blocks and do a dry run with the screws. The aluminum or plastic track may or may not have mounting holes that will fit the mounting block; drill and countersink new holes as needed (make sure the rail will slide smoothly fore and aft without getting hung up on the screw heads). When you are happy with the way the hardware works, remove it for varnishing the interior. Replace after varnishing and before gluing the deck into position (Photograph 12-20).

12-20

Rudder

There seems to be considerable debate over whether or not a rudder is necessary on a sea kayak. I wouldn't argue, because it really comes down to a combination of hull shape and how, where, and who will be using the boat.

Think twice about installing a rudder unless you are convinced that you really need one. A double or triple kayak could benefit from a rudder to designate who the captain is, but it can be a nuisance on a single if it is not working for you. The downsides of a rudder are higher cost, and more pieces to install, break, and maintain—not to mention added weight and spongy foot braces.

Rudders are used on sea kayaks to aid in directional stability and maneuverability, and occasionally to compensate for a poorly designed hull. The offshore sea kayaker will appreciate a rudder, while the serious inland tripper will find it a nuisance. If you are a paddler, you will already have a preference; if not, consider adding the rudder later, after you have acquired the experience to have your own opinion.

The rudder assembly is made up of the rudder, which is hung on the stern, the foot pedals that slide in the track to control the rudder, and the wires that connect them together.

Although the rudder is best installed while the deck is removable, it can be added later if a few of the hard-to-reach preparations are made before assembling hull and deck. Use a foot-brace system designed to slide, but hold off installing the sliding rail until it is needed for the rudder. While you can get at it, drill the necessary holes in the track and fit the track temporarily. Having the pilot holes in position and knowing they will work will take some of the frustration out of retrofitting later.

The stern should also be reinforced for the rudder attachment, as it will be extremely difficult getting in there later. The wire guides should not be a problem, as they may be rigged through the stern hatch and the cockpit opening.

The rudder is hung on the stern with a single pintle that fits into either a hole in the deck or a gudgeon that fits around the stem and back onto the hull. If you can find a gudgeon that is a close fit to your stern, it can be adapted with shims and will make the most secure mount. Provide the necessary backing block and do a dry fit before attaching the deck. If there is no gudgeon available, you could fabricate one out of wood, aluminum, or plastic, or you could drill a hole in the deck to accept the pintle.

A hole drilled through the deck will go into the end of the stem. The stem is a major structural component of the kayak and should be protected and reinforced. Glue in a corner block just low enough to clear the sheer clamp. When the deck is glued on, it will be glued to the block to further reinforce the joint.

The inside of the hole must be protected and made more durable. A pin working in a raw hole would first stick when the wood swells, and then the hole would wear quickly to a sloppy fit. There would be considerable lateral pressure on the pin, and at some point the stem would fail and additional damage could be done to the hull and deck.

A professional way of protecting the stem would be to line the hole with a brass, copper, or plastic sleeve set in epoxy. This would involve drilling or machining a standard-size piece of pipe to make a bushing that fits your pintle.

We have seen some success with drilling an oversized hole and casting a bushing using epoxy fortified with graphite powder. Graphite powder, which is available from your epoxy dealer, produces a slippery, self-lubricating surface when mixed in an epoxy binder.

To begin with, carefully drill a hole that fits the pintle, and use this hole to set up the rudder and install the related parts. After the deck has been glued on, redrill the hole several drill sizes larger—enough to let the epoxy-graphite mixture line the hole around the pintle. Wax the pintle well with paste wax or paraffin to keep it from sticking. To protect the bottom of the yoke, make a hole in the middle of a small square of plastic and slide it over the pintle.

To cast the bushing, saturate the hole with catalyzed epoxy resin, letting it soak up as much as it wants. The resin that soaks into the surface of the stem will increase the density of the surface, in effect beginning the bushing below the surface of the hole. Remove the unthickened epoxy that has not been absorbed before adding the graphite-and-epoxy mixture (add about 25% graphite by volume). To make this surface more durable, add 10% colloidal silica (stone dust).

Drilling a hole of this size in your beautiful deck may take some courage. Cover the end of the deck with masking tape and take your time laying out the position of the hole. It might be a good idea to get some help lining up the drill and bit. If you are working alone, make a guide block by drilling a plumb hole on the drill press to make the bushing. Position and stabilize the block with cleats on the bottom that fit around the edge of the deck; make sure it is level with the deck before drilling. Put a piece of masking tape on the bit to indicate when the desired depth has been reached.

Another way is to sneak up on the hole by beginning with a small-diameter bit, then work through progressively larger bits. To confirm the angle of the hole, drill the first hole the size of something straight that will fit snugly in the hole. Make this round straightedge out of a 12″ piece of straight coat hanger or a small wooden dowel. Fit the straightedge into the hole and stand back to check from all angles. Measure from the top to the edge of the deck on both sides to check for plumb. Correct the direction of the hole by reaming with the previous bit before going to the next larger bit.

There will be a final chance to make fine adjustments when the bushing is cast

to fit the pintle-and-rudder assembly.

The rudders that are available will have been designed for a production model boat and will require adapting to your kayak. Without specifics, there is no easy explanation of how to locate the position of the gudgeon, but there are several things to keep in mind. If a hole is being drilled through the deck, keep it as far forward as possible without interfering with the movement of the rudder. Examine the pitch of the pin in relationship to the rudder. Holding the rudder and yoke in position should give some clues. The rudder and pintle will generally be plumb to the level-sitting kayak. Check the height of the yoke if an external type of gudgeon is used. It will most likely be positioned as high as possible, but check the angle at which the wire control cables enter the hull or deck. I like the idea of the cable entering the side of the hull through the guard and sheer clamp. This keeps some of the clutter off the deck and allows the cable to enter the cavity at the straightest angle. If the rudder is hung on the deck, the yoke will be above the deck, necessitating the cables entering through the deck.

Lay out the straightest possible path for the cable to reduce friction and allow the cables to slide smoothly. The time to decide on the path of the cable is after the rudder has been temporarily hung. The cables will enter the deck about 24″ from the stern; it is important to have the exact beginning point at the yoke, and to know where to go. Whether the cable is entering through the hull or the deck, having it enter through the sheer clamp is a first choice, as it saves putting in backing blocks under the deck. But, if it looked like the entry would work better through the deck, I would not hesitate to fit a backing block.

Where the cable enters the kayak, it is enclosed in a plastic cable housing. This isolates the cable and the space it travels in from the sealed cargo area. Water entering along the cable will travel through the plastic tube and drain into the cockpit. Let the housing extend as far forward as is practical. When the housing enters the cavity, it travels along and is secured to the sheer clamp to a point forward of the seat. Exactly where the housing ends will depend on where the cable will best exit for the smoothest path to the pedal.

Drilling the holes for the cable housing is tricky and can be disappointing if done by eye. This is not to say that it can't be done with precision by eye, but there is a way to ensure first-time success.

To drill this hole under control, you will need a very long drill bit that is slightly larger in diameter than the housing tube, and a wooden guide bushing that you will make (Illustration 12-21). The success of the drilling operation will depend on the accuracy of the guide bushing. The 15° angle is not hard to drill, as being a little high or low will not make much difference. We are drilling from the underside of the deck, so it is to our advantage to plan a predictable exit through the deck. Keeping the hole plumb as it goes through the guide will influence the direction the hole takes from where it enters the sheer clamp to where it exits on deck.

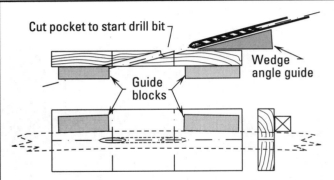

Cut pocket to start drill bit

Wedge angle guide

Guide blocks

Drill bit should exit the bottom of the jig on the marks. If the hole is not centered on the marks, remake the position of the hole for positioning on the deck.

12-21

Use a block about 4″ wide by at least 1″ thick and about 12″ long. To prepare the guide, draw a centerline down its middle and project the line down the ends. Then join these lines on the back. If the hole exits on this line, it will confirm that the bushing is plumb.

Prepare for drilling the hole by cutting a pocket where the bit will enter the deck. This will keep the bit from wandering and get it started on the centerline. Cut a block of wood at 15° to sit on the guide block to direct the angle of the bit. If you have a helper, he or she could stand to the side and confirm this angle. Now, standing behind the centerline of the block, line up the bit at 15° and directly over the centerline. Being plumb to the centerline is what will bring you out on the back centerline.

After drilling the hole and confirming that it exited in the right place, project a line from the center of each hole to the edge and up the side of the block. This will be a reference for lining up the guide on the sheer clamp. Because the sheer clamp is curving, we can't simply line up the centerline on the end of the guide with the middle of the sheer clamp and expect the hole to be centered. Draw lines the width of the sheer clamp parallel to the centerline on the bottom. Clamp the guide to the sheer clamp, lining up the business portion of the guide with the edge of the sheer clamp. If the guide has been prepared accurately, you can now drill the hole confident that the hole will exit without a surprise.

Be sure the hole is going in the right direction. Keep in mind, too, that it is a long hole and the chips will have trouble being ejected. Pull the bit out often enough to keep the bit clear and turning freely. If you run out of drill length going through both guide and sheer clamp, drill as far as possible with the guide, then remove the guide and complete the hole by eye. Be careful to keep the bit centered in the entrance hole. The shank of the bit lying on the side of the hole will cause a significant change in the direction of a hole this long.

Protect the deck from being damaged as the bit pushes through the surface. Clamp a block over the spot where the bit will exit to support the surface and keep the bit under control.

The time to make a permanent installation is after the interior has been varnished and before the deck is glued on, but have everything fitted and tested beforehand. The housing will likely have one end reinforced to provide additional wear surface where it enters the deck. Drill out the hole in the deck large enough to accept most of the reinforcement, but leave enough to file flush after installation.

When the housing is ready for installation, feed it into the hole, leaving the section of tube that will be inside the sheer clamp exposed. Spread compound bedding/adhesive on this part of the tube, and then draw it into the hole. This will put all the excess bedding on the outside, so it might be a good idea to cover the end of the tube. Pick up the excess adhesive and clean up with mineral spirits. Fasten the housing to the sheer clamp with plastic clips so it is out of the way and does not become kinked. To make sure water will not enter the hole from the inside, put a neat fillet around the tube where it exits the sheer clamp. After the bedding has set up, file the end of the tube flush with the surface of the deck and sand it smooth.

Install the rudder controls after all the varnishing has been completed, but do a dry run beforehand to be sure you have all the pieces and they work. We now have the rudder hanging on the kayak, so the next step will be to set it up to be controlled from the cockpit.

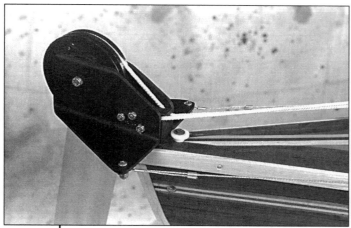

12-22

One small detail to look at before rigging the cables is some way of keeping the pintle from jumping out of the gudgeon. If you are using an off-the-shelf rudder package, it will most likely have a way of being secured. (Gudgeon-and-pintle units may have a cotter pin that fits through the pintle.)

The rudder we are using here (Photograph 12-22). is secured with a plastic spacer and washer that fits over the edge of the rudder yoke. The spacer must be long enough to raise the washer part slightly above the yoke. Screwing the spacer and washer to the deck should contain the yoke but not restrict the side-to-side movement.

This screw will have to be removed in order to remove the rudder, so the deck will take a beating from this much handling. Protect the deck by installing a brass threaded insert in the deck and using a machine screw in place of the wood screw. (Choose a common head for the screw, as the tool for removing it will have to be carried on board.)

The cables are attached to the rudder by looping them through the yoke and attaching them back to themselves with swage fittings. The swage fitting is a small metal clip that fits around the cable and is squeezed to capture the two parts of cable. While there is a crimping tool made specifically for the swage, vise grips will do the job. Slide a short piece of heat-shrink tube back over the end of the cable and swage and shrink with a heat gun (hair dryer) or flame. If using a flame, keep it back enough so that the plastic heats up evenly and not too fast.

Attach the other end of the cable to the rudder slide in the same manner. Before making the attachment, set the pedal sliders flush with the ends of the track and wedge them into position. This will make the cables the same length and the foot pedals parallel.

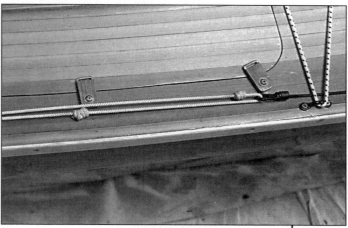

12-23

The next thing to set up is the rudder lifting line (Photograph 12-23). The line leads from the pulley on the rudder forward to the back of the cockpit and back to the pulley. Pulling one side of the line raises the rudder; pulling the other lowers it. Secure the forward end of the line to a hook or ring on a piece of elastic cord. This is necessary to allow the rudder to turn freely yet keep the line under tension. If there is a long run from the cockpit to the rudder, one or more fairleads may be necessary to keep the lines from getting fouled. Tie a knot on each side of the ring as a stopper; put an extra knot on one side of the line to identify which line is up or down.

When the rudder is raised up out of the water to lay on the deck, provision must be made to catch the blade so that it doesn't damage the deck—and to secure the blade in the centerline position. Mount the rubber catch block (which should be included in the rudder kit) on the deck as close to the stern as is practical (Photograph 12-24). The closer it is mounted to the pivot point of the rudder, the greater the chance of catching the rudder will be. Adjust the height, if necessary, with a wooden spacer. Rig a loop of elastic cord to hold the rudder blade in the catch block for transport.

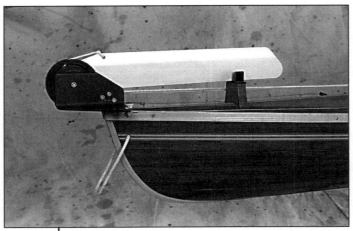

12-24

Hip, thigh, knee, and heel pads

To make the kayak a complete extension of your body, the body needs to be stabilized in addition to what the seat and foot braces can provide. Although where and how much is vague at the construction stage, padding is easy to locate after you have had time to paddle the boat and see what you need.

Padding may be made from dense foam such as Ensolite or Ethafoam depending on the thickness and density desired, or it may be purchased as an easy-to-install kit. Install and laminate the foam with contact cement; if a stronger glue or a glue with more body is needed, try an adhesive-sealant compound.

FINAL DETAILS
Varnish the interior

Although we will look at varnishing in detail later, there are a few items relating to varnishing the interior that are worth looking at now.

When varnishing the deck, mask off the outside edge of the sheer clamp to keep it from being contaminated with varnish. Also mask off the mating surface on the inside of the hull; the bond must be between the sanded epoxy and the bare wood. If a rigid bulkhead is being 'glassed to the deck, mask off the area to be covered with the fillet and 'glass tape.

Apply a coat of sealer to all raw wood surfaces such as the foot brace mounting block. Once sealed, the finish will build at the same rate as the sanded epoxy surface.

Apply three coats of varnish, minimum, to both the inside of the hull and the deck. It might be a long time before the interior is revarnished, so a fourth coat would be worth considering. It will never be easier than it is now; a little extra effort at this stage could pay off later.

Attach hull and deck

This is the moment we have been waiting for: all the bits and pieces have been installed, the interior has been varnished, and there is no reason to put it off any longer. This step is a culmination of all the patient work that has been done up to this point, so even though it will not take long to do, it is a significant step.

Unless the bulkhead is being installed at the same time, there is no reason why the hull and deck need to be assembled right-side up. On our boat, we set the deck up in the deck cradle forms and lowered

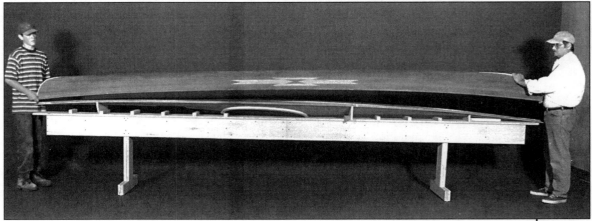

12-25

the hull onto it (Photograph 12-25). The big advantage to this method is that the excess epoxy glue either runs into the joint or is squeezed to the outside, where it is easy to clean up. When the kayak is assembled upright, some glue will run down the inside of the hull and will be awkward to see, reach, and clean up.

Spread an appropriate amount of thickened epoxy resin on both the sheer clamp and the lip of the deck. Because the glue is not going to soak into the epoxy-coated hull, it is not necessary to precoat the hull (Photograph 12-26).

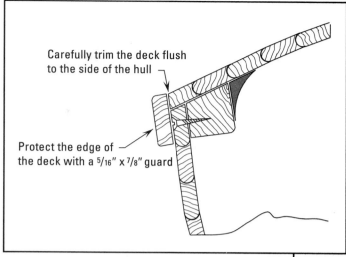

Carefully trim the deck flush to the side of the hull

Protect the edge of the deck with a ⁵/₁₆″ x ⁷/₈″ guard

12-28

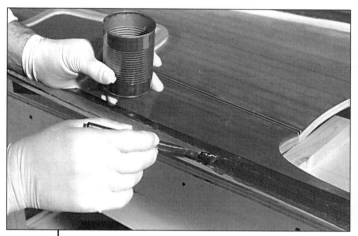

12-26

After placing the hull over the sheer clamp, replace the screws that you had been using to hold hull and deck together. If the screws are not drawing the joint together consistently all the way around, add more screws as needed. Drive the heads of the screws below the surface of the hull so they do not interfere with installing the guard. If you can't get them in far enough, remove them after the glue has set (Photograph 12-27).

Clean up the squeezed-out glue and

wait until the glue has set before turning the boat over.

Install the guard

The purpose of the guard is to cover the hull-deck joint, hide the screwheads, and protect the edge of the deck (Illustration 12-28). The ¹/₄″ or ⁵/₁₆″ x ⁷/₈″ guard is made of a hard or semi-hard wood and is glued to the hull. A wood species that contrasts with the planking color will visually break the hull from the deck and help define the shape of the kayak. If you are worried about it fitting, do a dry run with the screws only before committing to glue. The top edge should extend above the deck enough to be trimmed flush after the glue has set.

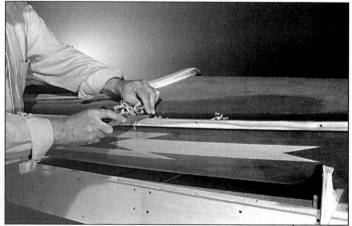

12-29

Take your time trimming the edge of the deck flush with the hull (Photograph 12-29). The idea is to project the shape of the hull up to the top corner of the deck. If you can do this, there will be a crisp line between the guard and the deck. Unfor-

12-27

tunately, while you are keeping the plane from digging into the hull or avoiding the screws, there will be a tendency to tip the top of the plane in more than necessary. Get as close as possible with the block plane, and finish up with 80-grit paper on a firm sanding block. You will notice that the 'glass will quickly take the edge off the plane, so keep an eye on it and sharpen when necessary.

After the glue has set, you might want to remove the screws and plug the holes. Then trim the top of the guard flush with the deck and round over the corners. Sand the hardwood trim to 180-grit, and clean it up for varnishing.

13 | Varnishing

There are some parallels between varnishing and human relationships, and these are worth noting. Both begin with your definition of perfection, a definition that is, one would hope, somewhat flexible. Between people, or varnish, and your expectations, are many variables that are not easy to control. There will be flaws that you will have to decide what to do with. You must, at some stage, realize whether or not there is enough inner beauty yet to be revealed that it is worth your effort. Ultimately, you will have to accept some imperfections, but this doesn't mean you have to lower your standards. Boats and relationships both work best when you can look past the things you wish were different, and appreciate the beauty and integrity that first attracted you. Fortunately, the odds of success for either improve with patience and thoughtful preparation. In spite of this, both relationships and varnish can be more satisfying than you can imagine—and more frustrating than you want to admit.

Dust-free varnish does exist, but it is elusive. We look at a piano finish and want the deck of our kayak to look just like that. But that piano's surface is an illusion, because the last coat of finish is probably not what you are seeing; unlike relationships, we do have control over the final finish because we can polish the surface to remove the imperfections.

Somewhere between flies in the varnish and a piano-quality finish is a standard of finish that is appropriate to you and your kayak. It is a good challenge to work towards a perfect last coat, but keep in mind that, while you'll focus on the dust when you're working in the shop, you'll see the kayak differently after a day on the water.

SAFETY

A significant percentage of the material that comes out of the varnish will evaporate, so having a good cross draft and a supply of fresh, clean air is most important. It is not necessary or desirable to have a rapid replacement of air. The flow should be gentle enough not to stir up dust but able to sustain a steady supply of fresh air. Think about the source of the incoming air and how clean it is. Working in a basement shop, the air would be drawn from the house and exhausted to the outside. By drawing air from the living area, there is little chance for fumes to invade the house.

Fumes should be respected. If you are sensitive to solvents, wear a charcoal filter respirator. Most people will be comfortable with a good supply of fresh air.

MATERIALS
Premium spar varnish

Use a modified oil-based varnish with ultraviolet inhibitors. Check that it is compatible with your epoxy and that it contains at least 3% UV inhibitor. (Note: A total of 12% UV inhibitor is required to protect the epoxy.) Some two-part polyurethanes are compatible with epoxy and make a hard, durable surface. The downside is that they are more toxic than spar varnish and harder to apply with a brush.

Varnish brush

A good badger-hair brush is a joy to use, but good results are also possible with a natural bristle or foam brush. Foam brushes are cheap, available, and disposable, and they don't shed bristles. Use a 1" brush for the trim and a 2" to 3" brush for the hull and deck. Because the varnish does not build as fast with a foam brush as with a bristle brush, consider applying an extra coat.

Even the best brush will lose a few bristles when it is new. Before using, remove the bristles that would fall out anyway by spinning the handle between your hands. If you take care of a good varnish brush, it will last forever and improve with use.

Solvent

Generally, paint thinner (mineral spirits, Varsol, etc.) will work with spar varnish, but check compatibility with your varnish. Sometimes when the instructions on the can specify the company's own thinner, they are serious, and not just selling product. Brushing thinner is a retardant and will aid in keeping a wet edge in a hot environment. Spraying thinner, as an accelerator, will speed evaporation, thus cutting down the working time window; but the varnish will be dust free in a shorter length of time. Never use lacquer thinner or acetone with spar varnish; it works as a mild paint stripper and will dissolve the varnish.

Tack cloth

This is a piece of cheesecloth impregnated with a sticky substance that will pick up and hold dust particles that you can't feel or see. The old-timers made tack cloths by working a mixture of varnish, boiled oil, and solvent into cheesecloth. Stored in a Mason jar, it had a reasonable shelf life and could be reused. But you can buy your tack cloth at most paint and auto supply stores. Count on dust settling out of the air continuously, so wait until you are ready to apply the finish before the final wipedown. Wipe easy when using the tack cloth; I have noticed that if the cloth is pressed down on the surface, the sticky residue will be transferred

to the surface. If this is not removed, the varnish will not stick.

Rags

Well-washed cotton makes the ideal rag. White is a good color, because it is easy to see what is being picked up. Fold the rag neatly so it is easy to expose a fresh face. As you wipe the surface, keep turning the rag to expose a clean face.

Paint filter

Use a paint filter to strain the varnish—even from a freshly opened can—to be sure there are no floating particles. Naturally, such particles are more likely if the can has previously been opened and used.

Varnish containers

Recycled clean cans, yogurt cups, and such make good varnish containers. To keep from getting your can-holding hand sticky, tie a rag around the top of the can to capture the drips.

Sweeping compound

Sweeping compound holds onto the fine dust that sweeping sends airborne or leaves behind. Try it, it does make a difference. All the compounds I have used have contained wax, some of which stays behind on the floor; watch your step, and slow down on the corners.

Masking tape

Use ½" and 1" masking tape. Peel it off as soon as the varnish has been applied. This will allow the varnish to flow out, leaving a soft edge that won't have to be feathered.

Brush cleaner

Even the best badger-hair brush must be well cleaned and maintained if it is to do the job. There are some good arguments for storing brushes in raw linseed oil, but we have always had good results with a water-soluble brush cleaner. After using the brush, wipe the handle, then scrape all the grunge into a can and rinse well in paint thinner. Shake the brush, then rotate the handle rapidly between your hands to spin the remaining solvent out. Soak it in the brush cleaner, then rinse with lots of warm water. Spin dry, arrange and smooth the bristles, then hang to dry in a dust-free area. When the brush is dry, store it in a plastic bag.

Lighting

An even light of comfortable intensity allows you to see what you are doing, but expect to control the film thickness mainly by feel. Fluorescent lights are great for finishing, as the bulb gives a nice, long, hot spot that will highlight any runs or holidays on the surface.

VARNISHING: THE PROCESS
Getting ready to varnish

Apply varnish when you are relaxed and unhurried and won't be interrupted. Forget about the world and focus on completing this magnificent boat with care. Varnishing is a special part of building. Take time to savor it.

Good varnish depends on three things: preparation, preparation, and preparation. Having control over the space in which you varnish and preparing the surface of the boat carefully will increase the odds of a good finish. A professional spray booth is not necessary for good varnish as long as basic good work principles are incorporated into the home workshop. Most environments can be improved enough to get a respectable finish.

Even though the last coat of varnish is the one that counts, the actual finish is the sum of all the buildup coats that came before it. If you treat each coat as if it were the last, problems will be identified early on and corrected, and you will be a pro when you get to coat number four.

Planning ahead

Break the surface of the kayak into manageable sections. Plan where to begin and how best to maintain a wet edge. Masking to an obvious break line is the only way to avoid the ragged double thickness of varnish between sections and sharp corners. Obvious divisions would be the hull-to-deck joint and the cockpit and hatch openings.

Varnish has a very short working time, so don't plan on going back after you finish the job to clean up the runs and holidays. Complete a section to your satisfaction, then leave it alone and move on. Once the surface has begun to skin over, anything you do to it will make it worse. The time in which the edge can be worked will depend on the speed of the varnish (how fast the solvent evaporates), which is influenced by temperature, humidity, and how much and what kind of thinner has been added. Five minutes will be a safe window, and will be convenient on a boat this size.

After sanding and shop cleanup, a change of clothes and a clean hat are a good idea before getting into the varnish.

- Give the shop a good cleaning using a sweeping compound to keep the dust down and pick up the fine particles.
- Vacuum the kayak and all exposed surfaces.
- Cover stationary power tools, shelves, and hard-to-clean areas with plastic film.
- Check out the ceiling in your work area. If you are working in a barn, or if there is a lot of hard-to-clean junk up in the ceiling joists, consider suspending plastic film over the kayak as a barrier against falling debris.
- Lock up the cat. She might have been good company while you were building, but she won't know the varnish is wet until she lands.
- In most locations, flying bugs are a problem, especially around dusk. To minimize the problem, pick the safest time of day, light one of those bug killing coils when you finish varnishing, and close up the room after you leave.
- Wet the floor down, if possible, to keep dust down and raise the humidity. If your shop is very dry, there will be a big problem with static electricity. If the surface is charged, it will attract dust particles out of the air. The old Muskoka runabout builders would put a chain over the boat and wire it to the steam pipe to ground the boat. We can do a lot by raising the humidity and carefully cleaning the exposed surfaces.

Preparing the kayak

If it has been a while since the epoxy surface was sanded, I think it is a good idea to run over it with 220-grit sandpaper to be sure the surface is clean. After cleaning, avoid handling the surface with sweaty hands, as oil from the skin will contaminate it.

After vacuuming, wipe the dust off the kayak with a water-dampened rag. This will pick up the fine dust and help to discharge static electricity. Some solvents, such as turpentine, increase the static charge. As the rag is wiped across the surface, you can hear the crackle and feel the sparks tickling your hand. Do what you can to keep this charge from building.

Mask off screw holes and any small, hard-to-clean openings that could hide dust that will be pulled out with the varnish brush later. If you have compressed air, blow the tight corners out before the final cleanup with the tack cloth.

Seal the bare wood trim parts first. The purpose of the sealer is to penetrate the wood to provide a deep mechanical bond for the later coats, and to limit further absorption of the varnish. Use a sealer that is compatible with the varnish you are using, or thin the varnish to 50%. Once the bare wood has been sealed, the varnish will build at the same rate as the epoxy-coated surfaces.

Preparing the varnish

The solvent in varnish acts as a vehicle for the solids that will be left on the surface. Shortly after the varnish has been spread, enough of the solvent will have evaporated that the surface will begin to skin over. This will continue until the finish is hard.

The amount and type of solvent in a can of varnish differs widely between brands. A clue to this is the price: a varnish with a high solids content generally costs more. It is to our advantage to have a high solids content to begin with, because it gives us the option of adjusting the viscosity and drying time to suit our needs. A brushable consistency will be as full-bodied as possible, yet thin enough that it will flow out of the brush without dragging; the brush marks should have time to level before skinning over. If you are unfamiliar with the brand of varnish you are using, try it on a test panel before deciding whether to add thinner.

Thinners control the length of time it takes for the surface to skin over. The rate of evaporation is influenced by temperature, so an accelerator could be used in cool temperatures to speed up the cure time, or a retardant in hot weather to slow things down. The balance we are looking for is enough working time to maintain the wet edge and have the brush marks flow out, but also to have the surface skin over as soon as possible. The sooner it skins over, the less dust will get stuck in the varnish.

Never add thinner to the whole can of varnish. If too much varnish is added, you'll need another can of unreduced varnish to thicken it. Mixing small batches will allow you to quickly adjust the mixture to suit the environment and the size of area you are working in.

Add thinner to the mixture a little at a time, then stir well before deciding whether you have the desired viscosity.

Applying the varnish

Expect to spend a lot less time applying the varnish than it took to prepare for it. The action of applying the varnish and smoothing it will be familiar to you after you have applied the last coat of epoxy. You will find the varnish easier to work with than the epoxy, as it is thin enough to flow freely out of the brush.

The first step is to transfer the material from the can to the surface and quickly spread it over an arm's-length section. If this is the outside of the hull, work from the keel line to the sheer. Be firm with the brush. Hold it at a high enough angle to push and spread the varnish evenly over the entire surface. A firm yet aggressive stroke will introduce less air and spread varnish better than a choppy, slapping motion. After spreading the finish in a fore-and-aft direction, work the surface on both diagonals to be sure that the parallel strokes have been blended together.

The next step is to work the surface in a careful and systematic pattern to smooth the surface and confirm that the film thickness is consistent over the entire surface of the section being worked.

A thick coat of varnish that has been worked to an even film thickness will have less chance of running than a conservative amount that varies from not very thick to thin. A thicker horizontal brush stroke on a vertical surface will run over the thinner area below it.

Make a full stroke with the brush as you draw it back and forth. The brush should land gently as it reaches the surface and lift off with the same grace at the end of the stroke. Work the varnish until you feel a consistent fluid drag through the brush, indicating that the material on the surface has been spread evenly over the area being worked. If you find that the varnish is harder to work than you think it should be, try adding a little more thinner before moving on to the next section.

When you do move on, be conscious of not building up a double thickness of material where the sections meet. It helps to brush from the wet to the dry and to pay particular attention to what the brush is telling you.

If, while varnishing, the brush begins to fill up with bubbles, scrape the grunge out of the brush into a clean can. The bubbles will eventually disappear, and the varnish may be reused after straining.

Sanding between coats

The purpose of sanding between coats is to correct any problems you might have had with the previous coat, to expose a surface that you know is clean, and to give the following coat something to hang onto. I think that 220- or 240-grit is about the optimal balance between efficient preparation and a scratch small enough that the varnish will flow into and level out to achieve a good and good-looking bond between layers.

When sanding between coats of varnish, try not to contaminate the work area; use a vacuum cleaner, fan, and sweeping compound to help control flying dust. Pick up the remaining dust with a water-dampened rag. If there is a chance that the surface has been contaminated with finger prints, degrease it with paint thinner.

The epoxy needs at least four coats of a premium spar varnish with ultraviolet inhibitors to protect it from sunlight degradation. Ideally, you should sand between each varnish coat, but you can save time if you apply the two middle coats

on the same day. Wait until the second coat has become firm but not hard before applying the third. Sand with 220-grit paper in preparation for the fourth coat, then apply the final coat with extreme care.

There is no reason why you cannot sand up to 400-grit wet before the last coat is applied. The reward will be a slightly higher gloss that will be appreciated by few; most people will not notice scratches from the 220-grit paper. Such a finish is respectable, and the last coat has a good bite into the previous varnish layer.

Well, the last coat of varnish is on, and you are happy with your work. The kayak is lit by one small light bulb, putting everything else in shadow. The smell of fresh coffee mingles with fresh varnish and you don't know if you should laugh or cry. It is an important moment in your life and your future. For me, it is a lot like having kids; although we have been intimately involved with the creation, what we see before us has elements beyond what we can take full credit for. This is the magic. And like kids, the kayak will continue to teach us things we need to know. When your kayak is launched, another adventure begins.

I have no doubt that building this craft has satisfied some basic need that is special to you, and that your life will be fuller, and perhaps make more sense, because you have built this kayak.

You can turn the lights on now. After you put all the fittings back on, she is ready to get her bottom wet.

Sources

ASSOCIATIONS

Trade Association of Paddlesports
12455 N. Wauwatosa Rd.
Mequon, WI 53097-2711
414-242-5228

**Wooden Canoe Heritage
    Association, Ltd.**
P.O. Box 255
Paul Smiths, NY 12970
www.wcha.org

GENERAL EQUIPMENT

spray skirts, foot braces, seats, foam for
bulkheads, rudder, foot brace, accessories

**Northwater Rescue and Paddling
    Equipment**
#5 2925 Oak Street
Vancouver, BC, V6H 2K7
604-264-0827
www.northwater.com/rescue

Chesapeake Light Craft, Inc.
1805 George Avenue
Annapolis, MD 21401
www.clcboats.com

**Feathercraft Folding Kayaks and
    Accessories**
4-1244 Cartwright Street on Granville
    Island
Vancouver, BC, V6H 3R8
604-681-8437

Dagger
319 Roddy Lane
P.O. Box 1500
Harriman, TN 37748
423-882-0404
www.dagger.com

North Shore Inc.
Hood River , OR 97031
800-800-7237
www.nsipadz .com

America Outdoor Products
Planetary Gear
6350 Gunpark Dr.
Boulder, CO 80301
800-641-0500

Kokatat
5350 Ericson Way
Arcata, CA 95521
800-225-9749

Perception, Inc.
111 Kayaker Way
P.O. Box 8002
Easley, SC 29641
864-859-7518
www.kayaker.com

Snap Dragon Designs
15862 14th Ave. N. E.
Seattle, WA 98155
206-364-1842

The Boundary Waters Catalog
105 North Central Avenue
Ely, MN 55731
800-223-6565
www.piragis.com

Cooke Custom Sewing
(Cockpit Cover, travel bag for kayaks)
7290 Stagecoach Trail
Lino Lakes, MN 55014-1899
651-784-8777

Magellan Systems Corporation
(GPS)
960 Overland Court
San Dimas, CA 91773
909-394-5000

Seairsports
(Air Support Seat)
2043 Main St.
San Diego, CA 92113
619-230-1167

Ritchie Navigation
(Ritchie Kayaker Compass #S-59W)
243 Oak St.
Pembroke, MA 02359
www.ritchienavigation.com

TOOL CATALOGS

CMT Tools
310 Mears Blvd.
Oldsmar, FL 34677
800-531-5559

Lee Valley
1090 Morrison Drive
Ottawa, ON, K2H 1C2
800-267-8767
www.leevalley.com

Garrett Wade
161 Avenue of the Americas
New York, NY 10013
800-221-2942

House of Tools
#100 Mayfield Common N.W.
Edmonton, AL, T5P 4B3
800-661-3987
mailorder@houseoftools.com

Highland Hardware
1045 N. Highland Ave. N.E.
Atlanta, GA 30306
800-241-6748

Klingspors Sanding Catalogue
Box 3737
Hickory, NC 28603-3737
800-228-0000
www.sandingcatalogue.com

MLCS
Box 4053
Rydal, PA 19046
800-533-9298
www.mlcs.woodworking.com

Woodworker's Supply
1108 North Glenn Road
Casper, WY 82601
800-645-9292

Woodcraft
Box 1686
Parkersburg, WV 26102-1686
800-225-1153

EPOXY

WEST SYSTEM Epoxy
Gougeon Brothers Inc. (United States)
100 Patterson Avenue
P.O. Box 908
Bay City, MI 48707-0908
517-684-7286
www. westsystem.com

Wessex Resins Ltd.
(Europe, Africa, and the Middle East)
Cupernham House
Cupernham Lane, Romsey
Hampshire, S051 7LF
England
44-1-794-521-111
www.wessex-resins.com

Payne Distributors Inc.
(Eastern Canada)
1173 North Service Road West
Unit D1
Oakville, ON, L6M 2V9
800-668-8223

Payne's Marine Supply Inc.
(Western Canada)
1856 Quadra Street
Victoria, BC, V8T 4B9
604-382-7722

MAS-Phoenix Resins
1501 Sherman Ave.
Pennsauken, NJ 08110
800-398-7556
www.masepoxies.com

System Three Resins Inc.
Box 70426
Seattle, WA 98107
206-782-7976
www.systemthree.com

WOOD AND MATERIALS

Anchor Hardwoods Inc.
6014 Oleander Drive
Wilmington, NC 28406
910-392-9078
www.anchor.wilmington.net

Edensaw Woods Ltd.
211 Seton Road
Port Townsend, WA 98368
800-754-3336

Robbins Timber
Brookgate
Ashton Vale Trading Estate
Bristol, BS3 2UN
England
117-963-3136
www.robbins.co.uk

West Wind Hardwood Inc.
P.O. Box 2205
Sidney, BC, V8L 3S8
www.woodworking.com/westwind.

Duck Flat Wooden Boats
230 Flinders Street
Adelaide, 5251
South Australia
618-223-6727
www.duckflat-woodenboats.com.au

Monaghan Lumber Specialties
R.R. #3
Davis Road
Peterborough, ON, K9J 8G0
705-742-9353
www.monaghanlumber.com

Canadian Canoes
7885 Tranmeer Drive
Unit #27
Mississauga, ON, L5S 1V8
905-676-1998
www.canadiancanoes.com

The Newfound Woodworks
R.R. 2 Box 850
Bristol, NH 03222
603-744-6872
www.newfound.com

Bear Mountain Boat Shop
Box 191
Peterborough, ON, K9J 6Y8
www.bearmountainboats.com
705-740-0470

Great Northern Craft
Suite 433
1641 Lonsdale Ave.
North Vancouver, BC V7M 2J5
604-983-3733

Noah's
54 Six Point Rd.
Toronto, ON M8Z 2X2
Canada
416-232-0522

Wermlandia Kanoter
Algarden 5
671 92 Arvika
Sweden
tel. +46 (0)570-34-170

VARNISH

Epifanes (gloss varnish)
58 Fore Street
Portland, ME 04101
800-269-0961
www.epifanes.com

Pettit Paint Co. (Easipoxy Hi-build)
36 Pine Street
Rockaway, NJ 07866

Interlux Paint Inc. (Schooner)
2270 Morris Ave.
Union, NJ 07083

Woolsey/Z-Spar (Captains Varnish)
36 Pine Street
Rockaway, NJ 07866
800-221-4466

PUBLICATIONS

Sea Kayaker
7001 Seaview Ave. N.W.
#135
Seattle, WA 98117-6059
www.seakayakermag.com
206-789-1326

Canoe and Kayak
10526 N.E. 68th Street, Suite #3
P.O. Box 3146
Kirkland, WA 98033-3146
www.canoekayak.com
800-692-2663

Kanawa
P.O. Box 398, 446 Main Street West
Merrickville, ON, K0G 1N0
613-269-2910
www.crca.ca

Wave-length
(604) 247-9789
R.R. #1 Site #17
Gabriola Island, BC, V0R 1X0
www.wie.com/~wavenet

River
P.O. Box 1068
Bozeman, MT 59771
406-582-5440
www.rivermag.com

WoodenBoat
Naskeag Road
P.O. Box 78
Brooklin, ME 04616
207-359-4651
www.woodenboat.com
Issue Nos. 110 and 111 include lofting instructions, with great tips and shortcuts.

BOOKS

Lofting
by Allan Vaitses
(Re-published by WoodenBoat Books
Brooklin, Maine, 1999)

The Kayak Shop
by Chris Kulczycki
(Ragged Mountain Press/McGraw-Hill
Camden, Maine, 1993)
Plywood kayak building, good ideas on home built seats, rudders, and accessories

Wood and Canvas Kayak Building
by George Putz
(International Marine/McGraw-Hill
Camden, Maine 1990)
Skin on frame kayak building, paddle and accessories you can make

The Aleutian Kayak
by Wolfgang Brinck
(Ragged Mountain Press/McGraw-Hill)
Skin-on-frame kayak building, paddle and accessories you can make

The Strip-Built Sea Kayak
by Nick Schade
(Ragged Mountain Press/McGraw-Hill
Camden, Maine, 1998)
Interesting planking patterns and coaming ideas

Baidarka
by George Dyson
(Alaska Northwest Publishing Company
Edmonds, Washington, 1986)
Skin-on-frame kayak building, excellent history of the kayak

The Complete Guide to Sharpening
by Leonard Lee
(The Taunton Press
Newtown, Connecticut 1995)

Building Small Boats
by Greg Rössel
(WoodenBoat Books
Brooklin, Maine 1998)
Traditional small boat construction, useful information on plans, tools, jigs and materials

Featherweight Boatbuilding
by Henry "Mac" McCarthy
(WoodenBoat Books
Brooklin, Maine 1996)
Strip-planked double-paddle canoes

Brightwork: The Art of Finishing Wood
by Rebecca J. Wittman
(International Marine/McGraw-Hill
Camden, Maine, 1990)
Marine wood finishing in easy to read detail

The Whole Paddler's Catalog
Edited by Zip Kellogg
International Marine/Ragged Mountain
Press, Camden, Maine 1997)
Sources and commentary on a wide variety of subjects relating to paddle sports

The Bark Canoes and Skin Boats of North America
by Edwin Adney and Howard Chapelle
(Smithsonian Institution
Washington, DC, 1964)
Kayak history

PADDLES

Barkley Sound Oar & Paddle Ltd.
3073 Vanhorne Road
Qualicum Beach, BC, V9K 1X3
250-752-5115, fax 250-752-1814
barkleysoundoar.com

Mitchell Paddles, Inc.
RD-2 Box 922
Canaan, NH 03741
603-523-7004

Werner Paddles
Northwest Design Works, Inc.
12322 Highway 99 South, Bay #100
Everett, WA 98204
800-275-3311

Grey Owl Paddles
62 Cowansview Road
Cambridge, ON, N1R 7N3
519-622-0001

Sawyer Paddles and Oars
299 Rogue River Pkwy.
Talent, OR 97540
541-535-3606

Shaw & Tenney
P.O. Box 213W
Orono, ME 04473
207-866-4867

PLANS

Bear Mountain Boat Shop
P.O. Box 191
Peterborough, ON, K9J 6Y8
877-392-8880 (toll-free order line)
www.bearmountainboats.com

Laughing Loon
Rob Macks
833 Colrain Road
Greenfield, MA 01301
413-773-5375
www.LaughingLoon.com

Woodenboat Store
Naskeag Road
P.O. Box 78
Brooklin, ME 04616
800-273-7447
www.woodenboat.com

The Canoe and Paddle Store/ Loon Canoes
Moenchstrasse 22A
70191 Stuttgart
Germany
711-256-9365

Hiro Wooden Canoe Shop
813 Higashi-Inbe
Matsue, 690-0036
Japan
81-852-33-2673
village.infoweb.ne.jp/~fwhe5508/index.html

Pygmy Sea Kayaks
Dept 25 P.O. Box 1529
Port Townsend, WA 98368
360-385-6143

Databoat International
1917 West 4th Ave.
Suite 23
Vancouver, BC, V6J 1M7
800-782-7218
www.databoat.com

West System Norge As (Norway)
Gjerdrumsvei 12
Oslo, 0486
Norway
47-22-23-3500

Duck Flat Wooden Boats
230 Flinders Street
Adelaide, 5251
South Australia
61-88-232-2344
www.duckflatwoodenboats.com.au

Guillemot Kayaks
10 Ash Swamp Road
Glastonbury, CT 06033
860-659-8847
www.guillemot-kayaks.com

Index